49/50

RELIGION
AS
STORY

Edited by James B. Wiggins

HARPER & ROW, PUBLISHERS
New York   Evanston
San Francisco
London

FIRST EDITION

Library of Congress Cataloging in Publication Data

Main entry under title:
Religion as story.
  (A Harper forum book; RD 103)
  Includes bibliographical references.
  1. Religion and literature. 2. Narration
(Rhetoric) I. Wiggins, James B., 1935–
PN49.R4   1975   809′.933′1   75–9339
ISBN 0–06–069353–3

75 76 77 78 79 10 9 8 7 6 5 4 3 2 1

Contents

Preface

THE MAKING OF A BOOK is often a complicated task which consumes considerably more time than one projects. This has been no exception, entailing as it has the coordinating of the work of persons hundreds of miles removed from each other, each of whom concurrently has had many other responsibilities. For the cooperation of the contributors in finally bringing this book to fruition, I am grateful.

My colleagues at Syracuse University, both faculty and student, have continually offered encouragement and generous assistance, as well as thoughtful critiques, at various stages. The dialogue with each of them as they have listened, read and constructively responded over the past months has been invaluable. The role of *provocateur par excellence,* however, has been David Miller's in the continuation of our conversations begun fifteen years ago during our graduate school years.

The editors have been patient. The typist of significant portions of the manuscript, Mrs. Dianne Wallace, has been unusually competent and prompt, even under the sometimes severe time limits which I have pressed upon her. Support for attending and holding conferences and colloquies related to religion and story has been generous from Syracuse University. My wife, Kay, and my son and daughter, Bryan and Karis, by their very being who they are, have constantly been sources of support and comfort.

Most of all, however, my part in this book is dedicated to the memory of my mother, Parley L. Wiggins, who in the living out of her death over more than a year demonstrated to me the power

of being utterly and without remainder committed to a story that
sustained her in her dying, as it had so long sustained her living.

James B. Wiggins
Syracuse, New York

Introduction

"GOD CREATED MAN because he loves stories." So says Elie Wiesel. The referent of the pronoun "he" is sufficiently ambiguous to allow us to suppose that both God and man are lovers of stories. The saying additionally suggests that interaction of the contextual story of God's creation of man with the stories man tells in the exercise of his proper vocation when he knows his own origins. Perhaps, even as a way of coming to know his origins. Paul Pruyser in his *Dynamic Psychology of Religion* wrote the aphorism: "Without stories, no religion." Coupling his observation with Wiesel's catches up a number of the motives which gave rise to this collection of essays.

Each of the contributors to the volume has previously written on the relationship between story and religion. A variety of auspices, in different combinations from occasion to occasion, have enabled face-to-face discussions between the contributors. The invitation to participate reflects the editor's judgment that each person from his particular angle of vision has a unique offering to make. And we come from six disciplines within the field-encompassing-field of religious studies. The collection further reflects the fact that "story" is a subject which joins scholars in a way that enables and facilitates conversation in spite of the tendency toward disciplinary exclusiveness which specialization in religious studies often fosters. When philosopher of religion, theologian of culture, specialist in religion and literature, biblical scholar, depth psychologist and historian find common cause on anything it is, to say the least, unusual. But such are the issues connected with the religion-story discussions which invite and elicit response from many different directions.

There are, to be sure, frustrations often connected with the varied interests concerned with this subject. For example, some participants are quite naive about the technical expertise which a religion and literature specialist brings and might expect others to bring to these discussions. So it is with regard to other areas of formal training and preparation. Counterbalancing the desirability of everyone already being so broadly prepared is the stimulus to acquiring such skills and sharpening sensibilities which might otherwise be ignored. Above all there is the growing realization that all our disciplines have an intimate stake in the realm of story.

One of the threads connecting the six pieces included is the attention given to imagination. Although literature pertaining to imagination is enormous, the task of incorporating and integrating imagination into religious studies—with the attendant risk of experiencing a transformation of our very modes of thinking—is even more enormous. If this collection stimulates even some readers to take up this challenge, that will suffice.

Each of the essays corresponds to its author's experience of stories. And, read with an even focus on various ways of storytelling, each tells a story. The explicit inclusion of one of Michael Novak's own short stories serves dramatically to underscore the implicit storytelling in the other contributions. Each of us indicates the way in which our thinking is being informed and in some important sense, transformed by encounters with stories.

Familiar modes of consciousness tend to become comfortable and often result in stultification and stagnation of thought. One of the challenges of stories, as Gunn demonstrates, is to imagine the "other." Habitual modes of perceiving and thinking are often disturbed by encounters with stories in a manner otherwise unlikely to happen. That is my hope. Further, as Crites says, our thinking frequently becomes "unpeopled" to the point that we preclude the possibility of hearing whatever angels would say to us. Stories may reopen our ears. Our cultural history leads us to assume that we have passed beyond the need for stories—an assumption questioned in my chapter. But accepting our need for story, William Doty sees in our present predicament the presence of not only *a* story but a multiplicity of stor*ies*. In this situation, Doty believes that we have little choice but to devise our own canon of authoritative stories. And Hillman circles round the soul's irrepressible storytelling activities, the demand within us for *poesis,* the imaginative making of stories, or soul making. This leads ineluctably, as he reads psychological stories, to encounters with the gods. Openings or clearings where gods come to play and where angels speak just may contribute to our collectively discovering the power in imaginative words. Such is the promise of stories.

RELIGION
AS
STORY

I

Within and Without Stories

JAMES B. WIGGINS

> We are what we imagine; . . . our very existence
> consists in our imagination of ourselves. Our best
> destiny is to imagine who, and what, and that, we
> are. The greatest tragedy that can befall us is to go
> unimagined. We live in an age that is marked in
> some measure by a poverty of the imagination.[1]

A HEIGHTENED SENSE of the importance of story (a word I shall
use throughout as synonymous with narrative discourse) is emerging today, not least in religious and theological circles. But why?
Whence? And, so what?

Nietzsche once caustically observed: "By searching out origins,
one becomes a crab. The historian looks backward; eventually he
also *believes* backward."[2] More recently Marshall McLuhan has
poked fun at people who race forward into the future with their
eyes firmly fixed upon the rear-view mirror. And, of course, the so-
called history which bears the brunt of such commentary richly
deserves such criticisms. Surely there is another way for the historian to do his work. Surely the predominant ways of doing history today do not exhaust the possibilities for historiography.

By these remarks I wish to forewarn the reader that I arrived at
my interest in story by a circuitous route over several years. English
literature was my major as an undergraduate; process theology as
propounded by one of its outstanding exponents, was my primary
seminary fare. That history and its multitude of related problems
beguiled me during graduate school came as something of a sur-

prise. The pleasures of the literary arts have long claimed a significant portion of my leisure time. In over a decade of teaching
in a university department of religion, I have tried time and again
to draw these influences and loves together in some fashion. An
interest in story in its relation to religion represents my most recent
enthusiasm regarding a possible unifying vision.

Aristotle established the frame of reference from which those
who try to re-vision the possibilities of historiography as a form of
narrative thinking and presentation must liberate themselves. I
refer here, of course, to the oft-cited passage in the *Poetics* in
which Aristotle contrasted poetry with history. He wrote that
poetry may treat what might have been and yet may be, whereas
history must confine itself to fidelity precisely and only to what
has been. Whether or not it is explicit therein, surely implicit in
such a distinction is the differentiation of fact (history) from fiction (poetry).

In a process which may be playing itself out in our time this
fateful distinction has dominated much of the thinking related to
these matters in the West for millennia. Many of our contemporaries have become skeptical of fact almost beyond recovery. Others
have relegated fiction to the realm of the imaginary (as opposed
to the imaginative, to which some in our time still at least give lip
service and others like N. Scott Momaday take very seriously).
In such a predicament it would be predictable that many who regard story as obviously fictive and therefore false should have lost
interest in it. Since the rise of history as an academic discipline
only a relatively short while ago, historians have created a pool of
"professional historians" to whom learned, factual, scientific and
abundantly footnoted tomes are addressed. But do nonhistorians
read these "histories" to any appreciable degree? And, concurrent
with the rise of critical history over the past centuries, has anyone
failed to note the vast amount of criticism among the literary artists to whom the realm of storytelling has been relegated,
which pronounces the novel passé? The Norman Mailers of this
world now write about Apollo moon shots and Marilyn Monroe,
of the Vietnamese War and contra women's liberation tracts. The
Truman Capotes recount the fascination of murder and the inadequacy of our system of justice in a form of literature for which

no really adequate nomenclature yet exists, unless it be called "contemporary history," which many professional historians disdain.

But Theodore Roszak, Charles Reich, William Irwin Thompson, Carlos Castañeda, Doris Lessing, Isaac Asimov, Arthur Koestler, Nabokov, Borges, et al., write different and strange books, sell them, and even apparently find readers. By metaphorical extension, I judge it appropriate to denominate what they are doing by the term William Irwin Thompson has used to describe his own work, *Wissenkunst*. Whatever else may be buried in this Germanism, one of the things it conveys is a collapsing of the barriers between fact and fiction. To understand the consequences of that, I must try briefly to tell the story of how it came to pass. Just when the times in some ways seemed least propitious for stories, they are reappearing. Just at the moment when we thought we could, because some had boldly declared that we must, live without stories,[3] we hear from many different quarters the assertion that to try to live without stories is folly. Further, it is contended that we are, in spite of ourselves, always living within stories, even within a story which some sensitive persons are letting come to expression through them. But what story and whence did it come?

1. *The Collapse of the Story to End all Stories*

Cartesian man had the audacity to think thoughts, in a remarkable stroke of boldness, which, if they were practicable, would have at one and the same time enabled and forced him to live entirely without stories. By mastering nature, industrializing work, rebelling politically, taming the unconscious, identifying man as but another of the evolving forms of life, an objectifying consciousness tried to leave behind modes of perception which are the fertile soil from which stories arise. Convert the venerable capacity for re-membering through historical inquiry into a neatly packageable academic discipline and it will become harmless enough. Relegate the arts— the literary along with others—to a cultural ghetto for the eccentric but socially irrelevant modes of expression, even though this may require a wink at the Bohemian lifestyles within that ghetto. Elevate scientific technology built upon the positivistic reductions of a Newtonian worldview, while demoting religion to the rank of a precritical stage of superstition, and stories of all kinds will safely be left behind. Fabrications, fabulations, legends, folktales, epics, histories, biographies, autobiographies, romances, didactic fictions, satires, myths, et al. It was indeed, as Stephen Crites so pungently observed, a story to end all stories.[4]

But something went awry in the grand strategy. Nature, though malleable, proved much more mysterious than the Newtonians, cum Comtians imagined—just as Bishop Butler had insisted in the eighteenth century. Pollution threatens the ecosystem when the process of industrialization runs rampant and no amount of attempting to extrapolate the limits of growth appears to bring forth much relief. Democratic and socialist revolutions leave much to be desired. Stalin followed Lenin with a vengeance and the American Dream was immolated in the napalmed countryside of Vietnam. The body refuses to be fully mastered by ego-consciousness. Freud gives ground to all sorts of projects aimed precisely at making the conscious unconscious. All of which says that counter-revolution appears to follow revolution as night and day. And suddenly, unexpectedly and quite dramatically, a widening interest in stories appears. The plot to end stories can now begin to be seen as the plot of the story about trying to end all stories. And since plots are forms, empty shells which must be filled out, fleshed out by the stuff of life—at least by some reckonings—we can see now that the power-lust which motivated the West for three centuries was empty formalism by which life could not be sustained precisely because it neither offered nor contained vital sustenance. Concrete human experience was subordinated to formal, critical thinking. The attempt to live without stories has revealed that in spite of our civilization's intention, we are willy-nilly within a story, but a story which offers precious little life support.

If such an account does justice to the course of the last 300 years in the West, no matter how imperfectly, then à la Vico we must now consider the communication which narratives have borne in our cultural and religious history. Here we reach a critical juncture. We dare not look back in order to go back. Regression will be no solution to this malaise. Rather, we must look back to see if we are able to discern those forces which, allied in ironic fashion with stories, bring us to the present threatened demise of all stories. Put differently, what we seek in casting an historical glance is a clue to where story went wrong and was shoved into a corner of cultural and psychic indifference—even irrelevance. If this can be discovered, then perhaps we may be able to discern present possibilities and to anticipate future ones.

2. Once Upon a Time

There was a time once upon a time when out of the combining of legends, folktales, and myths into epics man began to assert his will and consciously to bring the traditional stories (*mythoi*) into some degree of purposive control. The first expression of this willfulness took the form of epic poetry. This fateful step indicated two potent forces at work, which, so long as the one does not totally swallow up the other, can be allowed a variety of persuasive combinations. The interacting forces were, on the one hand, the self asserting itself and, on the other hand, the traditional stories— myths—as an inexhaustible source within which to be.

Some of the more significant and important of these combinations must be recounted, even if in a truncated manner. Robert Scholes' and Robert Kellogg's extremely helpful work entitled *The Nature of Narrative* (New York: Oxford University Press, 1966) has greatly facilitated the telling of this story. The epic itself, and I shall refer to the Homeric as an example contrary to some interpretations of Greek culture and thought, represents the incursion of a degree of skepticism and rationalism into the mythic consciousness of pre-Homeric Greece. By this reading Homer and Hesiod are as problematic to interpret as the more sophisticated Socratic and Platonic views regarding the limits of myth in favor of emergent logical rationality. One finds within the Socratic-Platonic axis that the appearance of myths at certain critical junctures in the philosophers' analyses provided a positive valencing of myth. At the same time, Plato's insistence upon *inventing* stories *de novo,* e.g., the allegory of the cave, is an index of how far and how rapidly the art of storytelling, self-consciously pursued, had already developed in Greece within a relatively short time.

Once the impulse to impose some fabricated order upon myths

had begun to find expression in the epic form, it was with considerable rapidity that storytelling branched into two distinctive types. In the broadest terms, it seems legitimate to differentiate narratives of an empirical kind from those which were fictional. Shortly these two branches further divided into pairs. Under the heading of "fiction" one may distinguish: (1) the "romance" from (2) the didactic forms of narrative. Under the heading "empirical" one finds the emergence of: (1) historical narrative as distinct from (2) mimetic kinds of stories. Here one must risk yet another generalization. Whereas the empirical narratives aimed at scientific (in the then understood connotation of the word) knowing, the fictional works gave expression to artistic knowing.

Further distinctions can be made between history and mimetic works. The concern of historical narrators was assumed to be with the *past,* whereas mimetic narrators centered upon *present* experiences of sensation and environment, i.e., upon how it feels to experience, think, understand, etc., in some particular here and now. The Romans further refined mimesis by developing their versions of biography and autobiography which were little concerned with history in any larger sense—as, for example, a contemporary historian today might be involved in the study of Hitler in order to understand Nazi Germany. The Romans rather aimed at presenting the characteristics of the life being celebrated and explored. Further, the Romans adopted the eyewitness point of view for some of their storytelling. This allowed, of course, much greater latitude for the insertion of ideas into the story by the narrator than the earlier impersonal or third-person point of view had permitted.

Fiction, free as it was to treat the ideal as envisioned by the narrator without claiming empirically demonstrable validity, accuracy, or even appropriateness, came to be separated into "romances" and didactic stories. The word *romance* in this context functions as a metaphor, since romances proper did not really appear until the Middle Ages as a designation indicating narratives written in the romance vernaculars of Europe. What is intended in calling these premedieval narratives romances is that they combined aesthetic and erotic concerns expressed in rhetorical language, and produced through this combination a form of mimetic narrative. This form predated romances in the technical sense.

Didactic narratives, e.g., *Aesop's Fables,* are typically moralistic and/or intellectual stories, both in tone and content. In historical and didactic narrative there tended to be a greater concern with plot than with character, whereas in mimesis and romance, plot was subordinate to characterization.

The preceding foray into genre development allows us to enter into the more important question of its contribution to the storyteller's ability to express meaning, and particular kinds of precise meanings, through these forms. There is much reason to believe, as the centuries passed and as the forms themselves assumed a kind of fixity if not rigidity, that storytellers acquired a great degree of self-conscious freedom in selecting the particular form they could employ on given occasions and for specific purposes. Assuming a clear-cut distinction between form and meaning, as so much of antiquity did, the storyteller so long as the forms were relatively stable and available could concentrate on meaning. Given the further assumption of the more or less adequate "fit" between form and reality shared by many thinkers in that time, the storyteller's primary task was to find the form of expression most appropriate for the content, i.e., the meaning, which he aspired to communicate.

But when a new meaning sought expression, there were sometimes possibilities but often real limitations placed upon storytellers operating under these assumptions. Perhaps reflecting briefly upon the emergence of Christianity in its particular historicocultural context may help clarify this. Christianity appeared within the insulated context of rabbinic Judaism. What it was culturally insulated *from* at the outset was the Hellenic world, and what it was insulated *by* was the mode of communication long developed and deeply cherished in the biblical, rabbinical tradition. The importance of narrative in that tradition, of course, was inestimable. But the veneration of Scripture which evoked commentary, and which made interpretation of already established texts the supreme task, was bound to give a different shape to the form which the narratives within Judaism would take. Whereas for the Greeks and Romans the forms tended to be givens into which the storyteller could mold content, for the Hebrew storyteller the content, as embodied in sacred writings, had to be adhered to faithfully. Though perhaps overstated, this point nonetheless had been insufficiently considered in studying Christianity's rise. The new religion was heir to both emphases—the formal and the contentual—and at various times in its odyssey elevated first the one and again the other to primacy.

The development of Christian biblical interpretation through the centuries was aided and abetted by its appropriation from the Greeks and Romans of the substantialistic, formalistic, rationalistic tradition with which Christian theology struck a most precarious alliance during its first several centuries of existence. But in its attempt to preserve its Judaic religious heritage, such highly influential thinkers as Origen, Clement, Jerome, and Augustine reflected their training in the rhetorical, satirical, and allegorical traditional forms of the Greeks, as well as an immersion in the stories preserved in the sacred writing. We have tended in historical studies to focus on the rationalistic theologizing through which the intelligentsia were wooed to Christianity. Correspondingly, we have been less sensitive to the quantitatively far greater tradition through which the masses encountered Christian communication—sermons, commentaries, romances, legends, lives of the saints, and histories, such as they were. To be sure these were all to some great or little degree informed by the theological thought of the Church, but it now appears to me inappropriate to think that these narratives were dominated by theological sophistication or that theology was what they primarily communicated, or even were intended to communicate.

Trusting this analysis to have touched some crucial points, it remains to make another foray into the ways in which meaning came to expression in narrative form in the late Middle Ages and the Renaissance. Over the centuries the mixing of Christian content into story forms, which were themselves often amalgams of the inherited Classical and Hebraic genre, produced some striking effects. As the Western world had become more "Christian" in its self-conscious religious identity, the Christian content and the classical forms proved to be remarkably adaptable. This resiliency was demonstrated as Celtic, Germanic, Nordic, and Muslim waves broke over Christendom through the succeeding centuries, each bearing its own legends, folktales, and myths which, at least typically, ran at odds with the Christian understanding of reality. Christian storytellers proved remarkably inventive in absorbing much from these encounters, yet retaining an identifiable continuity. As the potential audience for Christian stories became more cosmopolitan through the passing centuries, there was a significant shift at the center of the stories. The shift was from the *representational* concreteness of particular lives or communities of Christians told in empirical narratives—annals, chronicles, and biographies—to the *illustrative* generalizations in which characters lost concreteness and became symbolic types of mankind. The emphasis, in other words, was shifting from the empirical to the invented fictional character, and the latter tended to be either in stories governed by aesthetic concerns (romances proper) or in those communicating intellectualistic concerns (didactic stories). One of the major accomplishments of these centuries was the development, therefore, of skillful *allegories* as a self-conscious mode of combining both serious thinking and effective storytelling. The most remarkable example of medieval allegory, understood in this sense, is Dante's *Divine Comedy*.[5] In this work the poet's desire to capture an audience by his storytelling skill is balanced by and occasionally outdistanced by his conviction that narrative discourse could be a genuine instrument not only for the communication of already cherished truth, but also for philosophical discovery. From Plato through Philo, Origen, Clement, and Augustine, to mention but a few, the lineage of allegorical thought had been transmitted to the Middle Ages. Too frequently comments on allegorical thinking in Christianity are confined to the allegorical method of biblical interpretation. If left there, however, it is easy to ignore the much more pervasive mindset which *allegoresis* produced in medieval Christian thinkers. This capacity enabled Christians to baptize the gods of the Greek, the Germans, and other ancients, just as the prophets, indeed the whole of Hebrew Scripture had been Christianized before them. It was this allegorizing impulse which enabled Dante to make room in his vision of *paradisio* for some of the pagans he judged to be most estimable.

But when perpetuated into the Renaissance with its upsurge of critical rationality and growing skepticism regarding things Medieval and Christian, the allegorical mindset allowed the critical camel's nose into the tent. It became logical to explore whether the original meanings carried by the myths of earlier traditions might not be at least as interesting in their own right as the Christian meanings into which the myths had been forced to fit. Put differently, one can scarcely preserve the mythologems of another tradition without risking a resurgence of the power of the mythic view of reality from which those stories arose. Thus the attempt to force the *stories* of the Greek gods into the mythic structure of Christian consciousness, even if filled out by "Christian" characterization, risked the danger of having the Christian mythic consciousness displaced by that of the Greeks. When the process went a bit further there dawned the realization that expressions of mythic consciousness have varied significantly from time to time and place to place. In short, the Christian stories were not, after all, the only available stories, and perhaps not even the best among the stories. From such a realization the conclusion may be drawn that the expressions of Christianity have been but one more or less coherent set of stories, many borrowed and modified from contiguous traditions, which are limited in their power and persuasiveness to people who are within a particular segment of space and time. Such a conclusion was fundamentally at odds with the long-standing claim of Christians to have in their possession, or rather to be in the service of, *the* story for all persons in all times and in all places. Although the inadequacy and particularity of Christian consciousness and expression were thought to have been discovered, the desire for some universally significant basis for human life and understanding continued to burn brightly in the West. The advent of the seventeenth century's version of rationality represents the culmination of a certain revulsion which some minds felt against the extravagant claims of diverse groups which called themselves Christians engaged in the vilification of other groups equally sure that they, and they alone, were the guardians of unique Christian truth. Europe and the rest of the world had been exposed during the Reformation era to the spectacle of warring groups of Christians slaughtering each other in the firm conviction that the particular and peculiar vision and version of the Christian story for which they stood was the *only* version. Although judging Christian factionalism to have demonstrated the bankruptcy of any church's claim to universal truth, the new rationalists aspired themselves to discover and possess universally significant truth. To that degree Christianity's long-standing universalistic aspirations survived suspicions of the churches' credibility.

Contributing to the decline in confidence in the Christian mode of allegory was the rise of a more sophisticated form of historical empirical narrative during the Renaissance. For example, the metaphorical-mythical power of the papacy's role as the universal shepherd of mankind could not survive unscathed when Lorenzo Valla's researches revealed that the papal claims to ownership of large portions of the Italian peninsula were fraudulent. This had the effect of pitting one form of narrative—empirically based historiography—against another: the legendary, epical story used to establish and sustain a particular view of the Christian Church. A long-term consequence of this jousting between narratives was the attempt to reduce, and for some to eliminate, the role of narrative altogether from the acceptable, or at least important, modes of communicating truth. It meant, in short, a turn to the story of attempting to end all stories mentioned earlier.

Before returning to our present situation, we should recall that virtually concurrent with the beginnings of critical history in the Renaissance an early form of the novel, if one may so designate *Don Quixote,* can be found. In that marvelous tale one of the suppositions called into question is any facile distinction between truth and fiction. Positivist critics, of course, will bridle at such a suggestion, certain as many of them are that Cervantes was at pains to demonstrate that he knew the precise difference between the two. But is it really so nonsensical to suppose that Cervantes may have been challenging the easy differentiation between truth and fiction? In any case, however it may have been for Cervantes, an extensive list of practitioners of the literary art of novel writing since then can be compiled to indicate the degree to which many have felt in the post-Cartesian world that fiction is a more viable medium of communicating truth than any "empirical" account could ever be. And although admittedly a special case of storytelling requiring very different means of critical appropriation, the dramatists of the West, through the very finely wrought fiction of their plays, have taught us much that is not only beautiful but also true. A debate regarding the good, the true, the beautiful lies far outside the pale of this essay, but I do wish to call attention to the novel as a medium through which storytelling has remained a vital force in Western culture, even at the price of having to endure many seemingly sophisticates who remark, "So what? It's only fiction."[6]

3. *Here We Go Again*

In our searching backward, the challenge is to try to avoid both thinking and believing backward. Earlier I proposed that looking backward was necessarily not to be construed as an advocacy for going backward, i.e., for regressing. It has been asserted here that ours is a situation which can be described as having passed through the story of the attempt to end all stories. But leap-frogging back over modernity and the Renaissance to the belief-ful realism of classical and biblical stories is a luxury denied those of us who have experienced the loss of innocence regarding the relationship of stories to reality. No matter how bound we are to do our thinking out of the past, as Kierkegaard insisted, we must do our living in the present and into the future. The Buddhist sequence of: first, there was a mountain, then there was no mountain, now there is a mountain seems apt here. Today we are seeing again that there is a mountain, i.e., that our willful rationalism of the past several centuries did not eliminate stories or our need for stories. The question is what to do with such a realization and to what extent may the study of religion both contribute to and be enhanced by a consideration of storytelling? And another question might be how widespread is this realization among scholars in the fields of religion?

To the latter question it may be replied that it is quite widespread and increasing rapidly. Not only have the authors of the essays in this volume attended the many faceted relationship between religion and story in other of their writings, but interest in the subject is evident in other quarters as well. Though hardly conclusive regarding the quality or depth of this concern, it should be noted that at the Annual Meeting of the American Academy of Religion and the Society for Biblical Literature in 1974 no fewer than a dozen sessions of various subgroups were devoted to some aspect or another of the relationship between religion and narrative. Other auspices have sponsored more specialized occasions during the past three years. By now the religion and literature specialists have been joined by theologians, ethicists, biblical scholars, historians, psychologists, and philosophers of religion, in conversations on these matters. Given the recent history of fads in theology, one ought to be cautious regarding any emergent thematic concerns among scholars of religions for fear of being aboard yet another careening roller-coaster car. Nonetheless one senses the possibility that concern with religion and story may be of more lasting importance precisely because it taps basic religious roots.

It is too soon to attempt an etiology of rising interest. However, it will be perhaps fruitful to suggest what some of the contributing influences appear to be. Near the head of any such list must be the development of religion and literature studies. Persons such as Stanley Hopper, Nathan Scott, and Amos Wilder led the way in this discipline and by their erudition, energy, and insight have demonstrated the viability and fruitfulness of such study. Not only their sensibilities—finely honed and brilliantly polished as they are —but also the range of partners they have engaged in conversation has offered new insights into the study of religion during the past decades. Well grounded in the traditional sources—the Bible, theology, and philosophy—these thinkers also have explored minds of poets, dramatists, novelists, literary critics, culture historians, psychoanalysts, and depth psychologists, and to some extent non-Western religious thinkers. Such broad contacts have stimulated modes of seeing and thinking which seldom have been characteristic of "theologians." While they have encountered suspicions from their colleagues in other established disciplines within the study of religion, thinkers of the substance of these persons have not been stopped, but have continued to offer dramatic contributions throughout their careers. The openness displayed by these thinkers to literature as one field of creative response to human experience seems to have been predicated upon their recognition that art and religion may stem from common sources. It follows that students of religion then potentially would learn much by attending to the major literary works, as well as to the more traditionally designated religious writings. This is, of course, far different from supposing that theologians should "use" literature as illustrative of points which theology is trying to emphasize. (I worry whether the current interest in story among religionists is informed sufficiently by such wisdom.) Especially in the cases of Wilder and Hopper, one perceives their attending to the literary artists for correctives to the received ways of theologizing. The term *theopoesis* has been proffered as an alternative to *theo-logy*. When taken in the spirit proposed, it becomes clear that such an alternative points toward aesthetics and ontology and away from logic and metaphysics as the appropriate modes of appreciating religious language. In no sense is this a retreat from deeply reflective thinking, but calls for critical thinking in a new key in religion and in other disciplines, for the implications are far-reaching indeed.

From yet other directions—again I insist on eschewing any etiological claim—one finds theologians who have thought their ways through to points of view which, by their very presence, contribute to the *Zeitgeist* within which the interest in story springs. John Dunne, a provocative theologian who teaches at the University of Notre Dame, has written a number of books in the past decade which have unfolded a carefully exposited view of the relationship between religion and story. Beginning with *The City of the Gods* (The Macmillan Company, 1965) and continuing through *A Search for God in Time and Memory* (The Macmillan Company, 1969) and *The Way of All the Earth* (The Macmillan Company, 1972), Dunne has searched through an astonishingly comprehensive range of theological, religious, and cultural history. His method of "passing over" to other ways of experiencing reality has enabled him to appropriate insights and offer suggestions of profound significance for the study of and thinking within religion. The most recent of his books, *Time and Myth* (The Macmillan Company, 1973), probes the question "What story are we living now?" This makes explicit the implicit matter of story which informed his earlier writings.

Among scholars of religion who have contributed to this emergent concern one must also mention Sam Keen in *Apology for Wonder* (Harper & Row, 1969), Harvey Cox in his *Feast of Fools* (Harvard University Press, 1969) and David L. Miller in *Gods and Games* (World Publishers, 1970). Each of these works contributed to establishing a sensibility within which interest in story and religion could flourish. These three authors have subsequently written books which directly, in part or in toto, address the story issue. Keen wrote *To A Dancing God* (Harper & Row, 1970) and coauthored *Tell Your Own Story* (1973); Cox wrote *The Seduction of the Spirit* (1973); and Miller wrote *The New Polytheism* (Harper & Row, 1974). The lineage in each case has been characterized by the recognition that deep religion has historically marched to the beat of a drummer different than the one propounded by established theologies, particularly in the West. To the extent that the so-called "theology of play," which each of these men has significantly shaped, reawakens the repressed childhood capacity to hear and participate in the multivalenced, multimeaning resonances of stories, it will have been an invaluable prepatory movement.

More conventional and traditional theology has also cultivated the new ground. "Theology of hope," before its development into various versions of "liberation theology," reminded us of several highly important matters. By its emphasis upon eschatology and the future, this theology underscored the importance of temporality in religious consciousness and experience. In his *Theology of Hope* (New York: Harper & Row, Inc.), Moltmann quite self-consciously engaged the thinking of Ernst Bloch's *Das Prinzip Hoffnung*. In demonstrating that Christian theology could creatively engage the philosophy of a revisionist Marxist, Moltmann focused upon the future's centrality to theology in principle, and thus opened the way to a departure from a more substantialistic and rationalistic mode of theologizing into one which is attentive to process. In my judgment Moltmann did not move his own thinking far enough in that direction, but he did open the way to which a possibility of allowing process to gain greater attention. It remained to Walter Capps in his *Time Invades the Cathedral* (Fortress Press, 1972) to indicate explicitly the challenge that this opening presents to many traditional ways of theologizing. Capps

was properly cautious in not claiming theology of hope to be a
panacea for theology's diverse ailments, but by illuminating the
the inherent concern for temporality in the theology of hope, he
contributed to the making of a clearing within which the concern
for story might emerge. Surely it is the case that narrative thinking and utterance exist only to the extent that they body forth
temporality in human experience. Narrative is about time and it
takes time. In other terms form and content are mutually suppor-
tive.

Although it is much too large an area to be fully delineated in
this essay, the study of mythology by scholars in many disciplines
in the twentieth century has dramatically altered the study of religion. And it has contributed to thinking about the relationship between religion and story. The writings of Jung, Neumann, Kerenyi,
Campbell, Ricouer, Lévi-Strauss, Eliade and Frye, to mention but
a few have sensitized any number of scholars to dimensions of
religious thought and experience that were long ignored.

One should not overlook the explicit attention given to story by
established theologians such as Robert M. Brown, Hans Frei,
and Bernard Loomer. Brown recently presented a major paper on
"Story and Theology" and is soon to publish a book on the subject.[7]
Frei published *The Eclipse of Biblical Narrative* (Yale University
Press, 1974). Loomer in a recent article in *Criterion* entitled
"S-I-Z-E" wrote: "Increasingly over the years, I find myself moving in the direction of stories, rather than explications of stories,
that is, with the theologies and philosophies."[8] Perhaps it is not
surprising to find a theologian so familiar with process philosophy
and theology coming to this view. In any case his remark catches
the tenor of the thinking of many who reflect on the religion-story
concern.

Even with that much recounted, the question remains: "So
what?" What is at stake in all of this? One can only offer some
suggestions by way of commentary. Sam Keen has helped further
our thinking upon the matter. He has demonstrated in *To a Dancing God* a willingness to take some risks. He recognizes two signally
important things. First, the attempt to persuade men in the past
three centuries that we could live without sustaining stories was a
lie. Second, the stories which used to be culturally and spiritually
sustaining in the West prior to modernity are presently inaccessible

to many of us, at least as so often told. In such a predicament Keen proposes:

> For the moment, at least we must put all orthodox stories in brackets and suspend whatever remains of our belief-ful attitude. Our starting point must be individual biography and history. If I am to discover the holy, it must be in *my* biography and not in the history of Israel. . . . *I have a story.*[9]

Keen attempts to divert some attention from the emphasis upon *I and my* in this statement when he adds a little further: "The more I know of myself, the more I recognize that nothing is foreign to me. In the depth of each man's biography lies the story of all men."[10] The point where I diverge from Keen comes precisely in regard to the rhetorical effect of making the statements in this order. Had he begun with the last statement, relating life story to the story of all men, it would have suggested in my view, a more promising way forward. The problem with beginning with attention focused upon the Ego-I appears to be that it perpetuates the substantializing, objectifying tendency of the cultural malaise from which relief is sought.

One further caution must be made. What one most desperately wants to discover in one's life story is not that the story is everyone's story. Nor does Keen quite say that. His words are "In the depth of each man's biography. . . ." What one needs precisely is to come to the conviction that out of the myriad possibilities of a human life there is embodied in one's own story sufficient particularity to mark one as an authentic *individual* human being who does not simply replicate some inevitable round of existence. At the same time one longs to discover the universal dimensions embodied in one's story to a degree that marks one's life as an authentic individual *human* being. Without both distinctiveness and commonality the story will ultimately be unsatisfying and one will continue to retell it agonizingly until both dimensions are uncovered in some fulfilling fashion. Part of what experiencing that fullness requires is a sufficient recovery of imagination to allow a person to feel one's way into stories other than one's own—both of individual and collective kinds—in order to discover if in some deep, previously unrecognized sense they might turn out to be part of one's own story.

What is wanted, in other words, is the openness to the fluid interaction of reality and self which will allow a more articulate telling of that interdependent experience. In this regard I wish to affirm the passion for precision which the scientific method has fought to enhance, even if for the wrong reasons and, therefore, misleadingly. I am urging the abandonment of the metaphysical supposition that what I can be precise about is *either* only the inner, subjective world *or* the outer, objective world. What is called for, and what story may allow for in a unique way, is a kind of precision which may result from expressing the interdependence of inner and outer. Symbol, metaphor, image in incarnated speech and action must be cherished and honored as a medium for such expression, and these occur most frequently—though not exclusively—in stories.

Let us return, as an instance of this point, to the case of historical narrative where the passion for precision has reigned supreme for some time now. In thinking on this matter the following remark of James Hillman's has been helpful:

> The psyche is not isolated from history. . . . And just as the psyche is situated in an historical present that trails behind it the roots of a thousand ancestral trees, so does history have psychological existence. . . . Historical facts are secondary. . . . The historical "facts" may be but fantasies attached to and sprouting from central archetypal cores. Below the clouded and tangled pattern of events, and behind them, are experiences, psychological realities of passionate importance, a mythological substrate which gives the soul a feeling of destiny, an eschatological sense that *what happens matters*. And it matters to someone, to a person. Without the person, . . . we are simply pre-historic men with only collective destiny. Without the sense of soul, we have no sense of history. We never enter it. This core of soul that weaves events together into the meaningful patterns of tales and stories recounted by reminiscing creates history. History is story first and fact later. . . . Only that which is re-told, recounted, remembered becomes history. This remembrance of things past requires an experiencing *sinngebende* individual psyche.[11]

Although hardly providing a primer for how to do historiography, this comment surely suggests why people are or might again become interested in history if historians were to become sufficiently self-reflective about their tasks and opportunities.

Consider John Dunne, who, based on his reading of Goethe, has advocated in *The Way of All the Earth,* that life expresses itself through two processes: turning truth into poetry and poetry into truth. Although applauding the spirit of Dunne's concern, again I quarrel with his diction, although not with what I believe to be his intent. For me it seems that truth is poetry and poetry is truth; their identity may allow differentiating them on some occasions and for some purposes, but never will it grant the assumption that what is required is a volitional decision of an individual ego to join them as if they were discrete, distinct *somethings* which could be volitionally amalgamated. The altered consciousness which allows one to see the identity-difference of truth and poetry is a gift, a presence over which one does not have willful control.

Stories present us with gifts. We may choose to manipulate them by skillful interpretative devices, but stories that matter are greater than and outlive their interpretations. The temptation of theology has been to interpret the foundational stories given by religion and then to treat the interpretation as if it were that which was originally given. Perhaps that is what we have grown so tired of in theology and perhaps that is one of the contributing reasons for the return to stories in some quarters of the study of religion.

If it be objected that the turn to story is itself a regressive move which promises nothing because stories are inevitably shackled by bonds imposed out of some past, I must respond that the objection misses a fundamental point. Every encounter with a story is a *present* event. Stories which evince no response in the present will be abandoned as dead. By contrast, responses which are evoked in the present give testimony to the abiding power of living stories. But one dare not prematurely foreclose the kind, the intensity, or the response to a particular story. The stories which survive and the new ones which are born will take care of themselves. There seems to be no alternative but to open oneself to and to trust the process.

Finally, some may say that stories are demonic! They may be and have been used time and again in history for the most destructive purposes imaginable. And insufficient criteria for separating the creative story from the destructive one have been offered. This is a serious matter. At this point I am only able to offer a tentative response by way of an observation. Some stories—perhaps more accurately some storytellers—present themselves as the story to supplant, to superannuate, even to destroy all other stories. The responses solicited by such a story are responses aimed at leading thenceforth to regarding all other stories as false, wrong, misguided, erroneous, incomplete, etc., because this one story is the Truth of the matter. But a story to end all other stories must ultimately fail on the grounds that it appeals to criteria of judgment which emanate from other than narrative modes of thinking, which is to say, such a story finally defeats itself. A story of real importance is not an argument so much as it is a presentation and an invitation. It presents a realm of experience accessible through the imagination and invites participation in imaginative responses to reality, indeed to respond to reality as imaginative. A story invites one to tell one's own personal and collective stories in response. Stories evoke other stories. The importance of stories lies ultimately less in what is told than in how whatever is told gets told.[12] The temptation is always to stop—to stop listening, to stop responding, to stop storying— but premature death (and what other kind is there, at least from life's point of view?) is always to be mourned. Any story purporting to kill other stories and the storytelling impulse will lead, sooner or later, to its own demise.

First, there were stories. Then, there were no stories. Now, there are stories. For those who have ears attuned to stories, there *are* now stories. And there will be new stories, no matter how old they may sound to those whose hearing is either committed only to particular old stories or to those who have willfully deafened themselves to all stories, not noticing that by now that too is a story in a state of rigor mortis.

NOTES

1. Cited from a portion of an unpublished paper presented by N. Scott Momaday at the International Congress of Religion, Los Angeles, Ca., September 4, 1972. *See* Momaday's two books *House Made of*

Dawn and *The Way to Rainy Mountain,* coupled with the corpus of Elie Wiesel's writings as the most outstanding examples of attempts in our times to transform imaginatively an inheritance of historical experience into stories for a livable, vital heritage.

2. Frederick Nietzsche, *Twilight of the Idols,* no. 24. Quoted from Walter Kaufman, trans. and ed., *The Portable Nietzsche* (New York: The Viking Press, Inc., 1954), p. 470.

3. Cf. Ted Estess, "The Inenarrable Contraption: Reflections on the Metaphor of Story," *Journal of the American Academy of Religion* 42, no. 3 (September 1974): 415–435. This provocative article, largely based on Estess's study of Samuel Beckett, is one of the two best challenges to concern with the religion-story relationship with which I am familiar. The other is an essay by Patricia Berry, "An Approach to the Dream," *Spring, 1974* (New York/Zurich: Spring Publications.)

4. Stephen Crites, "The Narrative Quality of Experience," *Journal of the American Academy of Religion* 39, no. 3 (September 1971): 291–311. Although by no means was Crites's article the first writing to take up this subject, it remains a genuinely seminal piece and perhaps the best place to turn for an introduction to the topic.

5. Caution is due in this regard. In his *Convivio* Dante in reference to allegorical interpretation wrote: "The allegorical . . . conceals itself beneath the cloak of the poetic fable and points to a truth hidden under a pleasing falsehood. . . . The theologians indeed view this allegorical meaning differently from the poets" (II, 1). Quoted from Karl Vossler, *Mediaeval Culture: An Introduction to Dante and His Times* (New York: Frederick Ungar Publishing Co., 1929), p. 131.

6. *See* and ponder William G. Doty's chapter in this volume, "The Stories of Our Times."

7. Brown's paper was delivered at the Annual Meeting of the American Academy of Religion, October, 1974. My reservations regarding the views presented in that paper are not unlike those I feel regarding James McClendon's *Biography as Theology* (Nashville, Abington Press, 1974). Both of them it seems are searching for an alternative mode of theologizing in terms of a new form within which to present a particular version of theology, though not an identical version in their respective cases. But I believe there to be more risk inherent in the religion-story venture than they seem to acknowledge. Not only does form often modify content quite markedly, but also the criteria for responding to such a mode of theologizing will no longer be appropriately the same as those employed in defending and responding to other modes.

8. *Criterion* (Chicago: Chicago Univ. Press, Spring, 1974), p. 8.

 9. Sam Keen, *To a Dancing God* (New York: Harper & Row, 1970), pp. 99 and 102; emphasis added.

10. *Ibid.,* p. 103.

11. James Hillman, "Senex and Puer: An Aspect of the Historical and Psychological Present," *Eranos Jahrbuch* 36 (1967): 304f. Hillman has extended and amplified these observations in his contribution to the present volume, "The Fiction of Case History." Cf. also my article in *Theology Today,* June 1975.

12. Too much may be made, of course, of this "how-what" distinction. It does matter immensely "what" meaning a story wants to tell. The point to be emphasized, however, is that failure to attend to the "how" tempts one to respond to stories on grounds other than the most appropriate ones. The dynamic and inseparable interaction between what and how is so important that overemphasis must be risked here in an effort to counterbalance the opposite and more problematic response to stories.

II

Angels We Have Heard

STEPHEN CRITES

I HAVE BEEN COMPLAINING to my students for many years about the neglect of the science of angelology in the modern university. Since they have generally considered these rumblings to be among my lovable eccentricities, they have never pressed me on the matter. If they had, I should have had to admit that I don't know terribly much about angelology myself. I am familiar with biblical and apocryphal references to angels and I have read some of the speculations of Origen, Augustine, Pseudo-Dionysius, Thomas Aquinas, and other philosophical theologians on the subject. I have seen many artistic representations of angels and have sung a good many hymns in which they figure prominently, particularly around Christmas time, during which season I have also been nauseated by dimpled cherubs on display in department stores and churches. In my teaching, actually, the angelic hosts have mainly figured in my explanations of the Great Chain of Being. It is pleasant to chasten youthful pride by pointing out that humankind is far from being the most exalted order of creatures that the tradition could conceive. Otherwise I suppose that my practice has been typical of both modern learning and modern piety, such as they are, in discreetly ignoring the angels.

Belief in angels has never been formally renounced by ecclesiastical bodies. It has simply atrophied, and it is worth asking why. Further on I want to offer some tentative answers to that question. It may seem foolish even to raise it, when the existence of the good Lord himself has been so widely called into question. Even modern piety prides itself on being lean, if not muscular; its soul does not delight, as the psalmist's did, in fatness. Modern believers deter-

23

mined to cut away the accretions of traditional theological fat slice by slice are given to issuing solemn reports on what they are still able to believe, and these bulletins tend to be ever leaner. Some depositions still assert belief in some sort of Supreme Being but won't swallow any Christological nonsense, while others hang on to Jesus but dispense with God the Father; and still others cling to no more than the Spirit immanent in humanity. With the Trinity falling apart at the seams it may appear frivolous to haggle over mere angels, who were among the early casualties of the idealizing, humanizing, demythologizing propensities of modern theology. Not even the neo-orthodox were prepared to fight strenuous battles over *them*.[1] Fallen angels have admittedly continued to titillate the imagination, but those who remained steadfast have suffered benign neglect at best.

In these theologically lean times, of course, the interest in demonology is pursued in good part because of the entirely plausible suspicion that it may shed some indirect light on the human condition. Angelology does not seem so promising a source of such insight, at least not in the same psychologically obvious ways. Angels must first prove fascinating to us for their own sakes. But if that fascination can give us the stamina to pursue them through some philosophical detours we may at least also come across some important questions about ourselves. The philosophical detours I have in mind are not primarily the metaphysical ones of traditional angelology, to which we can give little attention here—which is a pity, since there is some splendid scenery along that route. But our even less traveled path will take us through some speculations on the aesthetics of traditional religious narrative. For that is where we meet the angels first of all. I want in fact to suggest a sense in which they are essentially narrative figures. It does not necessarily follow that they are merely fictional fancies. For we will wish to explore the possibility that narrative form is so integral to experience that a figure encountered in a story may choose its moment to manifest itself in the "world" of our life experience as well. Perhaps, indeed, we may actually hear the angels themselves in stories, and not merely hear about them. Possibly they are narrative figures even in that incautiously strong sense of the term.

Furthermore, they are narrative figures of an extraordinary sort.

That is obvious if we simply consider the way they appear in well-known stories. They bring about dramatic turning points in the destinies of human beings, transformations that were in no way immanent in what preceded nor the result of human intention as such. Gideon is made a peculiar hero, with no visible qualifications on his part and by means of the most unlikely tactics. The firstborn of the Egyptians are slain in a single night, while the Angel of Death (or is it God himself?) passes over the children of the Israelites. According to some traditions the Law was mediated by angels. They begin and end the gospel, announcing the coming of Christ and his resurrection. They will sound the trump of Last Judgment. In some circles they are understood to be the unseen guardians of ordinary individuals. As death-dealers and ministers of grace, angels seem to belong to the mystery beyond human volition that lies at the heart of human actions and identities.

But before speaking further of angels we must consider the significance of the narrative conditions under which we become acquainted with them.

1. *Attributable to I. B. Singer*[2]

Genuine stories are always primary sources. They invite interpretation, but the interpretations are commentary, secondary sources that come and go, generally according to the intellectual fashions of an age. Some ancient stories have spawned centuries of interpretation, philosophical, theological, allegorical, psychological, social-class, new critical, structuralist, whatnot. That is quite in order, representing the efforts of many generations of intellectually committed readers or hearers to understand a seminal story according to their various lights, and make it more fully their own. Every interpretation sheds new light and casts new shadows. Still the story remains, to lure new interpreters to try their hands. It cannot in principle be replaced or exhaustively explained by any of its interpretations, because interpretation is theoretical—we quite properly classify types of interpretation according to the theories that underlie them—and theory has a form of its own, abstract and generalizing, that is essentially different from the form of narrative.

An interpretation cannot be so definitive as to render the story it interprets superfluous, for there is a formal incommensurability between a story and any theoretical construction that prevents either from being reducible without remainder to the other. That is why a story resists interpretation as much as it invites it. Its validity does not depend, like that of a theory, on its explanatory power. It is a no less complete response to the life of experience, but its completeness does not consist in its generality. It consists, rather, in the immediacy with which narrative is able to render the concrete particularities of experience. Its characteristic language is not conceptual, but consists typically in the sort of verbal imagery we employ in referring to things as they appear to our senses or figure in our practical activities. Still more important, the narrative form aesthetically reproduces the temporal tensions of experience, a moving present tensed between and every moment embracing a memory of what has gone before and an activity projected, underway. A theoretical construction can of course be attuned to temporal movement, may presuppose it or undertake to explain it, but it cannot in its own formal structure reproduce the very feel of lived time in this way.

A story, furthermore, is populated. The agents who move its action are "persons," not mere behaviors or minds or motives or symptoms but characters that are mysterious and whole, undivided, underway. One might say that the characters in stories are always "embodied," though that can be as misleading as to say that they are always ensouled, since the notion of "body" is no less an abstraction from the personal totality of a narrative agent. A story, by its very form, can tolerate neither mindless bodies nor bodiless minds, since narrative action presupposes a personal unity that is prior to any of the factors into which interpretation can analzye its characters. It is tempting to speculate, indeed, that our very sense of "person" may be derived from the agents of narratives. However that may be, these "persons," the *dramatis personae* of the story, are typically but not necessarily humans like ourselves. If one wishes to deny personhood to human beings, one must break the story form as well, as some modern writers have understood. For even if it is a god or an angel who appears as a character in a story, he can appear only in the form of a person. To be drawn into a story is to be personified, someone who can be addressed, who remembers and responds, who is underway in action. Even what we would have to regard, outside a narrative context, as an abstraction or a general power, like Death or Eros, must appear in a story under a personal aspect. One thinks of St. Paul in the narrative-dramatic mode typical of him, snapping his fingers under Death's nose, taunting: O Death, where is thy sting! Paul, of course, also had a theology of resurrection. But its source, which his every theological utterance on the subject attempted to interpret, was clearly the drama played out before his imagination in the most concrete way: Death as the demonic-personified tyrant over the sons of Adam being overthrown by Christ the Lord, risen in power from the tomb. The agents of even the most extraordinary narrative action are personal, the setting presupposed or projected by the action is a world of concrete objects, and the action is temporalized in a manner akin to our most immediate experience. In fact, narrative doubly reflects lived time, by not only reproducing it in its story line but also projecting it in its characters, whose every moment of action is invested with memory and anticipation. It satisfies our sense of reality by registering the tensions of experience in a way that is irreducibly specific and complete.

The completeness of a good theory is of the opposite sort: it provides the explanatory power of abstract inclusion. What we gain from a fruitful interpretation of a story is a more general perspective on it, establishing historical, conceptual, or other relations that cannot be explicit in the particularity of the story itself. When even the least doctrinaire interpreter refers in the most minute detail to a character or an episode in the story, he must lift the character or episode out of the narrative tensions of the story and deal with it abstractly. He must dissect and generalize. The structure of his essay will have conceptual coherence rather than reproducing the sense of lived time. This will give his language a different tension.

This transposition of narrative materials into a different linguistic form is no doubt one of the reasons narrative writers tend to regard critics as their natural enemies. Literary critics, in turn, have been known to be no less hostile to unabashed theorists (philosophers of art, theologians, and such), whose abstractions

seem as unprofitably vaporous to the literator as his interpretations may seem to novelists and storytellers. How, the critic may
demand (to choose an example near at hand), can you talk use-
fully about things like narrative form in the abstract? What we
need is an actual text before us—to dissect in a manner that will
outrage the storyteller. Quite right, too. No one wishes his chosen
medium to serve as grist for someone else's mill. On the other
hand the pretensions of the poets to inspired wisdom will so in-
furiate an honest dialectician like Plato that he will ban them from
the ideal republic, and it will serve them right. But if we were
not all so perversely human we might be able (a theorist says,
plaintively) to take a more reasonable view of the matter: that
there are diverse ways of using language, each of which may have
its limited but quite legitimate functions. It is important to dis-
criminate them so that we can be clear about what can and cannot be done with each. Without attempting to be exhaustive, we
might for our present purposes establish a kind of continuum
from concrete narrative language through the more abstract language of commentary to the transparently theoretical language of
speculation.[3] To move along this continuum may entail some gains
and always entails losses. The theorist cannot improve on what
the poet has done or tell a better story than the storyteller. But
he may do something quite different with a story, perhaps placing
a single concrete detail or formal aspect of it into a conceptual
context where it can be related to other works of art or facets of
experience. He may thereby clarify a general issue that may even
have something to do with what was on the poet's mind, but gain
in this sort of insight is usually proportional to a sacrifice of the
narrative textures and tensions. The narrative images which the
theorist thus drains of their blood by his dissections, however,
will still thrive in rosy health in the story itself, which will survive
all its interpretations.

Some stories, to be sure, are really theories thinly clothed in
narrative form. Allegory (written *as* allegory, not to be confused
with a story someone undertakes to interpret allegorically) is the
most obvious instance of such a pseudostory. Again, it was the
fashion not long ago for stories to be written more or less as illustrations of psychological theories. It cannot be denied that such

pseudostories sometimes satisfy our sense of the textures of experience in the way that genuine stories do, but only to the extent that the narrative movement begins to run away with the theory that was meant to underlie it. A born storyteller who grimly sets out to tell a morally uplifting pseudostory, or one that illustrates one or another world outlook or theology or social theory, sometimes in fact writes genuine stories in spite of himself. In such cases there is a comic discrepancy between what the author meant to do and perhaps still insists he has done, and what he actually accomplished. On the other hand, the purer types of edifying pseudostories are largely of interest to interpreters already committed to their underlying theories, and in such cases the interpretation can be so exhaustive that one doesn't really need the story. Pseudostories begin in theory, and to theory they return, to the general boredom, in the end, of all concerned.

It is a mark of esthetic honesty in a narrative artist that his work registers much more than he can accommodate to the theories, pieties, or programs he professes. This is not to deny the importance, publically and privately, of his professions. But the stories that demand telling are in much more direct touch with the density of his total experience than his general opinions can be. That is why a poem or story can have the ring of authenticity even if its author holds opinions that seem to us to be trivial, outmoded, or downright execrable. Even if his opinions are admirable, it would be esthetic dishonesty to make his work their mere vehicle.

For the sensibility of a good storyteller is attuned not only to the nuances of language but also to the subtle modulations of experience. It is a delicate instrument that registers in language the complex movements and interactions of beings who are themselves possessed of memory, imagination, the power to hear and answer in language and to respond in action, while they are underway. There is no telling ahead of time how things will turn out, and in the story, too, both the characters and the storyteller are taken by surprise, and must improvise. Whether stories are "about real happenings" or are purely fictional, they must esthetically reproduce the pulse and density of personal life time. Fictional stories, just because they are not restrained by documentary sources, factual data, and such, may indeed provide greater scope for the ex-

ploration of more elusive dimensions of experience. The modern
fiction writer has shared with the ancient bard a freedom from
literal facticities that has perhaps made it easier for both to deliver
over in their stories what they knew in their bones. Insofar as their
stories have evoked a shock of recognition in the audience, it is
clear that this bone-knowledge is not a private idiosyncrasy of the
storyteller.

Realistic fiction, for instance, can give us the very grit and intonation of a whole social reality. In an Emma Bovary we meet a
person more vividly located in an actual social scene than we are
likely to meet in most histories or biographies. If we want to be
tiresome and insist nevertheless that Emma still was not a "real
person," the reason is not only that no personage of that name
and that precise career can be found in the historical records, but
also and more significantly that a novel, after all, contains words
and not flesh and blood. That more interesting problem arises,
however, in the biography of an historical figure as well (as the
Roquentin of Sartre's *La Nausée* discovers in his futile attempt
to write a biography of the Marquis de Rollebon). On the one
hand, neither the novel nor the biography can contain more than
the verbal evocation of a real person. But a camera could not necessarily have done better; celluloid is not flesh and blood either, and
the flesh and blood of actors on the stage is not that of the characters they render, either. On the other hand, however, the narrative form, whether it inheres in the plot of a story told or a
story written or a drama or film, is precisely what evokes for us
the sense that we are encountering real persons. There is more to
persons than flesh and blood. Persons are incarnate in the action
of stories. Let a genuine story unfold and the flesh and blood will
materialize of itself.

For narrative form is common both to stories told, enacted,
etc., and to the way we experience in everyday life. It is not that
"reality" in itself somehow has a narrative form, but our experience does have, as I have argued elsewhere.[4] For that matter, it is
only when we don the philosopher's cloak or the scientist's white
coat (or *some* special garment reserved for deep thinking) that we
make clear distinctions between "reality" and what appears in
"experience." Our common *Lebenswelt* contains what we en-

counter in immediate experience and deal with in our practical activity, to which narrative locution is our most direct linguistic access. When we speak to or of what is immediately real to us we tell stories and fragments of stories. "Ordinary language" is largely made up of the sorts of locutions we employ in telling stories. What we ordinarily recognize as real and attempt practically to cope with is what can be put in narrative language. That is why the more artful narratives of the storyteller and dramatist satisfy our sense of reality even if they do not necessarily belong to the self-consciously "realistic" genre employed by some novelists.

Of course we do sometimes don our white coats or philosophical mantles, and employ abstract language. Then we do not speak of things in our immediate experience, bottles, boards, or the neighborhood grouch, but of quite different kinds of things, e.g. the chemistry of the blood, Being Itself, logical fallacies, the genre of the realistic novel. But such second-order language is employed in order to interpret or explain phenomena to which we gain primary access in first-order language, in narrative language in particular. Even if a theorist is convinced that he penetrates, through a specialized second-order language, to a structure of reality that is more fundamental, of which the kinds of things that appear in stories are mere appearance, still, in the end, the validity of the more abstract categories must be measured by their plausibility in explaining what is merely apparent, usually with some special purpose in mind. Many modern theorists regard their categories as purely heuristic, as constructs that are useful within a limited frame of reference for understanding and manipulating some things. But there is no escaping the basically hermenuetical function of abstract language even if the metaphysical enthusiasm of the theorist should lead him to claim that his language reveals a deeper reality. Even if he should pronounce the whole order of things that appear in stories to be but a veil of illusion, the acid test of his ultimate principles will be their employment in interpreting or explaining the vivid appearance of the illusory phenomena we can tell stories about. For such phenomena are what we ordinarily mean by real things. Narrative locutions remain our primary linguistics sources if we are to concern ourselves with the question of reality at all. In stories we meet what is concrete in experience, in the most concrete language we have. We employ abstract language to *interpret* it.

Stories may also be said to be interpretive in a very broad sense. They are certainly artful, both rendering and subtly shaping our sense of social and private experience. Implicit in any story are definite readings of the world we are "in." We may even in a manner test them in relation to our more inchoate sense of our own experience: but that sense of our experience, to the extent that it finds linguistic expression at all, will already have assumed at least a crude narrative form. Narrative form is irreducible in language, and possibly in experience itself. If stories "interpret," still they differ from theoretical constructs in that there is no more elemental form of language of which narrative is the interpretation.

But is there possible experience that is entirely pre- or non-linguistic? A difficult question that raises a host of other difficult questions, which fortunately we need not try to answer here. If I were put to it I should argue that although most of what enters experience is not merely linguistic, whatever enters experience does so in and with language, that in this sense we inhabit the world linguistically. But even if we grant that we may experience something in the utter absence of language: still, if an experienced present is not simply a dissociated "now" but contains at least a vestige of memory and a leaning into anticipation, then an incipient narrative form will be implicit in it, of which narrative language is the irreducible linguistic expression. However we settle the question about nonlinguistic experience, there is still an intimate relation between storytelling and the esthetic form of experience itself.

Now angels appear in stories we have heard, however else they may appear. Since we hear about them in stories, we at least know what it would mean to have them turn up in our experience. Hearing the stories, indeed, is already a way of experiencing them. Simply accepting them as characters in stories is of course a far cry from the sort of explicit and anxiously considered professions of belief in them that might be elicited from the faithful when the existence of their gods or angels has been called into question. But this strong sense of belief is too defensive, too highly self-conscious, too obviously the product of a crisis in belief to disclose the living sources of belief. When belief is not yet shaken it already has the stories, and even after it is shaken by the most severe doubts we still have the stories. To the extent that a story about an angel has seized the imagination, we must find a place for him among the intentional objects that make up the world we inhabit, even if we assign him no more than a place among the fictive objects to which we refer only in a manner of speaking. If we are forced to puzzle about that story we may offer interpretations, moral, psychological or whatnot, but the interpretations cannot displace the angel of the story from his position in our phenomenological empyrean. We must cope with him somehow. Even if we incline to reductive or debunking interpretations, identifying angels with hallucinatory phenomena or pathological symptoms or with the superstitious credulities of our feeble-witted ancestors, still there they dance, big as life, in the story, with however much steadfast pedantry we may insist on saying, "i.e. the hallucination," whenever they turn up.

The Scrooge of Dickens' tale, not easily stampeded into the supernatural refused to believe in the Ghost of Marley even though it had appeared before his eyes. The Ghost asked why he doubted his senses. " 'Because,' said Scrooge, 'a little thing affects them. A slight disorder of the stomach makes them cheats. You may be an undigested bit of beef, a blot of mustard, a crumb of cheese, a fragment of an underdone potato. There's more of gravy than of grave about you, whatever you are!' "[5]

Actually the Ghost offered no very convincing refutation of this plausible argument. Instead, as ghosts will, he cut off Scrooge's interpretation with a hideous cry that brought the old reprobate to his knees. But this dubious tactic cannot divert the attentive reader from the suspicion that the ghost may well be nothing more than a gastronomic indiscretion returned to haunt Scrooge. Though he can so interpret the whole scene, however, he cannot simply replace the ghost with the underdone potato and still be within the frame of the story. Within that frame, at least, the very ghost himself stalks and clanks, regardless of our debunking interpretation.

This consideration, indeed, does not distinguish angels from the whole host of dubious characters that can appear in stories. We must attend more carefully to whatever is special about angels.

2. Wrestling Jacob,[6] Wrestling with What?

It is high time we listened to a story. We choose one that has spawned perhaps three millennia of interpretation, but since it is a genuine story it is as elusive as ever and still speaks directly to the imagination.

Jacob is returning to his native soil after having lived for many years among his mother's kinfolk in another land. He had fled there alone, to escape his brother Esau, whom he had tricked out of both birthright and paternal blessing. Now he returns with a considerable retinue, having prospered in his exile. He is terrified to learn that Esau is coming to meet him accompanied by four hundred men. Prompted as much by his own bad conscience as by the cunning that never deserts him, he sends waves of followers on ahead bearing gifts to propitiate Esau's wrath. Finally, during the night, he sends his family and his immediate entourage and his possessions across the Jabbok River into his native land. He himself remains on the other shore.

> Jacob was left alone. Then some man wrestled with him until the break of dawn. When he saw that he could not prevail over Jacob, he struck his hip at its socket, so that the hip socket was wrenched as they wrestled. Then he said, "Let me go, for it is daybreak." Jacob replied, "I will not let you go unless you bless me." Said the other, "What is your name?" He answered, "Jacob." Said he, "You shall no longer be spoken of as Jacob, but as Israel, for you have striven [śārītā, cf. Isra-el] with beings divine ['elōhīm, cf. Isra-el] and human, and have prevailed." Then Jacob asked, "Please tell me your name." He replied, "You must not ask my name." With that, he bade him good-bye there and then.
>
> Jacob named the site Peniel [the face (pny) of El], meaning, "I have seen God face to face, yet my life has been preserved."

The sun rose upon him just as he passed Penuel, limping on his hip.[7] Jacob goes directly from this harrowing scene to his meeting with Esau: who, contrary to all Jacob's guilty fears, beautifully climaxes the Jacob-Esau strand of the saga by embracing his long-lost brother and kissing him!

The scene on the bank of the Jabbok is in fact the turning point in the saga of Jacob/Israel. It not only furnishes a climax in the plot. Something happens there, embedded in the details of a story told with deceptive simplicity, that changes the character of the whole saga. It will serve our purpose to offer a few observations about this uncanny episode and its context. No biblical scholar myself, I will draw on some of the biblical scholarship of which I am a grateful spectator, but will leave learned or balanced commentary to those better qualified. It is Jacob's great antagonist who interests us. The whole saga, indeed, is as if electrically charged by his presence in this episode. But if we immediately follow tradition and call him an angel we will not yet know what we are saying. We have chosen this story, in fact, because it does not yet reflect a developed angelology, but lets us see this strange narrative figure emerging from the mists of an elementally primitive and powerful story.

I will introduce some possibly relevant concepts in the course of offering my observations.

A NEST OF STORIES: We notice first of all that our story makes up an episode in a larger story, the Jacob/Israel saga, which is itself only a story within a story within—like a nest of boxes. Scholarship has made us aware of the diverse origins of the stories that make up the opening books of the Bible, but even without the aid of scholarship a reader is aware of the tensions that give these books a certain density and roughness of texture. These stories have not been homogenized into a smooth-running narrative told from a single point of view, but they are not simply a linear procession of independent stories either. The story of wrestling Jacob nests in the larger narrative units, its significance affected by them but also projecting its strange accents into those in which it nests. For there is, so to speak, a release of energy in the particular movement of any story; the way it moves gives that story its peculiar tone. Nesting stories make up a complex and somewhat dissonant harmonic. The Bible is of course not unique in this respect. It is characteristic of many traditional folk epics, which have been built up from diverse sources and shaped in the retelling, that they exhibit this reciprocal flow of energy between the overarching stories and the episodes nesting in them, that still retain an independent resonance. This tension in the way a nest

of stories gets told, as well as the details of the plot and characterization, gives a folk epic its distinctive narrative texture and force.
It also stamps the epic as the cultural product of a particular
people, whose history and complex character is reflected not only
in the story that is told but in the telling.

The story of wrestling Jacob nests in the Jacob/Israel saga,
which in turn nests in the great cycle of stories about the divine
promise to the patriarchs that begins in Genesis 12. These larger
narrative structures provide its preconditions and outcome. Yet
our story is peculiarly climactic, too, for this is the episode in which
Jacob is transformed into Israel! and nothing that precedes quite
prepares us for the manner and atmosphere in which this transformation occurs. Furthermore, the great cycle of stories in Genesis, and indeed the whole Bible, is framed by the story of the
creation of heaven and earth at the sheer fiat of a God who exists
in solitary majesty. But what is loosely called biblical "monotheism" is not so simple or so monolithic as it is sometimes thought
to be. For instance, just what *does* Jacob wrestle with on the bank
of the Jabbok? With the very Creator himself? It would be rash
to say so without qualification;—yet equally rash to deny it outright. For Genesis offers no conceptual definition of the relation
between the Creator who fills the horizon in chapter one and
Jacob's antagonist. Rather, Genesis establishes the relation, in all
its conceptual ambiguity, through a dense nesting of stories.

NARRATIVE METAMORPHOSIS: It is widely suspected that our
story, which belongs to one of the most ancient strata of the
Hebrew Bible, probably derives from a still more ancient tale that
did not originate from within the tradition of biblical religion at
all. The dim *Urgeschichte* that still casts its shadow on our biblical
story may have told of the struggles of a forgotten hero with a
river spirit, the god or demon of a sacred stream. His impatience
to break free of Jacob before dawn may even suggest some sort
of night demon. However that may be, Genesis tells us quite a
different story. The hypothetical *Urgeschichte* seems not to have
disappeared without a trace, but it has been cast into a new mold
and has been nested in a vast new narrative context. For it has
been appropriated by a people that calls itself by the name "Israel"

—identifying itself precisely through this story. The story now prefigures the conferring on this people of a name signifying its role as the bearer of the peculiarly biblical faith, locked in unceasing combat and embrace with its Lord. In this narrative metamorphosis the elements of one story have become material for quite a different story with a climax that requires new structural stresses throughout. But the narrative "material" from which this new story is made is hardly inert. The uncanny nocturnal combat survives, and again the release of energy between this story and its larger narrative context is reciprocal. It imports a strange new tone and motif into the tradition that has appropriated it. The transformation is the more remarkable because it probably occurred, not at the hands of a theological censor determined to suppress an alien theology (and not quite succeeding!), but by the spontaneous artfulness of an oral tradition[8] spanning generations: an oft-old tale shaped in the retelling into a perfect new story emblematic of the community that had shaped it.

NARRATIVE AMBIGUITY: Readers with a low tolerance for theological ambiguity, however, may fret over the apparent carelessness of the storytellers. They will ask, as we already have, just what it was Jacob wrestled with on the bank of the Jabbok. At least the hypothetical river demon has been suppressed. But first the story says it was "some man." Then Jacob, now Israel, is told that he has striven with ʹelōhīm, itself a notoriously ambiguous term. Sometimes the word refers clearly enough to the Creator God, who is indeed called by that name in Genesis 1. But the form of the word is plural, and sometimes it does not bear that obviously singular meaning. The present instance is a case in point. Our translator cautiously reads, "You have striven with beings divine and human."[9] Finally, however, in connection with naming the site of the combat, Jacob declares outright that he has seen God face to face and yet has remained alive. Jacob indeed marvels at his survival, so positively is he now prepared to identify his antagonist with that God whom man cannot see and yet live. But how is one to understand these three quite different references to the great antagonist, who refuses to clear up his identity by divulging his name, and instead confers the new name on Jacob?

As we puzzle over this numinous figure, however, other ambiguities arise. He possesses so much power that Jacob is amazed
he got away with his life, and yet Jacob is able to wrestle him at
least to a standstill. And the blessing he bestows on Jacob with
the new name: Is it a gift or a trophy of combat that Jacob is able
to force from him? Has he merely been testing Jacob? But that is
not implied in the story; the combat has been in earnest. Jacob,
alone in the dark, seems to have been taken by surprise and sav-
agely attacked. This creature of the night may not be a river
demon, but he behaves like one. There does seem something
demonic about the antagonist, benign as he appears in the end.
Either the divine or the demonic can be unspeakable.

But the story is told with a deliberate reticence that leaves such
problems unresolved. They arise only when we puzzle over questions that plainly do not interest our narrator, who wants only to
tell the story without wasting words on anything else. The story is
in fact so complete in itself that we are untroubled by these ambiguities when we simply listen to it and follow the action. The
antagonist is just who he is and does just what he does. He is clearly
a personal agent, "some man," even if he is demonic or divine,
for even a god or a demon must appear on the scene as a person
in order to function as a character in a story. He attacks, he becomes anxious, he hears and responds, he moves the narrative
action. He appears so opaque to us when we ask what he is,
human, demonic, divine, or whatever, precisely because he functions purely as a narrative character. Within the frame of the story
his role is as transparent as it needs to be.

Still, there is no denying that he is a person of an uncommon
sort. We can perhaps bring out what gives this peculiar narrative
character his special aura in the story by contrasting his appearance in it with that of Jacob, who is unambiguously human, however ambiguous he may be in other respects.

NARRATIVE CONTINUITY IN TIME AND SPACE: By the time Jacob
turns up on the bank of the Jabbok we know him tolerably well.
We have been introduced to his forebears, Abraham and Isaac,
and have followed Jacob himself from the moment he was born,
gripping his brother Esau's heel. The adventures of the canny

heel-gripper unfold through his little tricks on Esau, deceiving his dying father in the process, and on through his years with his wily father-in-law Laban, a worthy antagonist in the lists of heel-gripping, whom he also finally gets the better of. Jacob's life is presented in a few episodes, but they are sufficient to establish the sort of narrative continuity that gives our particular story its context as an event in a man's lifetime. It is a continuity in time and space, from Canaan to Haran and thence to the bank of the Jabbok on his way back.

Now the ordeal he undergoes there is admittedly not merely one more chapter in the adventures of the heel-gripper. He enters this story as Jacob (meaning Heel-gripper, according to Gen. 25:26), and goes limping out of it as Isra-el, the wrestler with God and the father of the Lord's people. He emerges with a radically new character and destiny. As the dramatic turning point in the saga of Jacob/Israel, our story is invested by the larger story in which it nests with a weight that is felt in all its details.

Still, the continuity of his career in time and space resumes. Thereafter we will follow the movements of Israel, now suddenly become properly patriarchal, until he is laid to rest by his favorite son in far-off Egypt. By then, indeed, the interest of the saga will have long since shifted to his sons, the fathers of the twelve tribes. But the saga enables us to trace his full itinerary, and we are well aware that any hiatus could be filled by some more stories if they were relevant to the larger concerns of our narrator. For with Jacob and the other characters as well, our storyteller recognizes his obligation to get them from one place, one episode, to another.

But not in the case of the angel.

BREACH OF NARRATIVE CONTINUITY: We may follow tradition and call Jacob's antagonist an angel only insofar as we recognize that in this case "angel" is a term for a narrative ambiguity, difficult to resolve conceptually but functioning perfectly well in the story nevertheless. Angels have already turned up in the saga: When Jacob had set out years before from his native land he had had a dream of angels going up and down a stairway that stretched from earth to heaven (Gen. 18:12); and again there is a cryptic reference to an encounter with angels when he finally departed

from Laban (Gen. 32:2). These angelic visitations not only punc-
tuate important junctures in Jacob's pilgrimage, but seem in
Genesis to foreshadow the supreme turning point in the encounter
on the Jabbok.[10] This narrative link at any rate prepares us for
the demand our story makes on us to perceive this "angel" as an
extraordinary sort of narrative figure.

He appears on the scene suddenly and inexplicably, gives Jacob
the fight of his life, confers a stupefying new destiny on him, and
disappears in the morning mists, without a hint of whence he came
or whither he goes. It would obviously be absurd to ask after either
forebears or children in his case. For the breach of narrative continuity is clearly essential to the role he has to play. This breach
in fact serves the narrative continuity of Jacob's own story, since
the turning point that bestows on his whole people the name and
destiny of wrestlers with God requires the appearance of precisely
the sort of extraordinary character whose existence is not homologous with that of the other characters who move within the space
and time of the narrative. He receives his aura from the fact that
the narrative continuities are out of the question in his case. He
is a full, personal presence in the story, with hammer locks and
portentous words, yet otherwise is not situated within the narrative plane at all.

What sort of character is this, to have turning up in a story?

3. *A Musical Presence*

> *Jeder Engel ist schricklich. Und dennoch, weh mir,*
> *ansing ich euch, fast tödliche Vögel der Seele, wissend*
> *um euch.*
>
> —Rilke[11]

> Astonishment is an exponent of quick translation
> from one existence-world into another. It is the ac-
> companiment of discovery against the grain of antici-
> pation.
>
> —R. R. Niebuhr[12]

In many archaic stories "angelic" appearances are marked by
the same narrative ambiguity we found in the story of wrestling

Jacob. One thinks of the three mysterious visitors who appear at Abraham's tent to announce the birth of Isaac, and who then go go, bearers of doom as well as promise, to rain sulfurous fire on Sodom and Gomorrah: they are first called "three men," but one of them is later revealed to be YHWH himself and the others his companion angels (Gen. 18:1–29). Again, Gideon is led to perform feats far beyond his own powers by one variously identified as the angel of YHWH, as YHWH, and simply as God (Judg. 6:11ff). Whatever he is called in such cases, the action of the story is radically altered by a personal agent, human in form, who is also somehow a manifestation of unutterable power.

This narrative ambiguity was later resolved theologically. The figure who had been indifferently referred to as human or divine was rationalized into an intermediate being of a rather definite kind, neither human nor divine, but an instrument of the divine will that appeared in recognizably human form, so that he could still function in stories. But the narrative ambiguity could not be altogether dissipated so long as the angels did appear in stories, even when these stories were nested in larger narratives reflecting more developed theologies. Only when philosophers and theologians subjected them to entirely abstract analysis, lifted out of their narrative context, could their position in the hierarchy of being be calibrated with much precision. Even then, the narrative form of the sources from which these curious entities were derived continued to adhere to them; they still had to be regarded as personal agents, despite the theoretical difficulties of doing so. But the distinction between Creator and creature, for instance, can be made theoretically clear, and angels unequivocally identified as creatures of the highest order. In a story, however, such discriminations are not so easy to sustain. For strictly within the narrative frame, we are not dealing with the created order as such, theologically defined, but with an order of spatiotemporal reference constituted by the narrative continuities of the action; and when a numinous figure advances the action in a marvelous manner precisely by breaking these narrative continuities, it is not possible to rationalize his status fully and still remain within the frame of the story.

For angels do not have biographies, much less genus and species. They even transcend moral seriousness, at least of the human sort. They are gravity-defying. The moral gravity of the human situation is inherent in that temporality that gives our acts a definite weight in existence. Most narrative characters live as we do, with the consequences of their past and the anxiety of their future. Their very selves are formed in this tension, formed by their action. But angels, subject neither to mortality nor to fate, beyond folly or temptation or misjudgment, do not even have to live with the consequences of their acts. Untainted by historicity, they risk nothing in their marvelous deeds. Human characters live beyond themselves, haunted by memory, bedazzled by imagination, pulled apart by contrary impulses, threatened and lured by possibility: as Sartre says, they are what they are not, and are not what they are. But the angel is just what he is, imperturbable, gravity-defying yet in perfect balance, terrible—*schrecklich!* When Christ's birth is announced, both to his mother and later to the shepherds, the herald angel must first reassure: "Fear not." For the shepherds, who take the occupational hazards of wolves and lions in stride, are "sore afraid" at the appearance of the angel. He himself is without dread or desire, beyond the tension of past and future. He is the inexorable agent of the divine will just in his sheer simplicity, beautiful and terrible in the concentration of his existence.[13] The angel introjects the radically unworldly into "the world," into the narrative space and time of the story, breaking something into it that is not at all immanent in the previous course of events. He astonishes, "against the grain of anticipation"; he uncovers something that dislocates the whole "existence-world" of the story. He evokes terror and joy at such a pitch of intensity that they are indistinguishable. He sings.

Angels are persistently associated with music and song in traditional Jewish and Christian representations of them. The angel musician is a familiar figure in visual arts as well as in stories. There are of course plenty of references to angels that do not contain any explicit musical allusion, but there are enough that do to make one suspect that the association is more than casual. According to the most common and powerful image of the heavenly court, the angels make up a vast choir, singing perpetual praise of God. That is why the heavenly court is not promising material for narrative, unless some intruder can be introduced, as in Dante's *Paradiso* or the Prologue to *Faust*. When, on the other hand, an angel appears in a narrative he in turn seems to import something of the altogether musical-lyric quality of the heavenly court into the story. Not that that can really explain why angels so often appear on the scene singing or playing musical instruments or dancing on the heads of pins. One must account for the fact, after all, that it seems so fitting for angels to express themselves musically in their "normal" sphere of existence in the heavenly court, even when they are not interfering in the affairs of mortals. That perhaps seems fitting because of an inherently musical character that their appearance in stories has, even when there is no explicit reference to music in the story. Many writers and storytellers and pious stonemasons and painters seemed so to sense the musical atmosphere of *all* angelic appearances that they did make it explicit in their works.

For the angel must seize not only the hero but the story itself. His uncanny intrusion in a story seems to require or at least to imply an intrusion at the formal level as well: that a different order of duration, rhythm, tempo, intonation, has converged with the narrative line as a kind of counterpoint to it. Esthetically, something like the squaring of the circle must occur. The narrative form cannot simply be expunged. It continues to make its own demands. The one who appears must be a personal agent, capable of interacting with the other characters and moving the action of the story. It may be necessary for this episode to nest in an otherwise quite realistic narrative. Yet the marvelous manner in which the action of the story is moved or transformed in this episode calls for the temporary convergence of the narrative with a more lyrical form, in which a more rigorously patterned structure of sheer sound and rhythm gain the ascendancy. For the only alternative to narrative, as an esthetic formalization of temporal movement, is the much more transparent formalization of movement in the rhythmical succession of harmonically assembled sounds. There are of course intermediate positions between narrative and pure music; strict verse, for instance, still employs language, but the way its sheer sound is ordered becomes as important as its syntax and signification. So the most obvious ways to square this esthetic circle, immersing the narrative in musical form, are for the angel to break into song or the story to break into lyrical verse or the rhythm of the narrative itself to become more formally transparent. The musical presence of the angel is like the burst of light that is also persistently associated with his appearance, not so much highlighting the more mundane details of the scene as flooding it, dazzling us. The angelic manifestation imports something of both the divine light and the heavenly hymn into the narrative plane. The human characters may be momentarily so inundated by that light and that music that they lose themselves to it, falling silent in their absorption or themselves breaking into song or ecstatic utterance. For music can transcend the limits of personal identity without necessarily expunging it. The character retains the identity that has been established through narrative continuity, and yet can be at one with the angel precisely in his musical presence, moving with the same pulse and following the same intonation. In apocalyptic and in mystical literatures, which often employ a narrative form even though the story moves through fabulous regions, it is not uncommon for a character in the ultimate ecstasies to join fully in the angelic chorus of praise to God.[14] The consummating mystery in the great liturgical drama of the Mass is introduced by the congregation joining voices with angels, dominations, powers, virtues, blessed seraphim in their perpetual song of praise:

> Sanctus, Sanctus Sanctus Dominus Deus Sabaoth.
> Pleni sunt caeli et terra gloria tua.

We can sense the musicality of angelic visitations even in stories that do not express it by any obvious devices. When it is absent our narrator has failed to convince us that we are really dealing with an angel, whether he has employed the obvious musical or poetic devices or not. A storyteller or dramatist must in any case make use of available musical or poetic forms, that have arisen out of the cultural vitalities of particular communities. But the musicality of the angels is pure, it is music absolute, not directly heard by our human ears, but telegraphically transmitted through the available cultural resources, whether musical-poetic or not. For it is the ideal music of the heavenly court, or the music of the spheres, which according to some traditions is made by angel musicians attached to each of the celestial orbs. The presence of the angel imports this pure, unearthly musical duration into the mundane time and space of the narrative action. One is reminded of some nineteenth-century romantic theories of music, according to which all pieces of music played or sung were "pieces" indeed, fragments of the perpetual music enveloping all nature but generally unheard: the musician simply lets it sound for a while through his voice or instrument.[15] When the musical presence of an angel sounds in a story, it, too, is a kind of fragment, but of another sphere of existence that is otherwise unseen and unheard here below. The suddenness of his appearance is lyrical, terrible in its dislocation of the whole existence sphere in which we are situated, and at the same time creating an ecstatic moment in the narrative, its horizon touched by a nontemporal rhythm and a harmony neither organic nor mechanical. In this instant the angel transforms the situation: confers a new name, threatens with a flaming sword, announces the birth of Christ, and his resurrection from the dead.

Indeed, the position of angels is peculiar in the New Testament writings, dominated as they are by the incarnation of Godhead in a human being. His story can be told, because he is like us, and the gospel writers observe the narrator's responsibility to account for the origins of their hero and to get him from one place and one episode to another, establishing the narrative continuity. Christ is no angel. "The Letter to the Hebrews" in fact tirelessly contrasts him to the angels, showing how the new, paradoxical dispensation in Christ far surpasses any that has been brought about by angels. The discursive portions of the New Testament have little to say otherwise about angels, beyond occasional allusions. For in a discursive genre, such as an epistle, it is possible simply to state the paradox: that God himself, in his redeeming grace, should have appeared in a man, "tempted as we are" and mortal. But such a paradox cannot be so baldly expressed in a narrative. The gospel writers express his unequivocal humanity through the normal narrative continuities, but the divine presence is announced by the appearance of angels, who break into the human horizon at decisive points in the story. And of course they sing! It is hard to see how a story with such a theme could unfold without the appearance of these extraordinary narrative figures, who are also prominent in the continuation of the story in Acts. The nesting of these episodes in the gospel and in its sequels in the New Testament and beyond concretely expresses the divine intervention and lends a pervasive quality of the marvelous even to the mundane details of the Christian story. Only with what Hans Frei has called "the eclipse of biblical narrative"[16] in the Christian theology and the Christian imagination has the music seemed to stop. To the extent that it has, no amount of theological bombast can compensate for the loss.

For just because the angel is not subject to the narrative continuities, his musical presence introduces new beginnings and open possibilities into the narrative. Everything is changed, and both the characters in the story and the hearers who are drawn into it are released from themselves. The past no longer imposes its necessity, the future is no longer in the grip of death. The tension of consciousness between memory and anticipation is sustained, but the present in which this tension is contained has a certain elasticity. At the appearance of the angel a story becomes musically fluid, transforming it from beginning to end.

Such a highly charged story can draw a hearer into it in such a way that precisely in its musically liberated possibility he must acknowledge it as his own story. Just to that extent he may be said to believe in angels.

4. *An Unmusical Theory*

As we noted at the outest, however, angels seem not often to come within earshot any more. The leaner sort of believers, for instance, have quietly dropped the angels long ago from their inventories of things that still command sober assent. If it is the case that angels are seldom heard among serious people nowadays, it behooves us to offer an explanation, congruent with the foregoing analysis, of this apparent silence from on high. A plausible explanation in fact lies ready at hand. It is a fine explanation, actually, since it explains not only the apparent disappearance of angels but their appearance as well. That is, it is the sort of explanation that replaces what it purports to explain, and like other such explanations it is easily stated. We can be brief about it, since anyone who grasps the gist of it can readily fill in the details, and even begin to quibble about them. We choose not to quibble, since it is simply an historical explanation anyway, plausible so far as it goes, but all too human and not in the least angelic.

So let us say that the rise and fall of Western angelology represents the persistence and subsequent suppression of polytheistic vestiges in monotheistic religions. The angels, that is, represent the surfacing of more ancient, pluralistic patterns of religious imagination in the cultic life of Judaism, Christianity, and Islam, those latecomers on the religious scene with their peculiar fixation on the number one. As such, the development of angelology was no isolated phenomenon. We are well acquainted with the resilience of archaic polytheistic and even animistic forms of religious life despite their apparent suppression. Already in the early biblical period, the prophets give rueful testimony to the stubborn persistence of old Canaanite cultus even among folk who considered themselves faithful children of Israel. This largely concealed tension, which occasionally broke into open conflict within biblical religion, was repeated on a grander historical scale with the ascendancy of Christianity in the Hellenistic-Roman world, and later in northern Europe. The Christians zealously suppressed one form after another of old European paganism, but always unwittingly assimilated a good deal of what they had suppressed.[17] They may have intended to be intransigent, but they proved in fact to be so hospitable that by the High Middle Ages Catholicism was a splendid rainbow composed of the most diverse religious colorations. Even the theologians largely yielded to the charms of a popular religion shot through with survivals of the old cults, generations of learned men devoting their considerable ingenuity to rationalizing popular beliefs and reconciling them to the received tradition. Thus the veneration of the Virgin introduced a refreshingly feminine hue into the stark patriarchal colors of biblical imagery, wonders were performed with sacred relics, and the saints came to receive appeals for help in the practical affairs of life as had the old gods—this one granting safe journey, that one a successful harvest, and so forth.

It seems likely that the angels, too, were in some sense precisely the old gods, spirits, numina carrying on under new auspices, assimilated along with their devotees over a period of three millennia from ancient Babylonia to the last northern outposts of paganism, provided they were prepared to make an orthodox profession of fealty to the high God of the biblical tradition. We browse through the topic headings of Davidson's *Dictionary of Angels:* "The Angel Rulers of the Seven Heavens," "The Angelic Governors of the Twelve Signs of the Zodiac," "The Angels of the Hours of Day and Night," "The Seventy Amulet Angels Invoked at the Time of Childbirth," "The Archangels of Punishment," and so on and on.[18] Is the cat not out of the bag?

But there has been no conspiracy to subvert pure Judeo-Christian monotheism from within. What has occurred is a very complex historical development that has analogies in non-Western traditions as well. I do not pretend to understand its dynamics in detail, but I suspect we may be put on the right track if we bear two considerations in mind: In the first place, "monotheism" as such is an invention of scholars. It is an instrument of analysis and categorization which implies an opposite called "polytheism." These categories have their uses, but the rigid distinctions projected by them do some violence to the dynamics of actual religious praxis and its first-order language. It is important not to confuse the second- or third-order language of "monotheism," "polytheism," "pantheism," etc. with the direct expression of belief and praxis. Christians, for instance, have never believed in "monotheism" as such, at least not until recently. They have certainly not believed in a pantheon of different gods either, but the God in whom they have believed is not the absolute monad that has figured in some of the philosophical and even theological transcriptions of that faith. For nothing so abstract as the absolute monad can figure in the concrete imagery and first-order language of immediate experience and praxis. It cannot, for example, appear in stories or be expressed in narrative language. In that sense it is true that the God of the philosophers, particularly the more monistic philosophers, is not the God of Abraham, Isaac, and Jacob.

Indeed, the notion of "narrative ambiguity" that arose in connection with Jacob's harrowing antagonist may also be useful in this connection. When a sacred personage figures in such a story, the very clarity of his narrative function makes it difficult to name or otherwise classify him. This narrative ambiguity is a feature not only of traditional stories, but of the storylike quality of experience and praxis as well. Whenever the sacred powers are rendered in such a neat, hierarchical fashion that they can be unambiguously discriminated, this triumph of theological clarity is won by achieving a certain conceptual distance from the forms and locutions of its narrative sources. When, on the other hand, a numenous character appears in a story, inquiry about either his status in the chain of being or his genealogy in the history of religions seems distinctly beside the point. Nor are people ever so clear about what they are praying to as theological purists would like them to be. One has other things on one's mind. I think this narrative ambiguity helps account for the fact that supposed "monotheists" have proven so hospitable toward powers of uncertain origin. No doubt it has been the source of many heresies, but it seems inseparable from the historical dynamics of a living religious praxis.

Another of the concepts that arose in considering the "angel" of Jacob's ordeal may be useful in introducing the second consideration we want to put forward regarding the development of angelology generally: For I suspect that something very like our notion of "narrative metamorphosis" defines the process by which the pagan gods and spirits are transformed into more or less orthodox angels. An old story, or a type or a fragment of an old story, comes to nest in a different cycle of stories, subtly altering its own tone and some of its details but also importing a new strain into the harmonics of the cycle as a whole. People who experience their own lives as continuations of the sacred cycle or as plot structures typified in it will find these changes in the structural tensions of the narrative registering in the forms of their own experience as well. Sacred stories and their mundane recitations are the preconditions of experience to the extent that we move to their rhythms and they enter our dreams and ruminations, called to mind without our bidding, sometimes jarred into mind at unlikely moments by dramatically similar episodes in the broad daylight of our waking lives. But these very stories can be transformed in the

White Goat, White Rose... [margin annotation]

retelling to conform to a new configuration of the imagination. Sometimes, to be sure, the old stories are forgotten or suppressed, but the new stories that engage the imagination will turn up some startlingly similar patterns and episodes nesting in them. Something extraordinary may occur, in terror and wonder, and yet will wear a face that for all its uncanny strangeness is oddly familiar.

Reorientations of the religious imagination occur very slowly. For they are not the result of deliberate religious decision. They form its preconditions. Conscious conversion may in some cases be instantaneous. But when we consider what people immediately recognize as sacred and the ways they situate themselves toward it, or the kinds of stories they tell and the cultic patterns they find satisfying, or the tension points of their expectations and the music to which they modulate their voices and move their feet: changes at these levels occur, so to speak, in the bedrock of the religious life and at an almost geological pace, erupting on the surface only when the subterranean conditions have slowly moved into place. To speak of angels displacing the more archaic numina through the dynamics of narrative metamorphosis does not imply that they are mere fabrications of storytellers, much less pagan infiltrations into biblical faith. We do not simply make up the stories we tell, nor those we enact, and biblical faith itself was not decreed by theological censors. Rather, the tradition was simply alive, in its depths as well as on its historical surface.

So much for our plausible theory about the way angels came to be heard by orthodox ears. Of their apparent silencing we can be still more brief, since it is a process we hyperliterate moderns understand very well and only need to have called to mind. For it is more or less replicated in our own education.

Having entered our conscious horizon through the medium of a musically pulsed narrative, the angels and their like fade from that horizon when the religious consciousness turns away from its musical and narrative sources. That turning had perhaps already begun, at least among a theological elite, with the doctrinal rationalization of angelology. But even when speculative reason came to serve a type of spirituality that sought ultimate wholeness in an unmoving, closed archetype, it did not necessarily lose touch with the luxuriance of the religious imagination.[19] Only the most fastidious attempted to suppress visual, musical, and narrative images altogether; the iconoclast smashes the image in order to worship the most abstract thought he can conceive. But speculative reason was not always iconoclastic, nor did it generally prove so insensitive to formal distinctions among modes of language as altogether to impose its own purely conceptual order on the narrative structures native to angelic visitation. For all their differences over angelology as well as other matters, both a Bonaventura and a Thomas Aquinas in the High Middle Ages clearly still heard the music and remembered the story. So did Luther, almost three centuries later.

But to the extent that the narrative imagination is supplanted in a religious tradition, angelology necessarily loses its vitality. That did occur increasingly in later developments within the main streams of Protestantism, particularly within its theological elite, and to some extent in parallel developments within other Western traditions as well. One wished to express Christian belief in doctrinal propositions; moral teaching became of central importance, with biblical stories invoked for illustrative purposes only; along with this didactic use of biblical narrative there arose a literalism determined to prove by hook or by crook its historical accuracy; theological apologetics sought to appropriate current philosophical or scientific thinking to its own uses. Again, a rationality of an abstract sort, alien to the traditional religious imagination, combined with a characteristic spirituality which sought a purified fulfillment in the sober adoration of the high God alone. Recognizing that the medieval Church was pagan to the ears, but without recognizing in this fact the exigencies of a living tradition, Protestant iconoclasm set out to purge its own house of everything that moved. Angels became little more than Christmas decorations, their gradual flickering out accompanied by the outright banishment of the cult of the saints and of the Virgin, indeed the conscious or unconscious renunciation of any transcending figures that are concrete enough to appear in stories. The Protestant mind was no longer, in David Miller's sense of the term, "peopled."[20] Its horizon was not so much demythologized as depopulated and disenchanted. Never before had a large body of Christians broken so radically with archaic religious forms: the dimming out of angels was the real *Götterdämmerung*.

Of course this epochal development did not occur everywhere or all at once. Where storytelling remained a primary religious medium, and retained its musical vitality, the angels have proven irrepressible. One thinks, for instance, of popular Catholicism, or of the astonishing musical appropriation of Bible stories among Black slaves in America: when stories sing, angels appear. Storytelling also retains its hypnotic power in some Jewish circles; angelic figures turn up by a kind of necessity internal to the stories even of some contemporary Jewish writers. For that matter, the great tradition of Protestant church music from the sixteenth through the eighteenth centuries continued quite unselfconsciously to celebrate angelic visitation in hymns, anthems, and cantatas that powerfully rendered the traditional stories. But by the middle of the nineteenth century the music had stopped for established Protestantism, in more ways than one.[21]

In fact, it is only a slight exaggeration to say that in the more liberal, "secularized" wings of Protestantism, and of other Western traditions as well, the first-order language of religious belief and practice has been largely replaced by the second-order language of analysis and interpretations. That is, abstract language has been forced into service as if it could function directly in the living out of religious devotion. Things have come to such a pass that *monotheism* has actually seemed to become an appropriate term for the worship of the high God. Liberal Protestantism has largely relegated even trinitarian language to the theological dust bin. As for angels, even their decorative or purely metaphorical use is an embarrassment. When anything as tiresome and vacuous as "monotheism" is all that is left of the encounter with transcendence, the death of God seems not only inevitable but an act of mercy for all parties involved. *Monotheism* is already the name for a dead archetype.

Well, that is my plausible little theory about the rise and fall of angelology. No doubt it is overgeneralized, lacks sufficient evidence, and needs correction in detail, but these are corrigible defects, for which I freely invite those more learned than myself to supply the needed remedies. To my own mind, what it chiefly leaves out of account are the angels themselves. Like many another exercise in *Geistesgeschichte,* it replaces what it purports to explain, by treating it simply as an episode in the history of human consciousness. But that is to say that our historical theory is itself a symptom of the bleak historical moment with which it concludes, in which the life of experience has been alienated from its sacred possibilities. It is a self-referential theory. That is its strength as a theory, for it is a poor sort of theory that cannot account for itself, at least. But that is also its flaw as an explanation of angels, for it has precisely as little to do with the musical presence of an angel as "monotheism" does with the sublimity of the high God. Indeed, like monotheism, polytheism, pantheism and such, our theory may be revealing nevertheless, but primarily as a mirror of our own minds.

5. *The Austerity of Angels*

> I am one of you and being one of you
> Is being and knowing what I am and know.
>
> Yet I am the necessary angel of earth,
> Since, in my sight, you see the earth again,
>
> Cleared of its stiff and stubborn, man-locked set,
> And, in my hearing, you hear its tragic drone
>
> Rise liquidly in liquid lingerings,
> Like watery words awash; like meanings said
>
> By repetitions of half-meanings.
> —Wallace Stevens[22]

It may seem that we could remedy the all-too-human tendency of theory simply to mirror the mind of the theorist by addressing ourselves directly to the reality of things, asking, for instance, what angels really are, whether any such thing exists or not, and so on. But the very illusion that we can comprehend what is real by abstracting from the most concrete forms of our experience has the ironical result of turning theory in on itself and rendering its all-too-human egocentrism inescapable. For the esthetic forms

Symbol gives rise to thought...

of experience are not obstractions standing between the conscious ego and reality, to be by-passed or beaten down. They are precisely our openings into the flow that encompasses us, the medium, fluid but not amorphous, through which consciousness is carried into that flow. Cassirer says that "the special symbolic forms are not imitations, but *organs* of reality, since it is solely by their agency that anything real becomes an object for intellectual apprehension, and as such is made visible to us."[23] Not only are they the organs through which the real becomes visible to us, however; they are also conduits through which consciousness must pass in order to be in the midst of what is actually happening. The esthetic forms of experience take shape in experience itself. Consciousness awakens through them, and finds itself in a situation in which it is already actively participating.

That is nowhere clearer than in the case of narrative, considered as a primary form of experiencing. We awaken to ourselves as persons in a storylike situation, already involved for all we are worth with the other *personae* in our incipient drama. They become "visible to us" as persons precisely to the extent that our transactions with them begin to take on a narrative shape. But we also come to self-awareness insofar as our role in the story gets clarified in relation to them. Yet neither we nor they can simply make up or impose a plot on the story. The plot unfolds, partly, to be sure, of our own doing, but it is something we must struggle to comprehend, and indeed sometimes comically misperceive. For precisely as persons, mysterious and whole, who materialize in the story, each of us has an existential density that keeps him from being entirely transparent to the others or entirely malleable at their hands. He cannot be reduced to a character in a story someone else has made up. The rest of us must contend with him; the story is ours only insofar as it is also his. Even in a work of narrative art, the storyteller must respect this density in his characters, that makes the story theirs as well as his. The story makes its own demand to be told.

Now Jacob contended with beings divine and human, and prevailed. That is his story, and through its action he was transformed though he had not planned it that way. The story took a surprising turn. For the beings with whom he contended had density of their own, and put up a flight; Esau even forgave him, to everyone's amazement. The story was not only his. It is his because it is theirs as well, and therefore also ours, who hear and retell it. For all his density as a character in the story, we know who Jacob is at least to the extent of knowing his name. The change in his name, in fact, signals the transformation he underwent. But one character in the story, the name-giver, was himself unnamable. When we chose to call him an angel, we remarked that we did not know exactly what we were saying. "Angel" was the name we chose to signify a narrative ambiguity, for clear as his function was in the story, his peculiar density was such as to make him opaque and uncanny, to Jacob and to us.

We still do not know what we say when we speak of angels, apart from the stories in which they have been heard. For angels are essentially narrative figures. This is not to deny that anyone ever had experience of angels, but the experience, too, will have occurred within a narrative frame, radically altering the plot the person may have thought he was living out. A musical presence enters the story and breaks open its narrative continuity in space and time. Such a story defies reduction. It cannot be dissolved conceptually into a general theory of human behavior or religiously into a closed, motionless archetype. Least of all can it be reduced to the two dimensions of a spatiotemporal plane. Yet the angel appears in a story that is our own. He is a figure of our freedom, he registers the possibility of our self-transcendence, just because of his austerity, that does not permit us to deal dishonestly with him as if he were of our own making. Angels nest in the stories we tell and the stories we enact, but they fly, birds of the soul, to and from this nest. We hear them only in the stories, and if there is a sense in which such extraordinary stories may be called archetypal, the person who situates himself through such an archetype finds that it is full of movement and open toward transcendence. The austerity that does not permit us to name the angels fits them to bestow new names on us. That is why they are so terrible and so liberating.

The being and knowing of Stevens's angel are what he is and knows as one of us. Yet Stevens calls him "the angel of reality," "the necessary angel of earth" who delivers our seeing from its

"man-locked set" and our hearing from "it's tragic drone." He
delivers us over to our necessary reality by delivering us up from
the tyranny of our own thoughts and our all-too-human expectations. But in his musical evanescence he eludes our grasp.

                                        Am I not,
        Myself,
he asks,[24]
                only half of a figure of a sort,

        A figure half seen, or seen for a moment, a man
        Of the mind, an apparition apparelled in

        Apparels of such lightest look that a turn
        Of my shoulder and quickly, too quickly, I am gone?

NOTES

1. Barth, to be sure, did discuss angels, and brilliantly, in *Kirchliche
   Dogmatik,* III-3, but space has seldom been found for them in
   recent Protestant theological works that run to less than twelve
   volumes.
2. It is questionable whether the name of the great Jewish storyteller
   should be introduced in this manner, since I am not sure whether
   he would agree with a word I am going to say. On the other hand
   I would be ungrateful if I did not acknowledge my debt to him. My
   dilemma arose in this way: On February 23, 1971, Isaac Singer
   presented a reading from his works and some autobiographical
   reflections before an audience at Wesleyan University. A long-time
   admirer of his stories, I was not only present but was so enchanted
   that being present to the reading made me almost absent from
   myself. It was therefore jarring to have my professorial instincts
   revived and irritated by what struck me as a singularly obtuse question addressed to Singer by a student during the discussion period.
   But the worst questions are sometimes unwittingly so basic that
   they bring out the best answers, and that is how it fell out in this
   case. The question: did Singer really *believe* in the imps, angels,
   demons, and whatnot that populate so many of his stories? Singer's
   reply was gentle, extended, and magnificent, so memorable, indeed,
   that I believe I might have retained it almost verbatim were it not
   for the fact that his remarks set my own thoughts churning vigor-
   ously on a line of reflection that has continued intermittently from

that day to this. The present essay is in good part the result of these reflections. Meanwhile, however, I have lost any clear sense of where Singer's thoughts leave off and mine begin, and so cannot trust my memory of what he said on that occasion. Hence my dilemma, which I have resolved by following the example of Kierkegaard, who entitled a chapter of *Concluding Unscientific Postscript,* "Attributable to Lessing." In a similarly equivocal way, I should for my part be happy to have my reflections, particularly in this section, be "attributable" to Singer, though for his sake I do not want actually to attribute anything to what follows to him, since I am utterly unsure what the great storyteller might think of these speculations of an incorrigible theorist who has no narrative gift at all.

3. Typically, of course, artists, literators, and thinkers move at different times over a considerable span of this continuum; the critic may even try his hand at writing stories and poems, the poet at philosophizing (not often with impressive results in either case, to be sure), but to do so each must adopt a different use of language or a different way of situating himself in language. The differentiation in language, reflecting different levels of immediacy and abstractness in relation to experience, will remain in place.

The failure to observe this formal incommensurability among different kinds of language has also led to a good many futile religious debates. One thinks, for instance, of the dreary history of that egregious category mistake that was committed when the theory of evolution was pitted against the story contained in the opening chapters of Genesis. It was not even a case of comparing apples and oranges; it was more like arguing whether an apple doesn't make a poor sort of bullfight.

4. Cf. "The Narrative Quality of Experience," *Journal of the American Academy of Religion* 39, no. 3 (September, 1971): 291–311; of which the present essay is in many ways a sequel.

I do not mean to imply that this convergence of art and experience occurs in narrative form alone. I am in general inclined to think that enduring esthetic forms and genre have their correlates and indeed their psychic sources in our most basic forms of experience. I do not share a popular assumption that they are arbitrary historical products that artists have happened to stumble upon. Experience itself is mediated and conditioned at the root by esthetic forms that lend it whatever coherence it has. There is no experience so immediate that it can occur apart from *some* of those esthetic forms that are also employed (with much more formal purity and sophistication, to be sure) in the religious and cultural expressions of traditional societies and ultimately in high art. The aural dimension of experience, for instance, takes on rhythms and tonalities that also get expressed in music, which in turn, within a particular cultural context, will then shape the way people hear the ordinary sounds of daily life. The visual dimension will have the sort of spatial organization and color harmonic that also gets expressed in drawing and painting, which again will affect the way people see within a particular culture. Here, however, we are concerned with narrative form, which I have argued is implicit in the temporal tensions of memory and anticipation, in at least an incipient way. Narrative genre of course have a history, like those of the other arts; new genre may arise and old ones may differentiate themselves. If my general view is correct, this historicity of the arts implies that the forms or mediating conditions of experience will also differ in some respects in different times and places. Yet it would be an exaggeration to say that, for instance, our own characteristic ways of experiencing have nothing in common with those of other people in remote times and places. Some esthetic forms are so necessary for any possible experience that experience is no more conceivable without them than it would be if we were bereft of all our sense organs. It is true that we never encounter "narrative" in general, apart from the narrative genre current in a particular time and place, and for many purposes it may make a great deal of difference what sorts of narrative we are talking about. But it does not follow that it is always vacuous to speak simply of "narrative," since all the narrative genre have some formal features in common, apart from which neither stories nor experience would be possible.

5. *A Christmas Carol,* stave one.

6. "Wrestling Jacob" is the title of a fine hymn by Charles Wesley, long one of his most celebrated but now, to the reproach of modern Protestantism, no longer sung.

7. *Genesis* 32:25–32, in the translation by E. A. Speiser in *The Anchor Bible,* vol. I (Garden City: Doubleday & Co., Inc., 1964), pp. 253–54. I have inserted etymological material from Speiser's footnotes into the text in brackets. See Speiser's excellent notes and comments on the story.

8. In addition, of course, the text itself has probably been pieced together out of diverse documentary traditions, according to most biblical scholarship since Wellhausen. Our story is commonly attributed to the hypothetical "J" document, but was already adapted by "J" from still more ancient oral and perhaps written traditions.

9. Some modern translations, e.g. the RSV and the NEB, follow the King James version, which reads, "with God and with men." But Speiser insists, "Not specifically 'God'" and refers us to the allusion in Hosea 12:4–5 (*op. cit.,* p. 255).

10. Following Speiser's suggestion, *op. cit.,* p. 256. We also sense, how-

ever, that these two earlier episodes do not have the same literary provenance as our story. According to the documentary hypothesis they are both attributed to "E," who among other things is fond of appearances in dreams.

11. Rainer Maria Rilke, *Duino Elegies,* opening of the Second Elegy. It may be be translated roughly, with the poetry left out, as follows:

Every angel is terrible. And yet, woe is me, I sing to you, near fatal birds of the soul, though I know about you.

The recurring appearance of the angel in Rilke's *Elegies* is a rare instance in modern literature in which angels have something of their primitive energy and terror.

12. Richard R. Niebuhr, *Experiential Religion* (Harper & Row, 1972), p. 101.

13. To see the curious theoretical implications of the angelic mode of existence, for instance of the fact that angels are neither temporally nor corporeally situated, one can do no better than turn to Thomas Aquinas, *Summa Theologiae,* especially part one, questions 50–64. Since it is matter, for example, that differentiates among different individual members of a species and is also the condition for the change from potentiality to actuality (such that a human being must be a child before he can become an adult), each angel is not only a species in himself, but exists always in a full state of development (question 50, article 4). Angels, furthermore, are neither temporal nor strictly eternal; only God is *tota simul,* the immutable whole of all perfection, both in his being and in his knowledge. The conditioned fullness of angelic being, which simply is all that it can be in the order of nature, is neither that of time nor eternity, but of the *aevum,* a kind of created changelessness that is capable of direct commerce with changeable things (q. 10, art. 5; cf. q. 53, art. 3). The discovery of the *aevum* is surely one of the more brilliant strokes of scholastic ingenuity.

Hardly less ingenious is Frank Kermode's revival of the notion of *aevum* to denote the peculiar duration of a work of fictional art (*The Sense of an Ending* [Oxford: 1966], pp. 70ff). It would seem to follow that all fictional characters are in this respect like angels. They do not share in the temporality of actual human experience, but they appear to do so, an illusion created by narrative art. Now I do not think that narrative is such an altogether artificial construct as Kermode does, with his special accent on its essentially "fictive" character; and so I am more inclined to regard the succession of events in narrative as homologous with the temporality of experience. In neither case, indeed, is there a simple successiveness, since every event transpires in the tension of memory and anticipation, both in stories and in experience. Yet an

artful story does unfold quite independently of the time that elapses
in its telling, and its pace, the rhythms of language in which it
is told, the succession of its changing scenes, etc., do create an
ideal order of movement that is esthetically detached from the
temporality of experience. In that sense Kermode is surely right:
there is a need for a third sort of duration, neither temporal nor
eternal, to denote the ideal order of narrative movement, and the
aevum fills the bill nicely in a number of respects.

This way of employing the *aevum,* furthermore, particularly
serves our present purpose by suggesting another sense in which an
angel is an intrinsically narrative figure: even in his appearance
among us he moves still in the esthetic *aevum* of narrative form.
But I am going to suggest that the angel imports into narrative still
another sort of esthetic duration, for which the notion of *aevum*
might on better grounds be reserved: the much more rigidly structured durations of music, in which movement inheres so fully in a
changeless order that every ephemeral instant implies the whole
structure that contains it.

14. In *The Apocalypse of Abraham,* for instance, composed late in the
first or early in the second century A.D., Abraham joins in the
angelic song of praise upon entering the heavenly court; otherwise
known only to the angels, the song has been taught to Abraham
as one of the blessed by his angel guide. The text of the song appears in chapter 17. (*See* the translation by G. H. Box and J. I.
Landsman [London: SPCK; New York: MacMillan, 1919]). This
is one of many examples of such esoteric songs of angelic praise in
Jewish apocalyptic and mystical writings (e.g. cf. *II Enoch* 17–19)
furnished me by my colleague, Professor Jeremy Zwelling, who
also called my attention to Gershom Scholem's *Jewish Gnosticism,
Merkabah Mysticism, and the Talmudic Tradition* (New York:
Jewish Theological Seminary, 1960), which cites many angelic
hymns and discusses their uses in magical practices and in the
mystical ascent to the presence of God. Angelic song, "like the
sound of many waters" etc., also permeates early Christian apocalyptic writings, such as The Book of Revelation, the vivid imagery
of which is as musical as it is visual.

15. Some romantic composers, such as Schumann, produced "pieces"
without obvious beginnings or endings in order to suggest this sense
that they are fragments of an encompassing musical whole.

16. Hans W. Frei, *The Eclipse of Biblical Narrative: A Study in Eighteenth and Nineteenth Century Hermeneutics* (New Haven: Yale
University Press, 1974). Frei's splendid study traces in detail the
gradual "sea change" that occurred in the way the Bible was read,
in at least the intellectually elite circles of Protestant countries. The
religious imagination turned away from its narrative sources, a

turning that gave rise to the peculiar hermeneutical dilemmas of the past century and a half.

17. From its early days, for instance, the Church followed a fairly consistent policy of celebrating its own festivals and saint's days on the dates of old pagan festivals, thus endeavoring to expunge the latter from popular consciousness and at the same time to bring the festal celebrations into the Christian order of things. But such a strategy of assimilation generally turns out to be more reciprocal than the assimilator intends. The ironical consequence was that many of the old pagan practices were preserved in Christian amber for centuries after the old religions had died out as such. To this day, for instance, St. Valentine's Day has much more to do with the Roman festival for young lovers called Lupercalia than with the veneration of the third century martyr named Valentine that was supposed to supplant it: and Christian children celebrate Easter morn by gathering colorful baskets of old Germanic fertility symbols left by a totem animal of notorious fecundity. Indeed, the two great Christian festivals, Christmas and Easter, are veritable archeological deposits of pre-Christian symbols and practices.

18. Gustav Davidson, *A Dictionary of Angels: Including the Fallen Angels* (New York: The Free Press; and London: Collier-Macmillan Ltd., 1967), an entertaining and richly illustrated coffee-table volume.

19. There is admittedly something artificial about the hierarchial ordering of angels that developed in late antiquity, particularly in speculative religious systems of neo-Platonic cast, in which the ranks of angels constituted the order of ideal forms that mediated between the pure One and the "many" objects of the material world. Medieval angelology, particularly among contemplative writers, was enormously influenced by such a sheme spun by a fifth century Christian neo-Platonist who wrote under the name of Dionysius the Areopagite. In his works, *The Mystical Theology, The Celestial Hierarchies,* and *The Divine Names,* the hierarchy of angels figured in a total spiritual cosmology, with each rank of angels so positioned as to be able to aid the soul in its ascent through progressive stages to ultimate unity with superessential Godhead. Certainly the names assigned these ranks of angels were only arbitrarily related to any stories or scriptural references in which they may have figured. Still, particularly at the hands of his medieval commentators, the positioning of angels at each stage in the mystical ascent did serve to give the scheme something of a narrative structure, the spiritual order taking on the aspect of a narrative space through which the soul passed, encountering adventures with angelic guides and examiners at every stage in its pilgrimage.

20. In *The New Polytheism: Rebirth of the Gods and Goddesses* (New York: Harper & Row, 1974), p. 33, Miller calls on us to "remythologize" our thinking, "repeople it with Gods and Goddesses." While I do not agree with Miller that a revival of polytheism is the order of the day, I do want to acknowledge my debt to the analysis that underlies this startling suggestion. What is refreshing is the direct way in which Miller deals with the intentional objects of the religious imagination, attending to the esthetic forms in which they appear, without letting them become enmeshed in anthropological, psychological, or other reductive conceptual schemes. Indeed, he does a kind of switch on the psychological reduction: Though the life of the psyche is clearly his central concern, he approaches it "theologically," in a special sense of the term that his beloved Greek writers might have approved. While I cannot claim to be a theo-logian in quite that sense, the present essay has led me into some of the same hazardous regions of inquiry that I recognize in Miller's book.

21. For at the same time the angels faded from Protestant view, the great stream of Protestant hymnody stagnated into sentimentality, moralism, and bombastic triumphalism. Except for the spirituals and folk songs, there is hardly a Protestant hymn written between 1820 and 1920 that can be sung without the brain turning to mush. After that the stream mercifully dried up, except for some surprisingly good modern hymns that are seldom sung. I do not at all mean to imply any sort of casual relation between angelology and church music, but I do think they are esthetically conjoined.

22. An excerpt from "Angel Surrounded by Paysans." The whole poem has been reprinted in *Poems by Wallace Stevens, Selected, and with an Introduction,* by Samuel French Morse (New York: Vintage Books, 1959), p. 153.

23. Ernst Cassirer, *Language and Myth,* trans. Susanne K. Langer (New York: Harper & Brothers, 1946), p. 8. Cf. p. 28, for some parallel remarks on the constitutive role of language in presenting theory with its objects: "Before the intellectual work of conceiving and understanding of phenomena can set in, the work of *naming* must have preceded it, and have reached a certain point of elaboration. For it is this process which transforms the world of sense impression, which animals also possess, into a mental world, a world of ideas and meanings. All theoretical cognition takes its departure from a world already preformed by language; the scientist, the historian, even the philosopher, lives with his objects only as language presents them to him." Again, my only quarrel with this supremely important observation concerns the rigidity of the subject/object model of experience which is presupposed in the way the matter is stated. Like Kant, his great

master, Cassirer thinks of the world of objects as being constituted as such by the activity of a self-enclosed subject that gives its own form to the inchoate flow of sense impressions. But I should wish to argue that the esthetic (or symbolic) forms are themselves constituted by the free interplay between the imaginative consciousness and a world in which it is already situated.

24. In the conclusion of Stevens's "Angel Surrounded by Paysans."

III

American Literature and the Imagination of Otherness

GILES B. GUNN

IN THE TITLE of an essay published several years ago called "America the Unimagining," Benjamin DeMott, one of our best cultural critics, drew attention to a problem which none of us can afford to take lightly. Noting the frequent public utterance of such slogans as "do your own thing" or "find your own bag" and the increased prestige, especially among the young, of the contrary tendency to seek engulfment by and complete mergence in the communal en-masse, DeMott claimed that Americans today suffer from a distinctive, though by no means exclusively American, form of myopia. Our national commitment to the ideal of personal self-fulfillment, together with our equally strong counterdesire to achieve an ego-transcending oneness of identity with other people, are two sides of the same coin, he argued. Both represent a rejection of the idea that the realization of humanness, whether for oneself alone or for an entire group, "depends," as he put it, "upon my capacity and my desire to make real to myself the inward life, the subjective reality, of the lives that are lived beyond me."[1] Instead, we either prate rhetoric about the sanctity of the individual, or feed ourselves on fantasies of an undifferentiated sameness of feeling and response with other people, while remaining indifferent to or uncomprehending of modes of selfhood which take an expression other than our own. The problem is largely attributable to "obliviousness," he contended, "habitual refusal to harry private imaginations into constructing the innerness of other lives."[2]

In pointing to this failure of imagination, DeMott was hardly

65

citing anything new. More than half a century earlier William James had isolated the same problem in his essay entitled "On a Certain Blindness in Human Beings," when he noted our marked indifference to forms of existence other than our own, our habitual and pervasive intolerance of what is alien, in short, our characteristic inability through an act of the imagination to get outside of our own skins, to put ourselves in the place of others, to understand that the only hope of escaping from the prison of self-regarding egotism, without falling directly into the tranquilizing embrace of mobocracy is by learning how to imagine, acknowledge, and value what is distinctively individual and other.

These modern jeremiads might prove less disconcerting if they were not confirmed by so much social and political fact. Unfortunately, the evidence of our imaginative enervation and myopia is everywhere. Think only of the massive injustices which have been suffered by black people in this country, or the uncountable and unknown outrages we have committed against the American Indian, to say nothing of the discrimination we practice daily against everybody from women to homosexuals to Mexican-Americans. Sociologists and historians are currently fond of employing an economic argument to explain these related phenomena, insisting that they are motivated largely by greed and the concomitant desire for political and social advantage; but surely the reasons run deeper. If our inhumanity to minorities of all kinds in America is not to be dismissed as simply another example of our bondage to the primal curse, to something inherently perfidious in our nature as men and women, then it derives rather from our inability to see, much less feel, other people as real human beings. Anyone who deviates from the official norm, whatever that is, anyone who fails to bear a likeness to the Standard Product, is simply not viewed as fully human and then becomes at best invisible, at worst a threat to the national security.

James's prescription for this malady was slightly different from DeMott's. With the optimism of a man reared in the middle of the nineteenth century, James could still find Whitman's belief in the plentitudinous variety of common life a bracing alternative, and was thus inclined to exhort his audience to turn their attention to the sublime human effulgence in the world about them. Failing the possibility of this, he counseled remaining faithful to one's own opportunities and blessings "without presuming to regulate the rest of the vast field,"[3] hoping that a little modesty in such matters would eventually dispose people to be more receptive to one another.

DeMott is not so sanguine. Because of his more vivid awareness "of general, culturewide dimming of the lights of inward life,"[4] he is much more pessimistic about our capacity through imaginative vision to renew our saving contact with all that lies outside the perimeters of the self. Worse, he finds the past, and particularly the more notable cultural and intellectual representatives of that past, of little assistance in teaching us what it means "to grasp another being's difference from within."[5] As D. H. Lawrence showed more than half a century ago in his *Studies in Classic American Literature,* those of our writers like Whitman and Poe who have meditated deeply on the stunted quality of American lives have usually proposed as an antidote, not the need for an imaginative, sympathetic fathoming of individual differences, but rather some illusory fantasy of engrossment with or complete submergence in the life of the "other." "And whenever the engrosser or merger disappears from American letters, an even more frightening figure—the self-bound man (Captain Ahab is the prince)—stands forth in his place."[6]

Thus when DeMott scans the American past for usable intellectual and spiritual resources, he comes away largely disappointed. The only "countervoices" he can find to our national Emersonian inclination either to withdraw back into the private sanctity of selfhood or to relinquish that sanctity in favor of fusing with the All are few and far between. John Dewey is one, George Herbert Mead another, the sociologist Charles Horton Cooley a third among that relatively small group of representative American thinkers who have at least understood what James was talking about and have thus tried, with varying success, to keep alive a sense of the importance of individual differences, of the distinction between the self and the other.

In his statement of the issue DeMott is surely correct, but in his assessment of the cultural resources we possess for dealing with it, I find him considerably mistaken. If few of our classic writers and thinkers have provided us with any ready-made solutions to this problem—have shown us, for example, what it would be like to see, feel, experience other selves as real and distinct—nonetheless a striking number of them have been obsessed with its consequences, and in their obsessive ways have realized, perhaps almost in spite of themselves, just what kind of problem it really is. By this I simply mean that many American writers have clearly perceived—though by no means in always identical ways—that the problem of imagining and responding to that which is experienced as "other" is at once an ethical and religious problem—ethical insofar as it involves a question of the "right relation" to that which is experienced as "other," religious insofar as it also involves a question about the nature of reality so experienced. That is to say, they have conceived of what I shall call "the problem of otherness" as a problem pertaining not only to man's possibe growth and self-fulfillment, to his capacities for imaginative self-transcendence, but also to the nature and meaning of life when it is perceived to be ingredient with just such possibilities. Hence their characteristic metaphysical preoccupation with what Emerson called in *Nature* the distinction—indeed, the transaction—between the "Me" and the "not-Me," and their consequent ethical interest in determining, under the widest variety of circumstances, the moral norms which might be assumed best to govern and regulate this transaction.

To explore this ethical and metaphysical impulse which determines the shape and substance of so much American writing is to penetrate to the very core of the American tradition. It is also to repossess many of the ways in which that tradition may still serve as a resource for helping us cope with one of our most crippling and destructive problems as a people.

1

It must be conceded at the outset that Emerson's distinction between the "Me" and the "not-Me" has been formulated in very different terms by different writers in the American tradition. In Jonathan Edwards's theology, for example, this distinction is disclosed in what, at least from the human side of the equation, is the impassable experiential chasm between man's consciousness of himself as a wretched and unworthy sinner and God's absolute sovereignty and perfect love. In James Fenimore Cooper's fiction, on the other hand, it is expressed in the distinction between the ways of the world, of civilization, and the ways of the forest or nature. In the poetry of Walt Whitman it manifests itself in the difference between his "simple, separate self" and the "democratic en-masse." In the fiction of Henry James it is epitomized by the contrast between American innocence and aspiration and European sophistication and decadence. In the novels of Theodore Dreiser it surfaces as the polarity between the unformed individual yearning to achieve social outline and the brute impersonality of the city. Yet, however, the "other," the "not-Me," is conceived—whether as God or Being in Edwards, Nature in Emerson and Thoreau, Europe in Henry James, other selves in *Huck Finn,* the democratic mass in Whitman, or the city in Dreiser—it inevitably becomes that factor which, as Emerson said in "Experience," precipitates man's fall into existence and thus inaugurates his conscious life as an adult self. That fall can, of course, turn into a deadly plunge if the "other" exercises a governance over the self which is malevolent as well as pervasive, destructive as well as despotic; but without an experience of it man never passes beyond the state of dreaming innocence, of blissful but infantile ignorance, which, as the authors of *Billy Budd* and *The Golden Bowl* both realized, possesses a potential for evil all its own.

This is not to say that American writers have projected but one way of relating to the "other." Having defined it in a variety of ways, they have as surely portrayed a wide diversity of reactions to it. Melville's Ahab, for instance, experiences the "not-Me," that "other" epitomized so completely by Moby Dick himself, as a personal outrage, a gigantic affront to his sense of "Me." Thus when the "not-Me," the "other," turns against him in a seeming act of vengeance, Ahab is driven into a fury of mind-annihilating hatred and rushes headlong to destroy it. Whitman, by contrast, views the "other" as comrade and thus seeks a relationship of reciprocal coequality with it. Robinson Jeffers plays still another variation on this theme by opting neither for the self in opposition to the "other," nor for a relationship of harmonious coexistence

with it, but rather for the "other's" absolute dominion over the
self. What is needed, as Jeffers declared in his book of 1948, *The
Double Axe,* is a philosophy of "Inhumanism:" "a shifting of
emphasis and significance from man to not-man; the rejection of
human solipsism and recognition of trans-human magnificence."[7]

A survey of such reactions tells us nothing in itself; it is important only to the extent that it demonstrates the view shared by
so many of our writers, that man becomes fully human, or at
least comes fully into possession of such opportunities as are
afforded him to be human, only to the degree that he is willing
to acknowledge the "other" and then respond to it. At the very
most, as Melville knew, this can turn the life of the "meanest
mariners, renegades and castaways" into a subject fit for great
dramatic tragedy. At the very least, as the contemporary poet and
novelist James Dickey has shown, it can shock us out of the boredom and complacency of the daily round, out of the grim banalities
of everydayness, and thus retrieve for us some comprehension of
what Alfred North Whitehead meant by the word *importance,* that
root notion by which we distinguish between crude matter-of-fact
and its significance. In either case, the object of all such experiences remains the same. As Dickey reminds us in the title of his
first novel, the aim of all such experiences is nothing short of
deliverance.

Though I would hardly want to make any very large claims for
Dickey's novel itself, it must be acknowledged that Dickey could
scarcely have chosen a title for his novel better calculated to reso-
nate with our deepest sense of ourselves, even our religious sense
of ourselves, as a people. For in each one of its three meanings—
as a state of being in which one is freed from restraint or captivity,
as an act of transmitting or turning over something to an intended
recipient, and as a form of authoritative self-expression—the word
"deliverance" carries us all the way back to the motives which
initially propelled the first colonists toward these shores in the
beginning. As we now know after a generation of superb scholarship on the seventeenth century, deliverance is not only what the
first Puritans thought they were seeking for themselves and their
immediate posterity by, in Cotton Mather's words, "flying from the
deprivations of Europe, to the American Strand"; it is also what

they believed they could secure for all of Europe besides by erecting here a true theocratic society which might then serve as a model for the reformation of the rest of Western Christendom. Thus deliverance entailed not merely fleeing the restraints of the Old World for the freedom of the New, but also undertaking an experiment in theocracy truly expressive of the new faith to which they had been converted, which might then be perceived as an example worthy of universal, worldwide emulation.

Yet, as Perry Miller was the first to argue, the Puritans were largely deceived on all counts.[8] Not only were they unable to secure deliverance for the civilization they left behind, since Europeans generally failed to get the message; they had, in turn, no sooner gained a foothold on the edge of this new continent when for a variety of reasons the experiment itself began to turn sour. As so many Puritan historians have reconstructed it, this must have been a terrible moment in the history of New England. The Puritans' hopes for deliverance were inextricably tied to two propositions: first, that they could erect a civil state in the New World organized as strictly as possible according to theological principles derived from scripture and tradition; and second, that this new society could then serve as a redemptive beacon in the wilderness directing a fallen world back to the light of God's truth. But when European Christians failed to fix their attention upon any but the economic implications of this attempt to build, in John Winthrop's fine phrase, "a City upon a Hill," the American settlers were left alone with their theocratic experiment. And when by the second or third generation the experiment itself had begun to fail— for by then anyone could plainly see that the community was rife with dissension, backsliding, licentiousness, apostasy, or just plain apathy—the colonists were left alone, so to speak, with America herself, or, better, with the wilderness, since that was really all that the continent amounted to. The wilderness, in other words, together with European neglect, had taken its toll, and there was little choice but to come to terms with it or perish both physically and spiritually.

We know, of course, what happened. Rather than perish, those early Americans decided to come to grips, but the price was larger than they first realized. Having undertaken "an errand into the

wilderness," as Samuel Danforth described it, to secure deliverance
both for themselves and for the rest of the world, the original
Puritan theocrats discovered within several generations that the
nature of their errand had been so drastically altered by the "otherness" of New World conditions that such deliverance as they had
originally pursued could only be achieved by coming to terms with
the American wilderness itself. As the realm of the "other," of
the "not-Me," the wilderness had begun to force upon them a
redefinition of their consciousness as transplanted Europeans, a
reconception of their sense of "Me." Whatever they had once been,
they could no longer exactly remain. As with Kate Croy at the
end of Henry James's *The Wings of the Dove,* they were compelled to admit: "We shall never be again as we once were!"[9]

The religious implications of this shift in theological perspective
were enormous. Where in the beginning the wilderness or America
had been but the location of an errand of the spirit run for other
reasons altogether, by the end of the first century of settlement
the wilderness or America itself had somehow become the chief
reason for running spiritual errands at all.[10] The errand itself retained its theological impulse, the quest for deliverance, but the
terms in which that aim was now formulated and could be realized
had begun to change drastically. Deliverance, that is to say, was
now conceived less as a problem of coming to grips with the Christian witness of faith or the theocratic community than with the
American strand itself. Or, to put it slightly differently, America
—or at least that aspect of it which was most accessible to lived
experience—had now begun to supplant both the Christian scrip-
tures and the inherited faith of the fathers as the chief source of
meditation for that encounter with "otherness," with the "not-Me,"
which, to the degree that Americans remained religious at all, continued to be both the origin and goal of their experience as *homo
religiosus.*

2

In using this last phrase, I mean to suggest what historians of
religion have taught us about man's experience as a religious being. According to Mircea Eliade, for instance, man becomes re-

ligious to the extent that he seeks reunification with those trans-mundane elements of his experience which are perceived to break through the profane dimensions of his existence and to confront him with a sense of "otherness" over which he has absolutely no control. Yet since virtually any object of existence both can and does serve to mediate this sense of "otherness" to man, the words *sacred* and *profane* apply not to different kinds of objects which confront us in experience but rather to different ways of perceiv-ing and then relating ourselves to them. The clue to the distinction between these two differently perceived objects, then, derives from the power we impute to them and the point of origin we imagine for them. Even though sacred objects are accessible to us only within the world of profane existence, their liminal character and potency of expression make them appear to originate from beyond it. Man responds religiously to such objects, Eliade contends, only when he seeks through myth and ritual to repeat those acts *in illo tempore* by which their sacred character was first made manifest.

Joseph Bettis has illumined this distinction nicely when he writes that, if man's purpose in relation to things perceived as profane is to shape them according to his needs, man's purpose in relation to things perceived as sacred is to bring himself into conformity with them.[11] This is chiefly effected through what Eliade and others call the *mode of repetition,* that religious strategy whereby primi-tive man, in imitation of the divine acts of creation through which the sacred discloses itself, attempts to conform himself to and re-main within the sacred sphere, that realm which for him now constitutes the domain of the Really Real, and to extend its domin-ion over the ephemeral world of the profane.[12]

For moderns, however, this strategy tends to require modifica-tion. Even if modern man can still acknowledge the distinction between the sacred and the profane, it is clear that he is much too conscious of the historicity of all experience to believe that the dimension of the sacred points to any realm of being which is stable and fixed for all eternity and to which he can simply at-tempt to conform. Though history may not exhaust what for him is the element of the real, modern man knows—as the very terms of his identity as modern assume—that there is nothing real which does not change. Hence he is unable to conform himself to a model of the real which is fixed and timeless simply because he cannot believe that there is anything fixed, stable, and timeless. The result, in those cases where modern man retains, or strives to repossess, any trace of what might be called a religious orientation, is a marked alteration of his use of the *mode of repetition,* which is precipitated by an equally important alteration in his relation to what is experienced as "other."

Primitive man might be said to view the encounter with "otherness" as a mode of access to what Emerson called "a world elsewhere" which, though revealing itself within the sphere of the profane, is nonetheless assumed to originate from beyond it. Just because of its stability and perdurance, this "other world" is assumed to be the "real" one and thus serves as model and norm for all that transpires in the unreal and haphazard realm of historical time. Modern man, on the other hand, just because he knows of no world untouched by the vicissitudes of temporality, tends to view the encounter with "otherness" instead as a mode of access to possibilities of change and development within the self and the self's relation to whatever is experienced as "other." To put it another way, reality for moderns, even religious moderns, is generally not identified with any worlds which exist, as it were, elsewhere, but is rather associated, insofar as we retain any imagination of other worlds, of "otherness," at all, with the process by which we respond to their imagined incursions from "beyond" and then attempt to readjust and redefine ourselves as a consequence.

When this brief excursion into the history of religions is brought to bear upon the experience of those first American colonists, it becomes somewhat easier to understand how a shift in their perception of the location of "otherness," and the experience which precipitated and attended that shift, became an archetypal or paradigmatic one for subsequent Americans. Before the location of what was conceived to be "other" had shifted from scripture and tradition to the American wilderness, our forefathers had responded to the "Other" pretty much as archaic man always had. Their original encounters with "otherness" through scripture and tradition had convinced them that in order to reunite and conform themselves to its holy energies, they must repeat through myth (the rehearsal of the Word), ritual (the owning of the covenant), and, particularly, world-founding (the establishment of a theocracy) those divine acts by which life for the Puritan was revealed to be sacred both in origin and destiny. The keystone of the arch was the relation of the covenant whereby God had originally called Israel to be his people in seeking to establish his reign in history. The Puritans saw themselves as belonging to the same continuity of election and considered the erection of a theocratic society as its inevitable expression. The establishment of a theocracy which united the civil and ecclesiastical realms was conceived to be as perfect an imitation as man could achieve here on earth of that model of the God-man relationship which was fixed for all eternity in Heaven. In patterning their life on earth after the very letter of the divine model, they intended to preserve themselves, as primitive man always has, in the realm of the sacred, and to extend its hegemony of the whole of the profane world.

When the sheer intractability of the wilderness caused their experiment to go awry, however, this not only precipitated a shift in their understanding of the nature and domain of the "Other," but also began to alter considerably their mode of relating to it. To foreshorten and radically simplify, it would seem as though the original colonists came to these shores with something like a primitive or archaic religious orientation but within a relatively few generations had acquired something closer to a modern one, perhaps the preeminently modern one. The existence of the wilderness had confronted them with a fact of "otherness" which profoundly threatened their identity as transplanted Europeans. In throwing their former identity into serious question, it thrust them into a situation where they could no longer repeat the saving formulas of the past and hope to survive, where they could no longer simply attempt to imitate, as it were, what they regarded as fixed models of reality and manage to cope. Faced with the constantly fluctuating, frequently novel, and often unexpected conditions of the New World experience, it was therefore inevitable that an interest in discerning the order of being revealed by the "Other" and then attempting to accommodate oneself to it was slowly supplanted by a new interest in the actual process of response and redefinition itself.

The result, if I may borrow a phrase from Wallace Stevens, was nothing short of a revolution in the American "idea of order." Where the earliest Americans, say, from the seventeenth century to the beginning of the nineteenth, tended to derive their ultimate ideas of order from the order of being they imputed to the "Other" revealed in scripture and vouchsafed to the tradition, later Americans, certainly from Emerson and Whitman onwards, tended to derive their ideas of order instead from their own innately human (though for some simultaneously divine) capacities to redefine and regenerate themselves in response to their experience of it. In either case, however, the incitement was, and remains, the same. Suddenly brought, in F. Scott Fitzgerald's words, "face to face for the last time in history with something commensurate to . . . [their] capacity for wonder,"[13] Americans could no longer look for salvation, for deliverance, in the theological formulations and injunctions of the past, but were compelled to find it, if at all, in what they could make of their New World situation. And thus was born what I believe Perry Miller was the first to describe as the essential paradigm of the American experience.

Parenthetically, it is imperative to add that it took years, even centuries, for a recurrent element in the actual experience of so small a group of Americans as the New England Puritans to become in time a unifying, interpretive thread in the experience of us all. And it did so only because the Puritans' experience of America as a disproving ground for what Daniel Boorstin calls utopias and Perry Miller referred to as theocratic experiments was but the first in a series of jarring confrontations between the beliefs, dreams, and convictions of individual Americans (as well as American communities) and the "otherness" of the actual materials of reality in America. And, furthermore, it was only as this recurrent pattern then worked its way down over the generations into our national consciousness and was there found and eventually given imaginative release by certain of our classic writers and thinkers that the experience itself took on the shape of a fully developed paradigm.

Though the paradigm to which I refer has been revised and elaborated by such various critics and scholars as R. W. B. Lewis, Leslie Fiedler, A. N. Kaul, Leo Marx, and Richard Poirier, its essential character remains pretty much as Miller initially described it.[14] Reduced to its fundamental components, that paradigm depicts a single, solitary self who is either characteristically transplanted from another culture (and hence unfinished), or essentially unformed and uncultivated (and hence innocent), falling, so to speak, into experience and encountering there that ideal "Other" in response to which he must at the minimum redefine himself and at the maximum virtually recreate himself. Whether the ideal "Other" confronts him in the form of God, the wilderness, Nature, other selves, history, the city, or the machine, man's chief aim in response to this "Other" is neither, at least initially, to try to define it nor, necessarily, to enter into a relationship with it. Though both of these things may follow as a consequence, the essential purpose of man's encounter with "otherness" is to compel him however he responds—whether with love, despair, submission, recoil, outrage, or awe—into some new understanding of and relationship to himself. The desired goal, whether successfully achieved or tragically frustrated, is deliverance and new life, and the method is always some form of decreation, a sloughing off of the old ways in response to the encounter with something astonishingly new.

3

To give this all more concrete expression, I wish to examine in turn several short poems where some variant of the paradigm—indeed, what I shall later argue in each case is a historically significant variant of the paradigm—is presented in miniature. I have chosen poems rather than novels only because their brevity allows me to analyze in some depth the way the paradigm shapes their form and substance. But the paradigm itself, insofar as it constitutes our essential story, is no more restricted to the mode of poetry than it is, say, to the literary tradition which derives from our Puritan past. In point of fact, its chief exemplifications, as I shall presently indicate, are to be found in our longer fictions, where it has somewhat unexpectedly proven to be equally as useful in the ordering of Southern and Western experience as of New England and of black experience as of white.

My first example is a relatively little-known poem by Emily

Dickinson which, like those to follow, brilliantly exemplifies the decreative method. As will be quickly noted, the poem is concerned to describe a fundamental change in attitude, really a basic alteration of belief. The significance of that change, however, lies less in its specific nature and character than in the reasons for it and their consequent impact upon the shaken speaker. The perceptive reader will immediately discern that the speaker's ironic tone at the beginning of the poem becomes tempered and grave at the end. In the beginning the speaker is witty and knowing about the superficiality of conventional religious practice; by the end, however, her playful knowingness has been supplanted by an attitude which is more uncertain and circumspect. Where before she seemed at great remove from her subject, she now speaks from the immediacy of present experience. This alteration in attitude is caused by the sudden intrusion of the American landscape, whose striking images not only disrupt the poem but also transform the speaker's faith. Witty skepticism gives way to stunned belief as the American wilderness—but a trope for America herself—forces the speaker out of the complacency of diffident agnosticism and into a new attitude of religious wonder and awe. The poem is as follows:

> My period had come for Prayer—
> No other Art—would do—
> My Tactics missed a rudiment—
> Creator—Was it you?
>
> God grows above—so those who pray
> Horizons—must ascend—
> And so I stepped upon the North
> To see this Curious Friend—
>
> His House was not—no sign had He—
> By Chimney—nor by Door
> Could I infer his Residence—
> Vast Prairies of Air
>
> Unbroken by a Settler—
> Were all that I could see—
> Infinitude—Had'st Thou no Face
> That I might look on Thee?

> The Silence condescended—
> Creation stopped—for Me—
> But awed beyond my errand—
> I worshipped—but did not "pray"—

In the first two stanzas, the speaker is in complete control of the poem as she condescends to mock, however politely, the kind of civilized religion which approaches prayer as an exercise in spiritual artifice, requiring the proper tactics. God is merely one of the rudiments for a satisfactory performance, and, if he is sensed somehow to be missing, one simply looks for him in the usual place where people have always located the God made in their own image. But once the speaker steps out of the protected enclosure of her own mocking contempt, once she steps "upon the North/To see this Curious Friend," she quickly discovers that the American Landscape refuses to afford her the anticipated prospect: "His House was not—no sign had He—/By Chimney—nor by Door." The quaint "Residence" she had at least half expected to find, which would have kept matters comfortably domestic and therefore easy to ridicule, is suddenly swallowed up by "Vast Prairies of Air/Unbroken by a Settler." Though this marvelously native image, which conspires to fling open the doors of the poem onto the vacant and immense spaciousness of the American continent, is carefully prepared for by the speaker's ascent of horizons towards the American vista, it is still so striking that the third stanza needs the fourth to complete its thought, as though the speaker's rigid self-control were suddenly breaking down with the verse form. The "Creator" is no longer the familiar "Curious Friend" of stanza 2 but a featureless "Infinitude" who shatters the speaker's former self-assurance.

In the seemingly endless and unexplored open spaces of the American wilderness, none of the old names for the deity nor the old rituals for domesticating him any longer suffice. The traditional tactics of familiarity and the previous attitude of condescension, both of which came so easily and naturally at the beginning of the poem, have now been fundamentally altered by New World conditions. Contempt for the religion of domesticity and civility gives way to a recovery of the capacity for wonder and awe as the formerly sophisticated and faintly cynical speaker is stunned into silence and veneration before certain of the sovereign and totally unaccommodating facts of the American experience. Whether these facts promise life or death, felicity or failure, we are not told. All we can do is measure their effects. Suddenly brought face to face with what is not the self, or even any possible projection of the self, the speaker confronts the "Other," the "not-Me," and is left in a profound state of shock which is also a new state of being— "awed beyond my errand—/I worshipped—but did not pray."

This conclusion of the poem has a startling and unsettling quality about it, not only because it arrives so abruptly and unexpectedly, but also because it does and does not resolve the initial situation. Having originally set out to comment upon the termination of what is regarded as an odious kind of spiritual exercise, in this case prayer, the speaker is suddenly left at the end of the poem recalling the inexplicable commencement of different and wholly uncontrollable kind of spiritual experience called worship. In this, of course, the open-ended form of the poem bears striking affinities with many other American works. Whether one considers Hawthorne's *Scarlet Letter* or Mark Twain's *Huck Finn,* Fitzgerald's *Gatsby* or Hemingway's stories from *In Our Time,* Henry James' *Portrait of a Lady* or Ralph Ellison's *Invisible Man,* American writers display a penchant for bringing their characters to a state of sudden illumination and then leaving them, as it were, at the end of the book to work out their salvation in fear and trembling. The reason, I would submit, is a function of their interests and concerns as writers, and casts fresh light back upon the poem by Emily Dickinson.

Unlike their counterparts in English and European tradition, American writers often exhibit such interest as they have in human nature, not by inferring from the settled manners and morals of their characters the enduring qualities of their souls but rather by submitting their characters to sudden, often violent, confrontations with "otherness" to see whether, and, if so, to what degree and with what effect, they can change. Hence, their concern, and the Emily Dickinson poem is but a single, striking example of this, is not with everyman in his humor but with everyman, as Whitman would have said, on the road.[15] The issue is whether man can be transformed along the way, and the incitement to such transformations always springs from those startling confrontations with "otherness" which simultaneously threaten and promise to astonish man into what Emerson called "an original relation to the universe."

"The Most of It" by Robert Frost offers both a vivid illustration of this desire for "an original relation to the universe" and also an ironic comment on it. In the beginning, the all-too-recognizable Emersonian figure standing solitary in the midst of the natural world is almost tempted into the illusion that he is the sole proprietor of the scene he surveys. By crying out on life for a "voice in answer" which is more than "the mocking echo of his own," he would seek some reciprocal relation to the universe, in this case a relation of mutual coequality and comradeship—"not his own love back in copy speech,/But counter-love, original response." Yet nothing ever comes of what he cries, unless it is "the embodiment" that crashes "In the cliff's talus on the other side" and then, "Instead of proving human when it near[s]/And someone else additional to him,/As a great buck it powerfully appear[s]." This, to be sure, is a revelation of something and not nothing, and in the words of Gerardus van der Leeuw's definition of the primordial religious object, of something "that is a *highly exceptional* and *extremely impressive 'Other.'* "[16] At the same time, however, it is also a revelation of something which in the very alienation of its "otherness" undercuts the initial presumption of the figure's expectation even in the process of fulfilling it.

This ironic reversal of the protagonist's need and expectation, of an answering response which would signify recognition, community, even love, is then doubled by virtue of the images which the poet uses, remorselessly piling one on top of the next, to dramatize the nature of that which is made manifest. The epiphany which disrupts the protagonist's lonely vigil occurs in a natural setting, and yet the images employed to characterize its awesome, powerful movement through the water and then up onto land—"crashed," "splashed," "pushing the crumpled water up ahead," "landed pouring like a waterfall," "stumbled through the rocks with horney tread," "forced the underbrush"—make us think less of the noisy approach of a large animal than of something like the beaching of an enormous landing craft or outerspace machine. And this, as a consequence, only underscores the fearful strange-

ness of the apparition and the now even more terrible sense of
isolation of the lonely and impotent witness.

A third factor contributing to the protagonist's terrible sense of
isolation and loneliness is the speaker's own absolute neutrality of
tone. At no point does he intercede with a sympathetic aside
or an interpretive comment, but instead allows the twofold irony
of the protagonist's situation to work itself out to its merciless conclusion, a conclusion all the more merciless just because the final
phrase, "and that was all," allows no margin of response either for
the protagonist or for the speaker. What the protagonist wants is
an "Other" who is understanding and loving, a kind of comrade
and friend; what he gets is a Something which is brutally indifferent and unfeeling. The only antidote to an encounter with this kind
of "otherness," the poem seems to say, is the speaker's stoic neutrality of tone, a tone which refuses to sentimentalize the protagonist's situation because it would avail the protagonist nothing
in the face of the harsh truth he must simply learn to accept.

Yet, in a sense the speaker's stoic neutrality of tone *does represent* an intelligent and compassionate response, even if it comes
from the poet rather than from something within the presented
scene. The poet has put himself in the place of someone who
neither gets what he wants from reality nor even what he could con-
ceivably have expected; that someone, in turn, gets a sympathetic
and "original response," even though it is ironically conveyed
through the poet's reluctance to soften in any way the shock of the
protagonist's discovery. The poet's discrete neurtality constitutes
a kind of "counterlove" simply because it indicates the only way
in which the awful finality of the protagonist's shuddering discovery
may be borne.   "Spring and All"

William Carlos Williams's "By the road to the contagious hospital" begins almost where the Frost poem leaves off, in a world
which refuses to offer any accommodation to the self's desire for
an original and reciprocal relation with reality, but then discovers
through a new strategy of the imagination hidden resources in the
unaccommodating landscape which bring new life both to the
speaker and to the scene he surveys. One could say that this poem
is built upon a cliché, the transition from winter to spring with its
attendant emergence of new life out of death. But the power and

vitality of Williams's poem derives from the way this process of rebirth is effected, from the way it precipitates a marriage between the details which are seen and the quickened power of perception through which they are given new visual life, a marriage which ultimately unites the emerging details themselves with the power that enables all things to be.

Much of this is accomplished through what might be called an act of transcendence downward, where the eye of the observer is forced to make fresh contact with the actual and below that with whatever it is that pushes the actual, to reverse the spatial figure, back up both into being and into consciousness. Our eye, following the motions of the poem, moves from "the surge of . . . blue/ mottled clouds driven from the/northeast" above the landscape, down across a "waste of broad, muddy fields,/brown with dried weeds, standing and fallen," which is dotted with "patches of stand- ing water," and then, finally, to the objects nearest to sight along the road—"the reddish,/purplish, forked, upstanding, twiggy/stuff of bushes and small trees." We know that there is evidence of waste and death here in this barren landscape even before we are told of the "dead, brown leaves" under those trees and the "leafless vines" presumably clinging to them. This is a scene out of the modern wasteland whose presiding institutional symbol is the contagious disease hospital, a scene we might simply accept without further ado if our attention had not already begun to be drawn to some of the idiosyncratic features of the details we had been compelled to observe along the way. But once having been obliged to notice those features, we cannot help taking a new interest in the other- wise ironic announcement, made almost as a kind of afterthought, that "sluggish,/dazed spring approaches." "Lifeless in appear- ance," spring's approach is nonetheless felt as a reality. As the apparently lifeless details of the natural scene become more vivid, they begin to stir with freshening vitality. Suddenly the eye finds itself in the process of witnessing the revivifying of those details which, more than announcing the arrival of spring, appears to define, to enable, to constitute spring's very existence—the naked bulbs on bare branches, the fragile blades of grass beginning to tuft the dark ridges of mud, both evoking the thought of "tomor- row" and "the stiff curl of wild-carrot leaf."

As spring appears, objects "one by one" begin to be defined or, what is the same thing, perception starts to clarify. But by now the process of movement downward, far from slowing, has begun to hasten. The short, choppy phrases and flat, monochromatic rhythms at the beginning of the poem begin to give way toward the end to lines which are more emphatic, more tightly interwoven, more forcefully verbal and dynamic. The act of transcendence downward now enables the observer to see that within the new objects of his perception, as within his recovered powers of sight, bringing "clarity" and "outline of leaf," there exists an extraordinary Something—the only way to denominating what he sees is by reference to the impersonal pronoun "It"—which is known strictly because of what it does, an activity which can only be defined by the slightly archaic word *quickens*. Thus in the final stanza, with its heavy pauses and formal dignity, the eye actually permeates those objects, that scene, this vision and discovers that which enables the whole landscape to root, to "grip down and begin to awaken," an immanent Force which, though never visible as a thing in itself, now lends both to the objects themselves and to the quickened capacities of perception through which they are seen an unexpected, even numinous *hecceity,* or sheer thisness of being.

What the observer finally sees, then, and in his seeing for the first time knows, is not a wasteland at all but rather a fresh new world, which he discovers by releasing in himself, in the very act of transcending downward, that same power of life which at once quickens the vegetation into life and perception into vision. The experience itself finally takes on the character of a great pageant, a formal rite. What is being enacted is "the stark dignity of entrance" whereby spring is delivered from winter, insight from observation, life from death. The process, as always, is decreative; the result, in this case, is restorative. At the end, both the subject and its objects have become wholly transparent not only to each other but also to the power which holds both in Being itself. As J. Hillis Miller might well say, all exist in a new space of copresence in which the light reflected from each is the light of All.[17]

The pattern which is here illustrated, and illustrated as well in our foregoing examples, is the one which R. P. Blackmur defined some years ago in his brilliant essay on "Religious Poetry in the United States." It is the pattern of what I have termed the essential paradigm of the American experience, the pattern of the self's, and by extension the work's, relation with what I would call the experience of the ideal "Other" and what Blackmur called, more forthrightly, perhaps, "the numinous force; the force within the self, other than the self, greater than the self, which, as one cultivates it, moves one beyond the self." "Poetry," Blackmur said, by which he meant all literary forms, "is one of the ways of cultivation; and the harvest is vision."[18]

The problem, however, is not to isolate the pattern, or to define the paradigm; examples of it abound everywhere in American literature but tell us by themselves nothing more than that American writers have, from time to time, tended to order their experience in relation to a common set of terms, and beyond that in relation to a common set of premises about the possible relations between those terms which inevitably affects the variety of experiences which can be so ordered. To speak more plainly with the help of some formulations borrowed from John Lynen, the existence of something like a paradigm of the American experience tells us at most only that American writers, for a complicated set of reasons, have typically organized their fictions, or at least some of their more representative fictions, in relation to what Lynen defines as a describable "system of modes of experience which, though differing greatly, are yet related as alternatives within a single range of possibilities."[19] The paradigm itself, then, simply describes the single range or system of possibilities in relation to which individual writers have created various and alternative modes of experience. The question remains, what have they learned from their employment of this paradigm of the American experience? What new knowledge have they acquired from their utilization of this distinctively—though by no means uniquely—American idea of order, knowledge which has something to do with the lives we lead everyday and which might make those lives more livable, more valuable, more humane? More particularly, how does their work prove a resource for overcoming that curious form of spiritual myopia which seems to afflict us as Americans, what William James and Benjamin DeMott referred to as our insensibility to forms of life, of being, other than our own?

4

The answer, which can only be outlined in cursory fashion here, is closely allied with the ideal ways which American writers have proposed for responding to the "Other," and these in turn are to a large degree dependent upon the mode in terms of which the "Other" is experienced. The three poems by Dickinson, Frost and Williams illustrate, respectively, those three modes and thus serve to indicate the three ideal ways which our writers have devised for responding to one of the several, more representative modes in which the "Other" or "otherness" has been experienced in America.

To put this all in the form of a proposition, I would argue that American writers have tended to imagine the experience of "otherness" or the "Other" in three characteristic modes which turn out on closer inspection to be distinctive of, but by no means confined to, three successive periods in the history of American culture. Having imagined the experience of "otherness" in three different modes, I would contend that they have also proposed, respectively, three different ways of responding to it, have proposed, if you will, three very nearly generic definitions of what might be called "the nature of true virtue." In saying this I mean to suggest that an examination of the various modes in terms of which many of our more representative writers and thinkers have imagined and responded to that which is experienced as "other" affords significant insight into what Lionel Trilling has recently described as "the moral life in process of revising itself, perhaps by reducing the emphasis it formerly placed upon one or another of its elements, perhaps by inventing and adding to itself a new element, some mode of conduct or of feeling which hitherto it had not regarded as essential to virtue."[20]

Among those writers and thinkers who have experienced "otherness" in the transcendental mode, as the expression of a God, Power or Being who is reputed to dwell so to speak, above and beyond, it is either tacitly or overtly assumed, as Jonathan Edwards indicated in *The Nature of True Virtue,* that the appropriate form of response is some manifestation of "the consent of being to Being." This is the mode of experience and resultant ethical orientation which typifies most American writing from the Puritan period through the first half of the nineteenth century, and which finds representative expression in such diverse figures as John Winthrop, John Cotton, Anne Bradstreet, Jonathan Edwards, Benjamin Franklin, James Fenimore Cooper, and Ralph Waldo Emerson, though variations of the mode itself can also be seen in such later figures as Emily Dickinson, Edwin Arlington Robinson, and Robinson Jeffers. Whether their experience of it is a source of joy and renewal, like Edwards's and Emerson's, or more often a source of anguish and despair, like Dickinson's and Robinson's, most of the writers who imagine "otherness" in this mode comprehend the experience itself as some form of what M. H. Abrams, echoing Carlyle, has aptly named "Natural Supernaturalism."[21] And the exercise of consent in this case, or the withholding of it when the experience of "otherness" in this mode proves either too hostile or too empty, is viewed as affording the possibility, or destroying the possibility, of a kind of transcendence upward.

By the mid-nineteenth century, however, a subtle shift in theological emphasis began to occur in America which was accompanied by an equally subtle alteration in our idea of the nature of true virtue. One can discern intimations of this shift in the writings of Nathaniel Hawthorne, where a marked skepticism toward all forms of traditional belief and worship is coupled with an equally fervid conviction about the sanctity of the human heart, but it achieved its first full articulation in the writings of the elder Henry James. This was the shift in emphasis from allegiance to the God, Power, or Being who dwells above and beyond to belief in, or at least greater curiosity about, the God, Power, or Being who dwells both within and without, the ideal "Other" who meets one, if anywhere, in the form of what the elder James called, borrowing a phrase from Emmanuel Swedenborg, our "Divine Natural Humanity." Most of the writers who imagine "otherness" in this newer mode inevitably tend to reconceive the ideal way of relating and responding to it. Where those who imagine "otherness" in the transcendental mode define virtue as a form of consent, those who

imagine "otherness" in what may be described as the social mode
redefine virtue as a form of sympathy. The ethical ideal, in other
words, is not to consent to others nor even to feel for them but
rather to feel with them, to project ourselves so completely into the
interiority of their own distinctive inwardness that, as D. H. Lawrence once said, we "feel with them as they feel with themselves."[22]
And, correspondingly, the aim of all such efforts is not to effect a
kind of transcendence upward but rather a kind of transcendence
outward.

This is the ethical ideal or notion of true virtue which first begins
to show itself in Hester's relation to the townspeople of Salem at
the end of *The Scarlet Letter,* is explored more leisurely in Ish-
mael's developing experience of brotherhood with Queenqueg in
Moby Dick, becomes the great controlling theme of *Leaves of
Grass,* attains temporary consummation in the idyllic pastoral in-
terlude which Huck and Jim enjoy together floating down the river
in *The Adventures of Huckleberry Finn,* and then, finally, is realized both as an achievement of character and an achievement of
form in the great novels of Henry James's major phase. But, again,
this notion of virtue is recalled and partially retrieved as an ethical
norm long after the mode in which it serves as the ideal response
begins to lose its hold over the American imagination. One finds
variations of the idea of sympathy cropping up as the moral touch-
stone, for example, in such different works as Sherwood Anderson's
Winesburg, Ohio, Robert Frost's dramatic monologues, Willa
Cather's tales of frontier life, Ernest Hemingway's stories of love
and marriage, Nathaniel West's *Miss Lonelyhearts,* Bernard Mala-
mud's novels about the meaning of suffering, and, above all, in the
Yoknapatawpha saga of William Faulkner.

In the second quarter of the twentieth century, however, a second
shift in ethical and religious orientation began to occur in America,
one which I believe we are still very much in the throes of. This
new alteration in what deserves to be called, after R. P. Blackmur's
famous *Anni Mirabiles* lectures of 1956, the "irregular metaphysics" of the American experience, involves a discovery which many
of the great modern writers made close to the end of their careers
but which many of our best contemporary writers have accepted
almost from the outset as a working assumption. The discovery

itself is of the astonishing numinousness of things as they are, of
the rich liminality of, in Denis Donoghue's phrase, "the ordinary
universe."[23] Whether, like the later Eliot, they have made this discovery through the repossession of a traditional myth which puts
greatest emphasis upon the mysterious incarnate union of Word
and flesh, spirit and matter, or, like the later Stevens, through the
employment of a "later reason" raised to the level of metaphysical
speculation, or, like the later Williams, through a fresh plunge into
"the filthy Passaic" of crude fact, all are engaged in "the act of
finding what will suffice,"[24] and all must follow Theodore Roethke
in "The Abyss" past the surfeit of too much reality and the ex-
haustion of too close an immediacy until they reach, "beyond the
fearful instant," "A sunlit silence," where

> Knowing slows for a moment,
> And not-knowing enters, silent,
> Bearing being itself,
> And the fire dances
> To the stream's
> Flowing.

Is this moving "toward God," the poet asks, "or merely another
condition?" The only answer is the one found in the poet's images
as they rise dreamlike but clear from the fusion of his own inner
ambivalence:

> By the salt waves I hear a river's undersong,
> In a place of mottled clouds, a thin mist morning and evening.
> I rock between dark and dark
> My soul nearly my own,
> My dead selves singing.
> And I embrace this calm—
> Such quiet under the small leaves![25]

"Such quiet under the small leaves"; that "luminous stillness"
"in the eyeless seeking" of the fragile tendrils of young plants; the
enviable, innocent delicacy of "the child's hand reaching into the
coiled smilax"[26]—all these phrases, and the gestures of spirit they
represent, signify the mysterious recovery of a sense of Presence
which each of these poets achieve through an imaginative encounter with a form of the "Other" which is experienced as wholly

immanent. The ideal response to all such encounters with "otherness" in the immanental mode is neither consent nor sympathy but
rather transparency, a kind of reversal, as Geoffrey Hartman suggests in reference to Stevens, where we "become what we see instead of seeing what we are."[27] This is the strategy adopted by such
disparate characters as Stevens' Canon Aspirin, Saul Bellow's
Herzog, and Robert Lowell's skunk-watcher, each of whom strives,
however imperfectly, to become utterly transparent to the "other,"
to take their energy, courage, even identity from the "other's"
luminous reality, and each of whom achieves, as a result, a kind
of transcendence which is neither upward nor outward but rather
downward.

Such acts of transcendence downward are often hazardous and,
like the other strategies of self-transcendence we have mentioned,
are only undertaken in the most desperate of circumstances, when
there seems no other way of breaking out of what Stevens refers to
as "the man-locked set." But hazardous or not, they constitute one
of at least three ways in which American writers over the years have
attempted to keep alive our sense of "otherness," our imagination
of worlds elsewhere, beyond the perimeters of the self, by which
the self, through an act of recognition and response, can, as a
consequence, learn how to transcend its own perimeters. Such
knowledge may never save us, but it can at least make us a little
more human by teaching us how to respond both to the Me we are
not—to modify Emerson's formulation—and to the Me that we
are. This, clearly, is not all there is to life, but just as clearly is
part of the American heritage. Our problem is to learn how to use
such knowledge, and the question is whether, in the larger cultural
sense, we care enough to summon the critical energy to try.

NOTES

1. Benjamin DeMott, *Supergrow: Essays and Reports on Imagination
   in America* (New York: 1969), p. 93.
2. Ibid., p. 12.
3. William James, *Essays in Faith and Morals,* ed. Ralph Barton
   Perry (Cleveland: 1962), p. 284.

4. DeMott, *Supergrow,* p. 99.
5. Ibid., p. 93.
6. Ibid., p. 94.
7. Robinson Jeffers, *The Double Axe* (New York: 1948), p. vii.
8. *See* Perry Miller, *Errand Into The Wilderness* (Cambridge, Mass.: 1956), pp. 1–15.
9. Henry James, *The Wings of the Dove* (New York: 1939), II, p. 439.
10. Miller, *Errand,* pp. 1–15.
11. Joseph Bettis, ed., *Phenomenology of Religion* (New York: 1969), p. 203.
12. For the description of Eliade's understanding of religion, I am indebted to an extremely helpful and illuminating essay by Jonathan Z. Smith, "The Wobbling Pivot," *Journal of Religion* 52 (April, 1972): 134–149.
13. F. Scott Fitzgerald, *The Great Gatsby* (New York: 1953), p. 182.
14. In the great welter of material which constitutes his vast corpus, there is no single passage where Miller defines the paradigm exactly as I have formulated it. Nor is there any moment in the work of the aforementioned critics where the paradigm is explicitly described in terms parallel to my own. The definition I have provided is a personal reconstruction of various elements which I have found threaded throughout the work of many critics and can therefore, if found wanting, be held against no one but myself.
15. This is a variation on an observation by F. O. Matthiessen that American writers in the nineteenth century, in contrast to such English contemporaries as Jane Austen, Dickens or Thackeray, "were more concerned with human destiny than with every man in his humor" (*American Renaissance* [New York: 1941] p. 271).
16. Gerardus van der Leeuw, *Religion in Essence and Manifestation* (London: 1938), p. 23.
17. *See* J. Hillis Miller, *Poets of Reality* (Cambridge, Mass.: 1965) pp. 10–11.
18. R. P. Blackmur, "Religious Poetry in the United States," *Religious Perspectives in American Culture,* ed. James Ward Smith and A. Leland Jamison (Princeton: 1961) p. 286.
19. John F. Lynen, *The Design of the Present* (New Haven: 1969), p. 26.
20. Lionel Trilling, *Sincerity and Authenticity* (Cambridge, Mass.: 1972), p. 1.
21. *See especially* M. H. Abrams, *Natural Supernaturalism,* (New York: 1971), pp. 65–70.
22. D. H. Lawrence, *Studies in Classic American Literature* (New York: 1923), p. 185.
23. Denis Donoghue, *The Ordinary Universe* (London: 1968).

24. The phrase is Wallace Stevens's from "Of Modern Poetry," *The Collected Poems of Wallace Stevens* (New York: 1954), p. 239.
25. Theodore Roethke, *The Far Field* (New York: 1971), p. 53.
26. Ibid.
27. Geoffrey Hartman, *Beyond Formalism* (New Haven: 1971), p. 257.

IV

The Stories of Our Times

WILLIAM G. DOTY

"TELL ME a story, Daddy," probably asks more for an expression of who Daddy is than for a type or content of story.[1] Rilke's *Stories of God* disclose infinitely more about Rilke than about a deity. And *The Last Picture Show* was more a story of life in small-town, U.S.A., than about the closing of the local moving-picture theater in one such town.

Three examples of stories at work in our culture. In the stories to which we give our attention it is clear where we are and where we look for help, guidance, fun, profit. Stories that are explicitly fiction and those that may be called nonfiction stories (part 2). Features of storycraft that carry forward the storytellers' intentions can be explored (part 3). And finally, a few further reflections on the type of personhood represented by some of the stories, the new man and his interconnections (part 4).

1. *The Story and the Stories*

What kind of story are we in?—thus John S. Dunne, in a lecture at the 1974 Notre Dame conference on Jung and Education: Myth and Ritual, or in his latest book.[2] But I want to go further to ask about the stor-*ies* we are embroiled in and embroidered by, the narrative patterns and shapes and sizes that we tell and believe and participate. The shapes and sizes themselves speaking to a certain worldview and style of life: I think of literary quarterlies printed on loose pages that can be shuffled at will; or Cortazar's *Hopscotch,* the chapters of which can be read in any of several sequences; the fiction journal printed in large newspaper format, *Fiction;* or the

ten-part story by A. B. Paulson—printed on stiff paper, the reader
has first to cut it out and assemble it into a solid geometrical figure
before reading the ten segments in any consecutive sequence.[3]

The thesis is already stated in the first paragraph. We are what
we relate. Or, as another contributor to this volume puts it: "When
we tell our tales, we give away our souls.[4] But relating/storytelling
today is only rarely a lively oral activity, so we look not to the
spellbinders of traditional oral societies, but to the bookseller and
even (sigh!) to the publishers' charts, to see where our stories are,
which ones make it, and which do not. (The answer will not be
found only within the strictures of the formally defined "fictions:"
the reason is that short-story collections and novels have today a
terribly short shelf life. In mid-1973, I tried to get copies of
Barthelme's *City Life* for my parable class: published in paperback
in 1971, it was already out of print and unavailable.)[5]

Stories have to be told, to be expressed, for they are the part of
the narrative quality of existence[6] that can be shared and that
therefore compensate for all that cannot be shared. No matter how
jaded we are, we have our own stories to live out, and other
peoples' stories to hear. In our stories we extend ourselves toward
becoming other than we are; we learn to experiment with possible
futures as well as to gain perspective on where we have been. As
the rational rules us more and more—the cloture of science, the
emptiness of mass-speak—we need story to guide our emotions and
capabilities and morals.

Story has magic: *mu, mythos*—sound of the lips, into "world,"
"tale," and then "mythology"—the spellbinding of Hermes, who
like the shaman, like illness, "will surely take the mind/ Where
minds can't usually go."[7] The magic of spell-ing (Anglo Saxon
spel, a saying, tale, charm), the magical circle of protection:
"Neither ghosts nor demons shall have any power, whenever and
wherever these tales are told. And whoever relates with sincere
devotion even a single one of them shall be free from sin."[8]

"Sin" may not be our primary concern today, but we still know
the magic place of story as we seek to experience the shaman's
flight into fantasy, into story and dreams; to experience firsthand
the magical butterflies of Gabriel García Márquez (*One Hundred
Years of Solitude*), or the great fly of Carlos Casteñeda.

Dreams and fantasies feature strongly today, increasingly so, as other-than-strictly-Jungian analysts begin to work with dream diaries. The movement toward the interior (Erich Heller's brilliant title, taken from the essay on Hegel's influence and on Rilke: *The Artist's Journey into the Interior*); impelling more and more people, secondary school and college/postcollege age especially, toward Carlos Casteñeda's trilogy about the Yaqui shaman and his pupil; leading to T-groups, action therapy, and other interior-exposing methodologies. Having kept our lids on so tightly for so long, Americans now revel in exposure. (Or at least they have recently: I sense in many of my present students a turn toward content and substance, away from revelation and relevance.)[9] We have had to come to grips with our personal stories, and our *personae* have become us; we live out roles and then discard them in record-speed orgies of flip-flop: hair length, denim fads, and now Great Gatsby fashions rush by more quickly than we can internalize adequately. Our image is largely that found in the title of Richard Poirier's book of critical essays: *The Performing Self*.[10] At the same time, an internalizing trip: fantasy and mystical experiences, "doing your own thing," and "spacing out."

So stor-ies. Not a single story (and here I reveal my disagreement with many of the traditional "religion and literature" studies which claim to identify a paradigmatic model story for each age of man). A culture that lives in the midst of many stories, and from story to story. Is it so unbearable, this protean man of ours who shifts bases constantly and blows the minds of our parents and our colleagues?[11] Or are there bench marks even yet, road signs and way stations denoting some stability amidst the flux?

I think there are, and I guess I have learned not to be frightened by the paisley and the multiplicity—a long struggle toward a freedom that admittedly does not always work. Here I want to catch some of the markers, hold them up for viewing, and suggest that they are sightings relevant for 1974, at least. My sense is that the "new fiction" portrays a "new man," and that the artist sketches for us visions of the new men we are becoming. He stands on the borderline of the present and the future, and images the metaphors in which we come to experience the world.[12] At stake for most of us are the time-tested securities of the past—beliefs and structures that are directly challenged in literature today, even such basic elements as plot, sequential time and development, the third-person convention in writing, and others that we will describe in part 3. If the artists reflect the future that is now pushing the present, we need to find our place among the possible new metaphors; we need to learn to participate them and let them be our own.

The "religion" of the title of this volume I have to expand to its limits, or rather to its roots: I understand it in terms of its Latin origins: "to bind or hold together." The stories, then, that "work" for us—that hold together 1974-man in the moments when interconnection and continuity seem wise; the stories = life-expressions and life-affirmations for now.[13]

Whether also for tomorrow? I honestly do not know.

2. *The Writers, the Themes, and Modes of Acting*

To avoid wandering too extensively through the ranks of contemporary writers, we need a canon, a list of writers I take to represent aspects of "the new fiction." I do not aim here at the far-out for the sake of the far-out, at the aberrant or odd-ball, but at substantive performers whose works seem to me to have excellence and some lasting power. There is no attempt made to encompass everyone who comes to mind; and I run the risk of advancing favorites. My sensitivity to "the new" is not so much directed toward the chronologically recent as it is toward that which challenges the traditions of literature on which most of us were reared; and I am interested as much contentually as literarily, i.e., directed toward the story components that respond to or reflect upon contemporary existence, rather than toward the literary analysis of the college fiction course or recent structuralist analysis.

From writers earlier in our century, I want to single out only three: Camus, Kafka, and Hesse. Each of them represents for me a particular breakthrough. Camus's works showed my own late-1950s college generation that the Big Issues could be approached narratively rather than only discursively (remember this was still when fiction belonged only in the English department!). Other writers doubtless did this for others—I make no claim to superiority or priority here—but for me and my friends, Camus's

Plague and *Stranger* become modes of telling our stories in ways which even our beloved Kierkegaard, Nietzsche, and Sartre could not.[14] Hesse was "ours" long before the current vogue: it was his gift to embody pathos and feeling for us. We could be men and cry, and we did. There is in Hesse a pure sort of in-forming from his worldviews, a directness that can be bathetic, but also a bodying-forth that still amazes me, even when I am told that *Siddhartha* was constructed in twelve chapters, each corresponding to a phase of the zodiac.[15] And finally Kafka: earlier the *Castle*-Kafka, or the *Metamorphosis*- or *Amerika*-Kafka; now the Kafka of the stories and especially of the parables, which I see as structurally analogous to those of Jesus and Borges.[16]

Camus, Hesse, Kafka: three giants among other giants for whom there is simply no room here. Three artists whose stories worked for many of us to break through the school patterns, artists whose compactness, sureness of hand, and chiaroscuro were such a relief after Fielding and Scott, whose ultimacy suggested depth after Hemingway, and whose polish evoked greater admiration than did that of Lawrence or Greene or Lowry.

Fiction remained a pastime for me throughout six years of seminary and graduate school—I remember clearly only the James Bond series, in cheap British editions, before the American craze —and it was not until my first year of full-time teaching that I knew I had to become at least partly immersed in creative fiction again. To Giles Gunn, who also contributes to this volume, I shall always be grateful for introduction to John Hawkes. His *Second Skin,* and then as quickly as I could get them, *The Cannibal, The Lime Twig, The Beetle Leg, The Innocent Party* (plays), and *Lunar Landscapes* (stories and novellas), and to some extent Harold Pinter's plays, acted on me like an acid, cutting deeply, but structuring and clarifying much as had Camus earlier.

And since then, others, most notably Robert Coover, John Barth, Donald Barthelme, William H. Gass, and Jorge Luis Borges. A raft of others (Kenneth Patchen, Flannery O'Connor, Isak Dinesen, William Golding, Henrich Böll, Günther Grass) whose fictions also had that hard etching edge commingled with ironic and pathetic laughter and parody; I single out Coover, et al. primarily because I know them best. What was happening in literary terms will occupy us in the next part; that they were the ones whose writings "worked," I point out here to establish some canonical limits. The scope is expanded by inclusion of more recent journal and anthology fictions, especially from *American Review* and *Tri-Quarterly*.[17]

My situation, as a result of this confessional purview, resembles that of a mapmaker in a story by Borges whose title I have lost: having spent his life charting in minuscule detail the contours of the world's boundaries, he realized at last that the final map matched stroke for stroke the lines etched on his own face. I have reached toward those who have made me, and instead of showing you their portraits, find my own. But one has to start somewhere, and it is in the telling that one comes to recognize who she or he is. As the Ashanti conclusion to folktale hints, we are reconstituted by our own stories: "This, my story, which I have related, if it be sweet, or if it be not sweet, take some elsewhere, and let some come back to me."[18]

In addition to the writers mentioned, whose works will be discussed in part 3, there are writings that reflect our corporate face-map in other ways than do these American writers. Several modes and types of writing may be noted, only some of which are explicitly fictional. The first two, however, are so: the French "new novel"—and I'll single out only Robbe-Grillet—and Latin American novelists and poets. I do not sense much impact from either direction, although contemporary French fiction has indirectly made its mark on the cinema (so that, for instance, Susan Sontag has felt the importance of reaching on to films after her novels.)[19] Latin American writers are being published in translation now to a much greater extent than has been the case; I anticipate more public discussion and wider reception. That both French and Latin American writing should be mentioned is surely a sign that American fictionists are increasingly exploring cultures outside their own immediate heritage.[20]

Jorge Luis Borges's Argentinian stories and parables are a special instance of Latin American writing. His own heritage seems more Continental and British, due to his education, but South American themes often provide the raw materials for his stories. There is no way to convey here the magic of this writer; fortunately the newer secondary literature is helpful, and thanks to his collaborator, N. T. di Giovanni, and publishers, his work is now widely available in translation. Other Latin American writers are being published in this country, and perhaps the fiction and thought of tomorrow will more fully embody the Land and the sensitivities so warmly portrayed in the Indian American and Latin American creations that have been ignored for so long. We turn to our own soil as the analysand recreates his own past.

The third and fourth themes both have to do with human groups within our culture whose rightful shares of that culture have been strictly minimal: that we listen now to the *American Indians* or to *Women*—and listen intently to them—reveals an important recognition of the one-sidedness of our past. Fictional modes have not been the dominant modes of expression, and the explicitly fictional presentations (say, for instance, N. Scott Momaday's *House Made of Dawn* or *The Way to Rainy Mountain,* or Doris Lessing's novels) have made their way as fiction rather than as movement pieces. In either case, there is a need for a new story, a completing story, that will balance and complete the half-selves we now find so painfully unfinished.

One aspect of the inexpensive-book revolution of our times has a great deal to say to the kinds of "stories" that we are. I refer to the publication of large format paperbacks; these are now featured in every bookstore, and account, I am told, for an impressive sales volume. If that is the case, they must be meeting needs or desires for "telling it like it is," and will repay our scrutiny. I have a number of these books in my home, starting with the Sierra Club series published by Ballantine, which made it unnecessary to covet and to lug home their enormous prototype originals, and including the *Whole Earth Catalogue,* which was one of the biggest sellers of all. These books range now over an extremely varied field of topics, from George Downing's sensual massage books to the exquisite Avon/Thames & Hudson series that includes de Rola's *Alchemy: The Secret Art,* with its beautiful color reproductions.

Browsing through local bookstores, I was struck by several motifs that seem to indicate contemporary interests. I list them quickly, in more or less catalogue fashion, since my interest here is to indicate foci, rather than depth analysis.

a. Generally speaking, the *how to* books: ranging from explicit handicraft manuals; plant, cooking, clothing, and candlemaking guides; to handbooks for constructing whole buildings (*The Dome Builder's Handbook,* and *Domebook 1* and *2*—espousing a philosophy of life as well as building diagrams). There is a "back to the earth" movement represented here, a reflection of both ecology campaigns and the rejection of urbanization; *Natural Life Styles,* a book-magazine, is typical. A number have to do with "natural medicine" and body awareness: *Healing Ourselves, Bodymind, Body Music, How the Body Feels;* and others offer technical guidance to sex, for example, *The Joy of Sex: A Gourmet Guide to Love Making.*

b. *Picture books* (for want of a better name): these include collections of paintings or photography intended for pleasure in their own beauty, as well as illustrative volumes such as the *Alchemy* book already mentioned, or the Sierra Club books, which seek to evoke responsibility for the natural beauty they illustrate.

c. The *occult, mysticism,* and other *spiritual* concerns: including materials on magic, astrology, mystical body exercises, the Argueles's *Mandala,* mythology, and the *Spiritual Community Guide.*

d. *Nostalgia* volumes: poster collections, stills from old movies, histories of comic books, *The Fifties,* old mercantile catalogues, and the like. Three which are worth special mention: Jensen, Kerr, and Belsky, *American Album* (rare photographs illustrating both American history and the development of photography); Michael Lesy's *Wisconsin Death Trip,* "an exercise in historical actuality" that counterposes photographs and news clippings from a Wisconsin county seat from 1885–1900; and Kinser and Kleinman's *The Dream That Was No More a Dream: A Search for Aesthetic Reality in Germany, 1890–1945,* which works toward "an aesthetic analysis of social systems."

e. Additional books: movies and television (especially *Radical Software,* a book-journal of experimental television); schools (especially the Big Rock Candy Mountain series of educational experimentation guides); and psychological interests (*Psycho Sources: A Psychological Resource Catalogue* is typical). Then there are Gay Liberation books, Women's Movement resources, and ephemera such as *The Joy of Streaking: A Guide to America's Favorite Pastime*—published within three weeks of the first exhibitions.

The point of this section is found in the listing; the justification for its inclusion is that I think we must allow "story" its maximal inclusiveness. The books mentioned here are read and used in ways which fiction is read and "used," and on that basis alone we have to look beyond formal definitional limits to functional ones. Perhaps one of the most striking instances of a fusion between the two is the presence of a novel (*Divine Right's Trip,* by Gurney Norman —subsequently published separately), segments of which are printed on each double page of *The Last Whole Earth Catalogue,* in attempts, the editors tell us, at "making the *Catalogue* what it has longed to be, a work of drama."

We see several trends—toward the body, toward the inner self, as well as toward the self-created; toward the experimental, but also toward the past. It will be helpful to keep these trends in mind as we look at the explicit stories and ask what they are saying.

And finally I want to point to two thematic motifs that also reflect desires to complete and fulfill: *science fiction,* as exploring alternatives to the increasingly arid saturation of science proper, and *fantasy-mysticism,* as the complement to that part of ourselves that leads us, like Molière's Tartuffe, to speak only prose all our lives. Scifi has spawned its own secondary literature now, and is even threatened fundamentally by being made the subject of university courses, so we will leave it alone. Fantasy-mysticism is a tough breed that spans Tolkien and Casteñeda, Aleister Crowley and Alan Watts, and asks again and again about the "reality" that seems so real until challenged. I do not see either the joyful fantastic literature or the occult-religious-mystical materials as "flight from reality," although either can work like a damp sponge, drawing the aficionado deeper inside toward entropy. Both are important, rather, in placing the reality questions, in elaborating the colors of the spectacles with which we are all trained to perceive our experiences.[21] The borderlines between fantasy, dream, and reality may become stretched so thin that it is difficult to know which is which: Jerome, the male character in Elliott Anderson's story *"from* Virginia Flynn,"[22] starts out for the bank and home, only to be abducted, tortured, and finally bound to the stake and shot; awakening to the smell of an ammonia bottle, he hears his friends applauding, and realizes that his experience has been an elaborate theater piece.

I am not as convinced as are others that contemporary openness to fantasy, to magic or science fiction is such a "revolution of the spirit" (so David Adams Leeming),[23] since I think many of us have kept openings toward the fantastic all our lives. But it surely *is* striking that so many people are receptive in these directions now, and that so many alternatives are opened up all at once—in his anthology of nonfictional prose, fiction, and poetry, Leeming includes: magic, mysticism, shamanic accounts, classical mystical poetry, folklore studies, psychology, witchcraft, Taoism, Blake, the Old Testament, fantasy and fairy tales, and mythological studies! It is impossible to avoid comparisons with the increase in choices during the late Hellenistic period; and it is chastening to suspect that the contemporary man on the street is no better prepared to confront integrally all his options than was his late-Hellenistic equivalent.

Religio—tying *what* together? Or: How many and with what respect valences? We have paid dearly for theological denunciation of eclecticism and syncretism, and perhaps the future religious task is to forge the flow-patterns that can hold together originally disparate images, symbols, and values. What if the "apocalyptic novels" of our days, such as Thomas Pynchon's stunning tour de force, *Gravity's Rainbow,* were the models? Must Western man surrender his love of connectives and outlines and flow charts? Is the new image of man an adjusted model of Heidegger's image of *Lichtungen* (clearings in the forest where paths meet and cross, instants of sunny clarification amidst the forest coolness)?

3. *The New Fictions: Techniques, Patterns, Tensions*

Seeking *what* is being said, we turn from who and where briefly to the *how.* The impact coming through the new fictions is as much a feature of the kinds of writing being done as it is a matter of contents.

This is not the place to present a technical literary critique (nor do I have the skills for the task) and I am not concerned here exclusively with craft as opposed to subject matter, or with demonstrating in detail the ways we have to refer to a "new," "antimodernist" fiction, or a "surfiction"—all terms of recent critics. Instead, I have assembled some of the literary features that, it seems to me, enable our authors to make the emotional and affective impacts they make.[24]

Multiperspectival is the first descriptive adjective I find useful: and it is an adjective that allows of several nuances. The first usage might be the more graphic multileveled one, since the split screens at Canada's EXPO, or the sequential storytelling in the movie version of Heller's *Catch 22,* give us one important key. Kenneth Patchen's *The Journal of Albion Moonlight,* for instance, has three simultaneous stories being narrated in parallel columns (comparison with John Cage's meditations and lecture in *Silence* is ready to hand). Or a related second usage: Robert Coover's "The Babysitter" gives us a series of choices, as the story-stories are told and retold: Did the sitter get raped by the husband, who had left the party without his wife's knowledge? Or did she and her boyfriend have sex in front of the TV? Or did the only sex take place in the television movie she was watching? Or did she really drown the baby in the bathwater? Here and in "The Magic Poker," Coover never really tells us the answers, i.e., he refuses to choose *one* of the possible perspectives from which his stories may be realized. Albee's *Who's Afraid of Virginia Woolf?* and Ionesco's play *The Chairs* both introduced us to this disquieting ambivalence: In each the question remains unresolved whether the narrating couple actually did or did not engender a male child. Now George Blecher begins his "The Death of the Russian Novel," which has four parts corresponding to a final examination, with these instructions: *"Part I: Comparisons.* Select the paragraph or paragraphs which come closest to a complete answer."[25] And in Coover's "Morris in Chains," the media reporter's account is given in alternating paragraphs with Morris's own internal reflections.

We are faced with a different narrative dynamics, no longer listening to a narrator, but to narrations from the author, from his characters, from elsewhere. The frames of reference have shifted, are shifting, and the author may speak directly to the reader not as narrator but as author: "The muddy circle you see . . . represents the ring left on a leaf of the manuscript by my coffee cup. Represents, I say, because, as you must surely realize, this book is many removes from anything I've set pen, hand, or cup to." And near the end of the book (I cannot give the page reference since the pages are not numbered): "You've been had, haven't you jocko? . . . Really, did you read this far? puzzle your head? . . . Was it racy enough to suit? There wasn't too much plot?"[26] The last question is, to say the least, ironic, since the book has little resembling plot in the usual sense.

Richard Pearce analyzes what happens when the traditional perspectivism is shattered:

> The narrator is no longer situated between the subject and the reader, he no longer stands on a fixed vantage, and he no longer encloses the subject within the frame of his visual imagination. Indeed, as he enters the frame, the medium asserts itself as an independent source of interest and control. The narrative voice loses its independent and dominant status. And what the reader sees is no longer a clear picture contained within the narrator's purview, but an erratic image where the narrator, the subject, and the medium are brought into the same imaginative field of interaction, an image that is shattered, confused, self-contradictory, but with an independent and individual life of its own.[27]

If the stories are all there, and the reader must assemble his own favorite, *time* is also released from the clockcase: in Coover's "In a Train Station," one of the three characters resets the station clock at the "end" of the story, in order to return the story's action to its beginning point and replay its cycle from the beginning. (Not being a sports fan, I am not less disoriented by occasionally seeing television "instant replays" of crucial events.) The author-cum-narrator is clearly in charge, and we are not forced to discover the inventiveness of the author: he tells us!

> I wander the island, inventing it. I make a sun for it, and trees . . . and cause the water to lap the pebbles of its abandoned shores. This, and more: I deposit shadows and dampness, spin webs, and scatter ruins. . . . I impose a hot midday silence, a profound and heavy stillness. But anything can happen.[28]

We have a sort of *heightened realism,* or perhaps a *sur-realism,* if that term were not already used in the graphic arts: we have to agree to the author's conventions to create a time, space, and reality that exist only for this story. (Coover, "In a Train Station:" "Now assuming both Alfred and the Express Train to be real . . ." —but of course they are only real within this story.)[29]

We find ourselves in the presence of *self-made subworlds,* as in Coover's *The Universal Baseball Association, Inc., J. Henry Waugh, Prop.,* where Harry's universe is his only meaningful response to the tedium of his daily life. There is an *inextricability* involved: characters are often "locked in" situations from which they have no egress. We see it happening and want to cry out (Hawkes's *The Lime Twig*), but are not allowed to do so; we are only allowed to watch as characters are forced into playing out their roles.

Plot suffers. Or at least those of us who are accustomed to the traditional Western plot concept find it suffering: my suggestion is that we learn new things about plot and what its significance is. Perhaps it takes a certain sophistication to maintain interest in a story that doesn't look like a story![30] I am thinking of Hawkes's *The Lime Twig,* in which the hero is killed midway through the book, and yet our interest is not lost. Sequence of events, our usual linear logics: perhaps we should not demand of fiction the connectedness that designs digital computers and napalm antipersonnel weapons.

At any rate, *patience!* We may have to wait for pages and pages to learn the next part of a crucial sequence, and illuminations come not in clear-cut delineations of movement, but in quick jabs and flashes. Guerard, introducing Hawkes' *The Cannibal,* uses the image of: "a solitary flashlight playing back and forth over a dark and cluttered room; the images may be sharp ones, but a casual reference to some major happening may be clarified only fifty or a hundred pages later."[31] Already Hesse had a presentiment of this kind of story/life; in *The Journey to the East,* H. H. speaks of his happiness as: "the freedom to experience everything imaginable simultaneously, to exchange outward and inward easily, to move Time and Space about like scenes in a theatre."[32] I am reminded of Samuel Beckett's *Play,* where the actors remain submerged in large concrete urns, only their heads showing; the spotlights play upon each head in an apparently random fashion, controlling our listening to three related monologues in brief bits and pieces or all at once.

In contrast to the traditional novel or fiction, the scenes in the new fiction are not necessarily sequential, and the customary pattern of expectation-established to denouement, no longer applies; the "form" is sometimes that of the random selections in one of the old patchwork quilts of my childhood. Stevick comments on three authors only, but catches something vital for many contemporary writers:

> Both Coover's and Barthelme's fictions are alike in this respect: both share with Brautigan's a form in which images and events accumulate and sometimes gather great force but do not arrange themselves so as to demonstrate a theme or so as to gradually gratify the expectations and resolve the tensions generated at the beginning of the work.[33]

Patience, then, is often required; sudden and illogical shifts in person, rapid alteration of time perspective, layering of narrative from different characters' points of view. More of a demand is being made on readers, more necessity to hear and to tell our own story within and through the story we are reading.

Clearly *the past* is of almost obsessive importance; in fact I suspect that we are in a phase of fiction where there is more than ordinary concentration on man's utilization of the past, of history, of The Tradition. Two primary options can be noted: historical revision, and a turn toward the mythologies of the past.

We have, for instance, Milton Klonsky's long piece which reconstructs history, relating Dostoevsky to Casteñeda, interwoven with antique drawings of fleas.[34] Or there is Alvin Greenburg's "The discovery of America,"[35] in which Amerigo Vespucci is reincarnated so as to explore his personal problems and views of society; or Coover's "The public burning of Julius and Ethel Rosenberg: *an historical romance,*"[36] reflecting on the moods and decision-making process of the President's Cabinet members; or John Bátki's "Two pieces,"[37] in which Rimbaud and Mallarmé are given "human interest story" treatments that would fit the daily news-paper. A reconstruction of history for the purposes of making sense out of it; of imagining it (giving it the images by which we come to comprehension), and enabling an appropriation of its meaning —I think immediately of Hawke's *The Cannibal,* Jerzy Kosinski's *The Painted Bird,* and the writings of Elie Wiesel; these authors are more adept than the academic historians at revoicing the World War II period. Kafka had reimaged history, as in his telling the possible alternative endings to the Abraham and Isaac stories, or the variations on the Odysseus myths, and Borges followed the model when he reported the death of "an old soldier of the king," Don Quixote, or when he speculates three responses Don Quixote might have made upon discovering that he had killed a man.[38]

Somehow there is a felt necessity to gain the boons of the past, to utilize and to internalize, *to learn from;* it is not just the reaction to the entrapment of existentialism, the inability to face the present, like Saul Bellow's *Herzog,* or the need to overcome the lack of being able to pull it all together, as in Coover's novel: "History is like a big goddam sea, Sal, and here we are, bobbing around on it, a buncha poor bastards who can't swim, seasick, lost, unable to see past the next goddamn wave, not knowing where the hell it's taking us if it takes us anywhere at all."[39] Nor is it simply the sense of the irony of history—as seen in William Golding's *Lord of the Flies,* where the stranded boys are "rescued" from their war games by a battleship.

John Barth is probably the author best known for turning to past mythologies, especially Greco-Roman mythologies, to find frame-works, themes, and characters for his fictions,[40] but he is not alone in the sort of consciously hip dalliance with the classical tradition. The hero of Robert Bonazzi's story, "The ancient tragical motif as reflected in the modern,"[41] thanks both Aeschylus and Abner Doubleday (inventor of baseball) for leading to his encounter with his "Cassandra."

The mythologies are to be reimagined as well as the histories; if on the one hand mythological themes and characters appear with-out belief, simply as reverse literary allusions, on the other hand there is a receptivity to the classical stories and archetypal narratives—witness the interest among writers in Frye's mythological criticism and in the crosscultural comparative work of Mircea Eliade or Joseph Campbell.

We might contrast use of mythological themes and characters with use of mythology as it functions as "social cement," to paraphrase Durkheim. Interest in broad social questions is notably lacking, however, and unless I am wrong, the new writers are turning to the classical mythologies for personal, almost existential, gain rather than a way out of the present social chaos.

One live option as a life-style or way out (or *in,* or *through*) is the *epigrammatic* as opposed to the mythically coherent; the fragmentary, the fragmented—and echoes of the style of N. O. Brown's *Love's Body* float through many recent writings. "Alice," by Barthelme, may provide an example:

> yellow brick wall visible from rear bedroom window of
> the rented house
> I see Alice walking away from me carrying a Primary
> Structure . . .
> Alice's husband Buck calls me will I gather with him
> for a game of golf? I accept but on the shoe shelf
> I cannot find the correct shoes distractedness stupidity
> weak memory! I am boring myself what should be the punish-
> ment I am forbidden to pick my nose forevermore
> Buck is rushing toward me carrying pieces of carbon
> paper big as bedsheets what is he hinting at? duplicity
> bleep! it is the tipped uterus from Carson City calling[42]

The same author's "Bone Bubbles,"[43] and other similar pieces, take the style to its extreme: groupings of sentence fragments ("paragraph" no longer applies), few verbs, mostly adverbs, gerunds, adjectives; almost total lack of punctuation, no capital letters.[44] His "Sentence,"[45] is literally, for all its length, one continuous sequence of clauses and word phrases (in this case the grammatical term "sentence" no longer applies, or is radically redefined).

Typographical experimentation—*poésie concret* in prose—appears and reappears, partly as a reaction against the boredom of our usual printed page, more significantly as a form of experimentation, seeing what contemporary media forms can contribute to the prose word. Perhaps the most attractive of these experiments is *Willie Master's Lonesome Wife,* written by William H. Gass and designed by Lawrence Levy.[46] Only a few pages in that volume appear in straight type; most employ a series of different fonts, lines of print that wiggle over the page (or, in the case of the title, over a nude woman's body), and brown smudges represent marks made on the manuscript by the author's coffee cup.

There is a *playfulness,* then, that can only be experienced in the reading. It appears frequently, often in rhythm with sadness, irony, or profundity. In Alfred Jarry's "The Supermale," a "machine-to-inspire-love," when hooked up to André Marcueil, is itself electrified and driven by his supernormal energies—reversing an eleven-thousand-volt dynamo.[47] The hero of Barthelme's "The Glass Mountain," ascending a slick mountain made of glass to rescue the stranded princess, pauses:

81. I was afraid.
82. I had forgotten the Bandaids.
83. When the eagle dug its sharp claws into my tender flesh—
84. Should I go back for the Bandaids?
85. But if I went back for the Bandaids I would have to endure the contempt of my acquaintances.
86. I resolved to proceed without the Bandaids.

And sometimes the playfulness becomes macabre or grotesque:

97. I approached the [beautiful enchanted] symbol, with its layers of meaning, but when I touched it, it changed into only a beautiful princess.
98. I threw the beautiful princess headfirst down the mountain to my acquaintances.
99. Who could be relied upon to deal with her.
100. Nor are eagles plausible, not at all, not for a moment.[48]

The macabre can be shown with a touch of humor—sick humor, perhaps, but nonetheless playful—as in Coover's "The Pedestrian Accident," where the entire story takes place over the fallen and tortured body of Paul, who "stepped off the curb and got hit by a truck." More of the story involves the truck driver's protestations, and Mrs. Grundy's flirtations with the policeman, than in rushing aid to the victim, who remains supine during the entire action.[49]

LeeWillie, in Ellison's "Cadillac Flambé," interrupts the Senator's outdoor barbeque by dousing a white Cadillac with gasoline and setting it on fire—a protest against the Senator's explicit racism, but a humorous ploy that soon becomes comitragedy of a unique sort.[50] And there's the young woman in Ursule Molinaro's "Chiaroscuro: a treatment of light and shade," whose Sunday morning bump on her forehead has by midday developed into a third, Cyclopean eye that smiles back at her.[51] More frequently it is brutal, as when a twenty or thirty pound green iguana fastens itself onto the naked back of the pregnant Catalina Kate who loved to dig herself a hole in the damp sand and sleep in it, or the horrible beating of a male teacher at a school for the rehabilitation of criminal female minors—both in fictions by Hawkes.[52]

In addition to the supercharged symbolism that many of the writers like to use, this sort of macabre, grotesque element is often combined with an extreme concern *to list* and *to provide detail* that almost seems a talisman against a society that has classified itself into absurdity. It may be a device for packing information into short compass: compare these opening paragraphs from Hawke's newest novel:

> Ursula is leaving. Dressed in her severe gray suit, her gardening hat, her girdle, her negligee, her sullen silk dress, her black blouse, her stockings, her red pumps, and carrying a carefully packed straw suitcase in either hand, thus she is leaving me. . . . With her skirts awry, her elegant tight black military coat draped to within inches of her ankles, and with her hair blowing, the black bun sculpted at the back of her head, a cigarette lighted between pale fingers, and with belted valises lightly in hand, thus she is leaving. . . .[53]

And sometimes the lists are devices of rhythm and of sensuousness:

> COLLARDS. Winter greens. Rosettes on the cracked lapel of soil. HEAD CABBAGE from green to red. Ai! Red cabbage cooked with a slice of apple to preserve its color, served with pork sausage. CAULIFLOWER, who curdles her atrophied flowers into succulent clusters soothed by liquid cheese. Rare and most ancient BROCCOLI who gladly foregoes her bloom and allows her green virginity to grace my plate. Delicate dainty BRUSSELS SPROUTS, skittish as a filly, obstinately refusing to firm your

tender heads unless raised in cool districts spiced by the sea.
Yeah, even KOHLRABI, of thee I sing. The turnip cabbage.
Cavoli rape. Chou-rave. Koolraap. Grown for stock feed. But I
found thy flesh sweet and mild and much too good for swine.
Cabbages! They do not heart, neither do they sing. But I say unto
thee, they are kinder to man than man is to his own kindred.[54]

Explicit sexuality and *allusive sensuality* are often found in combination, and I sometimes have the impression that this may be the
first post-Freudian generation of writers for whom sex is treated as
casually as other life acts. Sex is hardly "dirty," and more often
than not it is unselfconscious without losing its sacredness. Its
bluntness will offend only those who have not experienced the
poverty of writing in recent American pornography.

I have the impression that many contemporary writers are not
overly impressed with the exaggerated explicitness that has come
to be *de rigueur* in student and underground "creative writing"
magazines. Randall Reid, at least, gives us a taste of the bitterness
of "a semiretired roué" after thirty years of hyperactive sexuality:
"My orgasm is like a gun going off in another room; I scarcely hear
the report."[55] The mechanistic Love Manual approach leads his
character to suggest that: "Before long, someone will be selling
blueprints for orgies, and the guests can fit themselves together like
prefabricated pieces in the latest erector set."[56]

Already Hesse had explored human relationships instead of—
and alongside of—explicit sexuality (*Narcissus and Goldmund*),
but his sort of ambisexual identity does not appeal to many more
recent writers.[57] Sexual identity is part of personal identity, and it
is—we are told—to be celebrated and lived, not to be isolated and
idolized.

Humor about sexuality is not lacking. Without a doubt one of
the funniest parodies I've ever read, Kenneth Bernard's "King
Kong: A Meditation," overlooks few possible questions about
Tarzan and Kong's sexual makeups, including the length of the
gorilla's penis ("There is, however, some slight indirect evidence of
size. When Kong storms the walls that separate him from the
savages, seeking his stolen maiden, with what does he batter them?
It is definitely a possibility"),[58] and leading to reflection on the
despair of Fay Wray when she is abducted by "the savages": "Fay

Wray is feeling totally *abandoned* by her world. . . . Not even
the females look familiar to her or reachable. . . . Needless to
say, she also feels existentially abandoned by her god. Where can
God be if there are black fingers in her private parts?"[59]

Or there's the hilarious account of the aristocratic Brewster
Ashenden, who finds himself cornered so that he must have inter-
course with a rutting she-bear![60] Perhaps that which can be paro-
died and laughed at is no longer something awkwardly clandestine
and sacred. But perhaps we learn also that the sacred includes the
humorous, that the intensity of sexuality must be balanced by an
appreciative risibility to engender love.

4. *The Images of Contemporary Personhood*

As I reviewed my notes for this fourth part,[61] it became increasingly clear to me how much of the concern of the writers I have
been discussing is focused on anthropology, i.e., on contemporary
comprehensions of what it means to experience vital, living, personhood. There are responses to the machine and especially to
communications media;[62] there are stories that seek to come to
grips with the terrors and the pleasures of the future. But the
unifying thread seems to be the question of person: how to become,
how to find identity, how to remain authentically personal.

So there is an introspective flavor, a turning in to the self-
contained and self-created, a reduction of the social universe to
couples and families and individuals. The hero still lives: but he is
more likely than his earlier American prototypes to find himself
suspended, less capable of decisive moments of heroism that solve
group dilemmas or forge new breakthroughs (compare the iguana
scene in Hawkes's *Second Skin* mentioned earlier: Skipper can
only wait for the iguana to release its claws; in Coover's "Morris
in Chains," Morris is finally led away in chains). The hero takes
up the trials we each face daily, not the dramatic redeeming-the-
world quest, and finds himself confronted with seeing through,
with the necessity for resignation rather than heroism. This is not
so much existentialism's turning toward one's own navel: rather
an acceptance of life as it is; not moodiness or anger, but waiting
it out and surviving with the integrity of the moment; "Dancing"

—so Barthelme's hero in "Can We Talk"—"on my parquet floor in my parquet shorts. To Mahler."[63]

A shift from commitment to resignation. Published in 1927, Hesse could still call for transcending exertion:

> Who today wishes to live and have joy of his life must not be like you or me. For he who demands music instead of tootling, enjoyment instead of pleasure, a soul instead of gold, real work instead of activity, true passion instead of dalliance, this pretty world is no homeland.[64]

But Hawkes's hero, whose wife has left him, whose cruise lover has jumped overboard, and whose friend (and wife's lover) Peter has died of a heart attack in the sauna, concludes his story:

> Perhaps I should commit myself to Acres Wild [a psychiatric "home" run by Peter]. Perhaps I should go in search of the village of my youth and childhood. Or I could ask the international telephone operator to locate Simone [an earlier lover]. Or I could lock myself in Peter's frozen car and submit to asphyxiation, in which case I could no doubt join my departed friend on the island of imaginary goats. But I shall do none of these things.
>
> Instead I shall simply think and dream, think and dream. I shall dream of she who guided me to the end of the journey, whoever she is, and I shall think of porridge, leeks, tobacco, white clay, and water coursing through a Roman aqueduct.[65]

Not that the in between time is all roses—it can be shallow or painful; it can be the entrapment of playing it cool and bumbling through:

> Games were what kept Miller going. Games, and the pacifying of the mind and organs. Miller perceived existence as a loose concatenation of separate and ultimately inconsequential instants, each colored by the actions that preceded it, but each possessed of a small wanton freedom of its own. Life, then, was a series of adjustments to these actions and, if one kept his sense of humor and produced as many of these actions as possible, adjustment was easier.[66]

But the negative side of turning to fantasy, to fun and games as escape, is balanced and redeemed by its positive side: a sense of playfulness, celebration of the sexual and the sensual. We enjoy and create, find delight in the simple things (remember the rhapsody to cabbages quoted earlier), and provide space for anticipation; for, as Barthelme reminds us:

ANATHEMATIZATION OF THE WORLD IS NOT AN ADEQUATE RESPONSE
TO THE WORLD.[67]

The lines of connection are no longer stable; but don't all patterns emerge mostly through hindsight? The tyranny of definitions and dogmas is hardly preferable to the magnificent freedoms of our own age. To be able to challenge the definitions, to seek their revision, is to begin to take responsibility for the future: "Trying to break out of this bag that we are in. What gave us the idea that there was something better? How does the concept, "something better," arise? What does it look like, this *something better?*"[68] What do they look like?—for now our very own educational system has inculcated (at least in a pro forma way) the philosophy that "the unexamined life is not worth living," and our most recent experiences with the corruptions of American politics lead ever more quickly to asking fundamental questions of the consensual "something better."

And so there is a commitment to living out, to trying possible roles, to imaging alternatives even before they have been defined. Or: we hear of alternatives to the technocratic injection slipped to us along with grammar school polio vaccines, and we gain a sense of the "fate" of classical tragedy. Ancient myths seems suddenly less ancient, and we realize the turn forward may be informed by the looking backward.

The myths playing themselves out in us: so Lévi-Strauss in his own technological manner; and the poet Robert Duncan ("The surety of the myth for the poet has such force that it operates as a primary reality in itself, having volition. The mythic content comes to us, commanding the design of the poem; it calls the poet into action.");[69] and David Miller and James Hillman remand our religious and psyche stories to mythological first creations.[70] Mythic man, not the demythologized man of Bultmann, but mythic man now in a plurality of mythic motifs, tensions, desires, and partial completions. Not *The Myth,* but the myths, the stor*ies* that *together* inform and conform us in ageless patterns. So the incorrigible

Norman Mailer, reflecting for a moment, balancing the public psyche of film with the interiors of the actors' selves:

> We are always looking for real stories to ensue which never exactly enact themselves as we expect, yet we still work at such times as actors in the real story of our life, pursuing roles which can become our life at any instant the psychological can become real—as occasionally it will.[71]

Looking, waiting "for real stories to ensue" . . . but I think also seeking the true stories, the archetypal threads in our psychohistories.

We are our stories. We become our stories. And sometimes these stories are taken from the communal imaginings that have been disciplined for public sharing. As public, they are visible psyches to us, alternatives and visions, projections and reflections that are our contemporary mythologies, and that may seed our own future imaginings.

It would be naive to suppose that personhood should be imaged no differently in different times. Surely our own futures promise and threaten communal forms and existential shapes that can only be dimly grasped ahead of time—but they will certainly be different from what we now know. Contemporary fiction provides some of the imaginings upon which our own futures will be established. Our own disciplined imaginings may at least rebound partially upon them, as we set out to become the stories we are.

NOTES

1. Now I discover that the poet Robert Duncan has said this more clearly: "Like the poet, the child dwells not in the literal meanings of words but in the spirit that moves behind them, in the passional reality of the outraging or insidiously rationalizing adult. He hears not what his parents mean to say, but what that saying is telling about them." *The Truth and Life of Myth: An Essay in Essential Autobiography* (Fremont, Mich.: Sumac, orig. The House of Books, 1968), p. 13.
2. *Time and Myth. A Meditation on Storytelling as an Exploration of Life and Death* (Garden City: Doubleday, 1973).

3. A. B. Paulson, "2," *TriQuarterly* 26 (1973): 192 ff.
4. James Hillman, *The Myth of Analysis: Three Essays in Archetypal Psychology* (Evanston: Northwestern, 1972), p. 182.
5. See Charles Newman's ruminations on the problems of "literature as a commodity," in "The uses and abuses of death . . . ," *TriQuarterly* 26 (1973): 3–41.
6. The phrase alludes to Stephen Crites's article, "The Narrative Quality of Existence," *Journal of the American Academy of Religion* 39 (1971): 291–311.
7. "Amazing Journey," from the rock opera *Tommy,* by The Who.
8. Conclusion to the title story, Heinrich Zimmer, *The King and the Corpse: Tales of the Soul's Conquest of Evil,* 2nd ed., ed. Joseph Campbell (Princeton: Princeton, 1956), p. 215. The sense of the marvelous protection of the story—especially the old, the founding story—is found in a Navaho saying: "Knowing a good story will protect your home and children and property. A myth is just like a big stone foundation, it lasts a long time."
9. This impression is at least partly informed by reading student class journals, in which students reflect and respond to course readings. As can be imagined, the exercise becomes a means for them to share their own stories as they integrate or reject the moral formal scholastic stories of our culture.
10. The subtitle is also instructive: *Compositions and Decompositions in the Languages of Contemporary Life* (New York: Oxford, 1971).
11. Cf. Robert Jay Lifton, "Protean Man," in B. B. Wolman, ed., *The Psychoanalytic Interpretation of History* (New York: Harper and Row, 1971), pp. 33–49: "The protean style of self-process . . . is characterized by an interminable series of experiments and explorations—some shallow, some profound—each of which may be readily abandoned in favor of still new psychological quests" (p. 37). "Until relatively recently, no more than one major ideological shift was likely to occur in a lifetime, and this one would be long remembered as a significant individual turning point accompanied by profound soul-searching and conflict. But today it is not unusual to encounter several such shifts, accomplished relatively painlessly, within a year or even a month; among many groups, the rarity is a man who has gone through life holding firmly to a single ideological vision" (p. 42).
12. For development of this view of the artist, see chapters 18 and 19, Walter Abell, *The Collective Dream in Art: A Psycho-Historical Theory of Culture* . . . (1957; reprint ed. New York: Schocken, 1966).
13. I could also be happy with David L. Miller's thesis that "Religion means being gripped by a story," *The New Polytheism: Rebirth of*

the Gods and Goddesses (New York: Harper & Row, 1974), p. 30; on the same page he suggests that monotheism is being "gripped by one God at a time" as opposed to polytheism, where the stories of many gods have compelling attraction. "A polytheistic theology," he writes later in the book, "because it makes contact with the immediacy of life out of the depths, is itself a religion with no scripture, but with many stories" (p. 76, partly in italics in original). Instead of seeking The Story, then, we seek the stories that inform and mold us; "holding it all together" becomes more than a hip slogan, and we work toward Job's balance—Job, whose tension spans two conflicting stories in a painful dialectic (I am indebted to Karen Brown for this reading; conflict between *belief* and *experience* is sighted as the fundamental conflict in Robert Polzin's structuralist reading: "The Framework of the Book of Job," *Interpretation* 28 [1974]: 182–200.)

14. Although I cannot say why, Sartre never—except perhaps in *No Exit*—had for me the magic of Camus; his fiictional exercises struck me as just that, exercises; so too with Genet, although there is a magic in Sartre's *Saint Genet!*

15. Gary Greer, "Siddhartha: An Astrologic Parable; The Twelve-Step Cycle of Spiritual Development in Hesse's Famous Novel," *American Federation of Astrologers, Inc. Bulletin* 36 (1974): 26–32, 12–19.

16. William G. Doty, "The Parables of Jesus, Kafka, Borges, and Others, with Structural Observations," to be published in *Semeia* 2 (1974).

17. Up to issue 16, the title was *New American Review,* published by Simon and Schuster; from issue 16, the title became: *American Review: The Magazine of New Writing,* published by Bantam; all issues to which I refer were edited by Theodore Solotaroff, with others. In subsequent notes, I will use *NAR* and *AR* instead of the full references. *TriQuarterly* is published at Northwestern University, Charles Newman, editor.

18. Paul Radin, ed., *African Folktales and Sculptures,* 2nd ed. (New York: Pantheon, 1964; Bollingen Series 32), p. 27. Compare also the concern of the narrator in Rilke's *Stories of God* to know about the reception of his stories by the children.

19. Cf. also independently Norman Mailer, who reflects on the making of his "Maidstone" in "A Course on Film-Making," *NAR* 12: 200–41, and Robert Coover, two of whose stories ("Love Scene," *NAR,* 12: 91–104, and "Lucky Pierre and the Music Lesson," *NAR* 14: 201–12) are built around theater production.

20. Hardly coincidentally, new literary journals, *New Literary History* and *Genre,* have been started in attempts to deal more effectively with world-cultural literary forms. See also the attempt to formu-

late a modern theory of comparative literature (*vergleichende Literaturwissenschaft*) by Ulrich Weisstein, *Comparative Literature and Literary Theory: Survey and Introduction* (Bloomington: Indiana Univ. Press, 1973; earlier ed. in German, 1968). It would take me too far afield to mention the literary impact of others such as the Japanese novelist Mishima.

21. See Casteñeda's remarks on "sorcery in terms of Talcott Parsons' idea of glosses," in Sam Keen, "Sorcerer's Apprentice," *Psychology Today,* December 1972, p. 95. And Daniel C. Noel comments: "What he gives us . . . is a lesson in 'lived hermeneutics,' the actual *experience* of interpretation's role in interpreting experience so as to constitute what we know as 'world,' 'reality,' 'meaning'." "Makings of Meaning: Carlos Casteñeda's 'Lived Hermeneutics' in the Cargo Culture," *Listening/Current Studies in Dialog* 7 (1972): p. 85.

22. *TriQuarterly* 29 (1972): 167–72.

23. Editor, *Flights: Readings in Magic, Mysticism, Fantasy, and Myth* (New York: Harcourt Brace Jovanovich, 1974).

24. The critic Albert J. Guerard, writing in "Notes on the rhetoric of anti-realist fiction," *TriQuarterly* 30 (1974): 3–50, notes four characteristics of what he calls antirealist fictions; while I focus explicitly only on his second item, the list is a good starting point, and the article itself extremely insightful. His list (in italics in original): Self-consciousness and anxiety over the fiction-making process, and over the relation of fiction to reality: Nabokovian involution; Formal discontinuity: the impulse to fragment form, consciousness; Absurd reasoning. Eruption of the absurd among the banal, or vice versa; phenomenological fiction: notation, meditation, monologue. See also the article by Philip Stevick referred to below, *TriQuarterly* 26 (1973): 332–62.

25. *NAR* 14: 142–61.

26. William H. Gass, *Willie Master's Lonesome Wife* (New York: Knopf, 1971, with photography by Burton L. Rudman; originally *TriQuarterly* Supplement 2, 1968).

27. Richard Pearce, "Enter the frame," *TriQuarterly* 30 (1974): 71–82; quotation from p. 72.

28. Robert Coover, "The Magic Poker," in *Pricksongs & Descants* (New York: Dutton, 1969), p. 20.

29. Ibid., p. 99.

30. Obviously the therapist must excel in this type of sophistication; and a second-level sophistication is indicated by Jonathan Baumbach's "The traditional story returns," *TriQuarterly* 26 (1973): 184–91, which begins with a sort of parody of those who complain about lack of plot: "Too many times you read a story nowadays and it's not a story at all, not in the traditional sense. A

traditional story has plot, character, and theme, to name three things it traditionally has. The following story, which contains a soupçon of mood in addition to the three major considerations named above, is intended as a modest 'rearguard action in the service of a declining tradition' " (p. 184).

31. (1949, reprint ed. New York: New Directions, 1962), p. xi.
32. Translated by Hilda Rosner (New York: Farrar, Straus & Giroux, 1956), p. 28.
33. Philip Stevick, "Scheherazade runs out of plots, goes on talking; the king, puzzled, listens: an essay on new fiction," *TriQuarterly* 26 (1973): 332–62, quoted from p. 348.
34. "Art and Life: A Menippean Paean to the Flea; or, Did Dostoevsky Kill Trotsky?", in *AR* 20: 115–88.
35. *TriQuarterly* 26 (1973): 104–18.
36. *TriQuarterly* 26 (1973): 262–81.
37. *TriQuarterly* 29 (1974): 180–82.
38. "Parable of Cervantes and the *Quixote*," p. 242, and "A Problem," pp. 244–45, in *Labyrinths: Selected Stories and Other Writings,* ed. D. A. Yates and J. E. Irby (augmented ed.; New York: New Directions, 1964).
39. *The Origins of the Brunists* (New York: Putnam's, 1966), p. 330. Cf. Hermine's statement in Hesse, *Steppenwolf* (1929; reprint ed. New York: Holt, Rinehart and Winston, 1963) p. 153: "Ah, Harry, we have to stumble through so much dirt and humbug before we reach home. And we have no one to guide us. Our only guide is our homesickness."
40. *See* for instance "Menelaiad," or "Anonymiad," both in *Lost in the Funhouse: Fiction for print, tape, live voice* (Garden City: Doubleday, 1968), or *Chimera* (New York: Random House, 1972).
41. *TriQuarterly* 29 (1974): 157–63.
42. In *Unspeakable Practices, Unnatural Acts* (1968; reprint ed. New York: Bantam, 1969), pp. 113–23, quoted from pp. 121–22.
43. In *City Life* (1970; reprint ed. New York: Bantam, 1971), pp. 125–34.
44. I do not mean to imply that Barthelme is the only writer using such experimental patterns—far from it, as a glance through any contemporary anthology will prove.
45. In *City Life,* pp. 113–21.
46. *See also* Kenneth Patchen, *Wonderings* (New York: New Directions, 1971); but this has become a picturebook primarily, like his poster collections. Ferdinand Krivet discusses and illustrates the development of the *Sehtext, Schreibtext, Rundschreiben,* and other forms in "Decomposition of the literary unit: notes on visually perceptible literature," *TriQuarterly* 20 (1971): 209–52.

47. Translated from the French by R. Gladstone and B. Wright, in J. Laughlin, ed., *New Directions in Prose and Poetry 18* (New York: New Directions, 1964), pp. 71–148.

48. *City Life*, p. 70 and p. 71.

49. In *Pricksongs & Descants,* pp. 183–205.

50. *AR* 16: 249–69.

51. *TriQuarterly* 29 (1974): 41–52.

52. John Hawkes, *Second Skin* (New York: New Directions, 1964), pp. 103–09; Hawkes, "The Universal Fears," in *AR* 16: 108–23.

53. *Death, Sleep & the Traveler* (New York: New Directions, 1974), p. 1.

54. E. M. Beekman, "Cabbages and Death," in R. Kostelantez, ed., *In Youth* (New York: Ballantine, 1972), pp. 12–31, quoted from p. 21. One indication that this convention has worn itself out already is the parody, "Suspension Points . . .," by Meyer Liben. Reflecting on buying a newspaper, the narrator realizes "that I could, if I so wished, spend a good part of the rest of my life describing this act," and then proceeds to list all the aspects of the transaction that could be listed—we are saved in *medias res* by suspension points (ellipsis marks); *NAR* 14: 88–94; quoted from p. 88.

55. "Detritus," *NAR* 14: 11–33; quoted from p. 14.

56. Ibid., p. 21.

57. Cf. Harry Haller and Hermine in *Steppenwolf*: their lack of explicit differentiation reflects more intense Nietzschean dualisms than sex, however. To refer to *Narcissus and Goldmund* as being about "homosexuality"—so one edition's book jacket—surely reflects a lack of sensitivity toward the novel itself.

58. *NAR* 14: 182–98; quoted from p. 187.

59. Ibid., p. 195.

60. Stanley Elkin, "The Making of Ashenden," *TriQuarterly* 26 (1973): 42–103.

61. Initial impetus toward this essay came from teaching in a college preparatory summer course on "The Contemporary American Scene;" subsequently, parts were reworked for several student orientation programs, and for a Hillel Free University program at Princeton. I am indebted to participants' suggestions in the lively discussions that followed my presentations.

62. See especially the writings of Kurt Vonnegut, omitted here because of personal bias. See also "Monitor" and "Rotinom," by Frederick Barthelme, in *In Youth,* pp. 10–11, and Barth's *Lost in the Funhouse: Fictions for print, tape, live voice.*

63. In *Unspeakable Practices,* pp. 97–102; quoted from p. 102.

64. *Steppenwolf,* p. 150.

65. *Death, Sleep & the Traveler,* p. 179; cf. the almost identical ending to *Second Skin,* p. 210.
66. *The Origins of the Brunists,* pp. 141–42.
67. *Snow White* (1967; reprint ed. New York: Bantam, 1968), p. 178.
68. Ibid., p. 179.
69. *The Truth and Life of Myth,* p. 21.
70. Miller, *The New Polytheism;* Hollman, *The Myth of Analysis.*
71. "A Course in Film-Making," pp. 239–40.

V

The Fiction of Case History: A Round

JAMES HILLMAN

1. *Beginning with Freud*

An imaginative Italian writer, Giovanni Papini[1] published in a British intellectual journal, *The Colisseum,* in 1934, a curious interview with Freud. It is presented as a straight-on dialogue, as if Freud were privately confessing just what his work was all about. This is what that "Freud" says:

> "Everybody thinks," he [Freud] went on, "that I stand by the scientific character of my work and that my principal scope lies in curing mental maladies. This is a terrible error that has prevailed for years and that I have been unable to set right. I am a scientist by necessity, and not by vocation. I am really by nature an artist. . . . And of this there lies an irrefutable proof: which is that in all countries into which psychoanalysis has penetrated it has been better understood and applied by writers and artists than by doctors. My books, in fact, more resemble works of imagination than treatises on pathology. . . . I have been able to win my destiny in an indirect way, and have attained my dream: to remain a man of letters, though still in appearance a doctor. In all great men of science there is a leaven of fantasy, but no one proposes like me to translate the inspirations offered by the currents of modern literature into scientific theories. In psychoanalysis you may find fused together though changed into scientific jargon, the three greatest literary schools of the nineteenth century: Heine, Zola, and Mallarmé are united in me under the patronage of my old master, Goethe."[2]

I think Papini not off the mark. The Freud he offers in this interview reveals more of that master, and consequently of what psychotherapy is actually doing, than do the elaborations of Freudian
theory.

I am suggesting that psychoanalysis is a work first of all with
imaginative tellings and that therefore we must first of all regard
it as an activity in the realm of *poesis,* which means simply "making," and which I take to mean making by imagination into words.
Our work more particularly belongs to the *rhetoric* of poesis, by
which I mean the persuasive power of imagining in words, an
artfulness in speaking and hearing, writing and reading. However I
do not mean to go along with those who place depth psychology
under the aegis of communication theory or structural linguistics.
Neither of them takes enough into account the stylistics, the
rhetoric, the literariness of what is said, how it is inflected, and the
ways in which all things said are heard and, in hearing, organized
again into new tellings.

The subject, depth psychology and rhetoric, is so mammoth, so
ancient, tusked and hairy, that there is a massive psychological
literature upon the theme of psychology and literature in all their
interconnections. A proper investigation of the rhetoric theme is
beyond this essay's compass and its author's talent. Nonetheless I
do want to locate this limited paper within that larger perspective,
which means wrenching the whole business of psychotherapy,
depth psychology, psychoanalysis (terms used here interchange-
ably) from its supposedly empirical framework, whether as applied
medical science, sociology, education, or pastoral religion, so as to
connect it again with the tradition of rhetoric and poetics, disciplines whose concern it was to understand and differentiate the
effects of speech on soul.

By placing depth psychology within a poetic and rhetorical
cosmos, I am taking the consequences of a move I had already
made in my 1972 Terry Lectures.[3] There I essayed a psychology
of soul that is also a psychology of the imagination, one which
takes its point of departure neither in brain physiology, structural
linguistics, nor analyses of behavior, but in the processes of the
imagination. That is: a psychology that assumes a poetic basis of

mind. Any case history of that mind, even if disturbed in a medical sense, will therefore have to be an imaginative expression of this poetic basis, and therefore a piece of poesis, an imaginative making, a poetic fiction, disguised, as Papini says, in the language of medical science, both by the teller in his tale and the hearer in his recording.

That is my horizon. With the reach and haze of its threatening implications hanging over this entire paper, let us work away at the first matter to hand: Freud's case histories as fiction—Papini's thesis.

In the prefatory remarks to his famous 1905 publication, "Fragment of an Analysis of a Case of Hysteria"[4]—the Dora story—Freud writes: "I am aware that—in this town at least—there are many physicians who . . . choose to read a case history of this kind not as a contribution to the psychopathology of neuroses, but as a *roman à clef* designed for their private delectation." He also imagines "unauthorized," "nonmedical readers" turning to this story.

Already the "reader" was figuring in Freud the writer's fantasy. And how often in his subsequent work we come upon these Victorian, these detective-story style appeals to the reader, reminding him of what was said some pages back, or cautioning him that a point is worth holding in mind for it will appear again later, or showing concern for his wonder, confusion, perplexity—and maybe even shock at the bold frankness with which a matter is being exposed.

In this introduction to the Dora story, Freud's association to the elaborate disguised secrecy he employs in publishing this case is not to sexual psychopathology (Kraft-Ebing had not felt this sort of concern for the reader or the cases), not to household medical advisors (Tissot published his dreadful warnings on masturbation with plenty of cases), not to forensic psychiatry, or to medical *Krankengeschichte* with their illustrations of naked ladies and gentlemen standing full front and white, masked only with black rectangles over the eyes (as if they can't see us, so we can't see them).

No. Freud's associations are with literature, for which he uses

—always a sign of affective importance—a foreign term *roman à clef,* meaning "a work which presents real persons and events, but disguised by the author." Now isn't this precisely what Freud did do, and so of course the nonmedical reader comes to his mind, because in his mind Freud was already associating himself with the writer of novels. The fantasy of the two kinds of readers— authorized and medical, unauthorized and literary—refer to two figures in Freud's own fantasy.

Why did Freud get himself into this tangle between the medical and the literary when trying to write psychological case reports? Was he not struggling with a form of writing for which there were no existing models? His mind moved back and forth between the two great traditions, science and humanities, an oscillation that had to occur—not merely because the medical was a cabalistic disguise for his literary vocation, finally recognized ironically by Papini, fraternally by Thomas Mann, and officially by his being awarded a Goethe prize for literature—but more likely the dilemma had to occur because Freud was in process of inventing a genre, the very vehicle that was going to have to carry his new vision into the world. His psychoanalysis could make no further headway in the world at which he aimed it, medicine, unless it could find a suitable form of "telling" that gave the conviction, if not the substance, of medical empiricism. Freud tangled the two because he was en- gaged in both at once: fiction and case history; and ever since then in the history of our field, they are inseparable, even if we engaged in this field have lost touch with this double fact, this duplicity (which Freud did not), that our case histories are a way of writing fiction.

The analysis of this first major psychological case history—the *Iliad* of our field—*as a text* has already been done by newer Freudians, especially in France. Still I would draw your attention when reading the story to its literary technique even while it pre- sents itself as a medical technique. By *technique* I mean "style as a deliberate procedure, craftsmanship,"[5] and I follow T. S. Eliot's notion of technique which shows the writer as a "cool scientist" rather than as a "disheveled madman" (and is it not just this literary question of technique, "cool" or "disheveled," which distanced Freud from Stekel and Reich and Gross, drawing him closer instead to Abraham and Jones?).

Technique also refers to formal rather than to expressive values. Look at Freud's form in the case history of Dora. First the story as such. E. M. Forster[6] says: "The basis of a novel is a story, and a story is a narrative of events arranged in a time sequence"; we read on in a story in order to find out "what happens next?" Simple primitive curiosity, says Forster. And Freud meets us on this level, at the same time sophisticating the telling with artfulness—suspense, hints, concealments, and a setting which evokes curiosity par excellence: the clinical consultation (part one of his case is called "The Clinical Picture"). There we are drawn in by another narrational technique, one we find in Joseph Conrad for instance: the incoherence of the story, needing the author (and the reader) to piece it together, and that it is being told by the main character (Dora) on two levels at once.

Freud uses other devices: the modesty of the humble narrator in the background compared with the momentousness of what is revealed in his presence and to his reflection; the deepening of discoveries in answer to "what happens next"; the time limits pronounced at the outset, "only three months"; the enticement in the preface to forthcoming revelations of sexual details ("I will simply claim for myself the right of the gynecologist" with its pornographic echo of the "young-girl-and-the-doctor"); and then the sensitive apologies vis à vis the medical profession: no possibility of other specialists checking the results; not a verbatim report but written at the conclusion from memory; "the shortening produced by the omission of technique" (i.e., what he actually did in treating the case).

These last apologies are of no small order! For just here, despite showing his awareness of the requirements of empiricism, our author begs off that method of writing in which he was thoroughly competent from his earlier work in brain pathology and cocaine experiments. A case history as empirical evidence in science would have to offer some means for public verification. It could not be merely a record from memory, unless it was to be taken only as anecdotal reminiscence (like the unverifiable cases of the parapsychology of the time). And the whole technique employed—Freud's main omission—would have to belong to the record. Medical case histories tell us mainly about course of illness in relation to treatment; what the dosage, measures and procedures were, and why, and what then resulted. We expect to learn exactly what the doctor did. Freud tells us only darkly and in part.

When setting out to show "the intimate structure of a neurotic disorder" (for that was his intention with this case), Freud could go the way of Vesalius or Balzac,[7] the anatomist or the moralist, the one revealing the intimate structures of physical morbidity, the other those of mental, moral, or psychological morbidity. He could approach the matter from the outside or the inside, or as the French writer Alain[8] puts it:

> The human being has two sides, appropriate to history and fiction. All that is observable in a man falls into the domain of history. But his romanceful or romantic side [roman as fiction] includes "the pure passions, that is to say the dreams, joys, sorrows and self-communings which politeness or shame prevent him from mentioning"; and to express this side of human nature is one of the chief functions of the novel.

Where Alain speaks of "politeness and shame," Freud writes: "Patients . . . keep back part . . . because they have not got over their feelings of timidity and shame."[9] Freud's histories are the stuff of fiction; they express the fictional side of human nature.

In the double dilemmas between history and fiction, outside and inside, Freud prestidigitates the compromise that becomes his case style and our new genre of psychotherapeutic writing. He gives us the "pure passions . . . the dreams . . . the self-communings" but from the outside as the medical pathologist of morbid structures, his first vocation. We do not enter into the inside of the case as we do in a novel, sympathizing with Dora, but outside laying bare tissues, analyzing with Freud. As readers we identify with the main character, but not with her subjectivity, her feelings and torments. We identify rather with the "intimate structure of a neurotic disorder," the *idea* that the character embodies sexual repression and its dynamisms. For the focus of our interest imperceptibly shifts from a subject being revealed to an object being exhibited, from the study of character to the analysis of character, and to a demonstration by means of character of the author's tendentious aims. (Thus he tells us less about her person than about her dreams, her material.) Our interest may be caught by what happens next and held by the author's subtleties of technique, but it is not the *story* that Freud is as much concerned with as it is the *plot* (to which we come in a moment).

Compromise was Freud's formula for the nature of the dream, of the ego, of the symptom, and it was also the way he built his own dream theory as a compromising integration of the conflicting theories in the field at that time.[10] And because his case writing was a compromise we cannot follow either those who say Freud was "really a physician" with a fortunate literary gift, or "really a writer" who happened to appear in the field of medicine.

His double movement is best put in his own terms. It is a compromise between an *unconscious* literary presentation (the style of the *romancier*) and the *conscious* analogy with physical medicine (the gynecologist simile). The manifest material was medical; but the latent intention, which necessitated the transfigurative suppression of medical, empirical methodology, was that of the poetic art. His case histories are brilliantly successful symptom formations, sublimated, transfigured into a new genre of narrative; they are like dreams: and all—art, symptom formations, and dreams, are, in Freud's theory, compromises between two irreconcilable demands, providing defenses against awareness of what he was most deeply engaged in—fiction writing. Ever since him we are all in this field of psychotherapy, not medical empiricists, but workers in story.

2. *Theory and Plot*

Alain[11] gives another important difference between history and fiction. The first is dominated by external causes, "whereas . . . in the novel . . . everything is founded on human nature . . . everything is intentional, even passions and crime, even misery."

Plot reveals these human intentions. Plot shows how it all hangs together and makes sense. Both history and fiction can be narrative stories, one event after another in a time sequence. But only when the narrative receives inner coherence in terms of the depths of human nature do we have fiction, and for this fiction we have to have plot. Forster[12] explains plot like this:

> We have defined a story as a narrative of events arranged in a time sequence. A plot is also a narrative of events, the emphasis falling on causality. "The king died and then the queen died," is a story. "The king died and then the queen died of grief," is a plot. A story answers what happened next; a plot tells us *why*.

To plot is to move from asking the question "and then what happened?" to the question "and why did it happen?"

In our kind of fictions the plots are our theories. They are the ways in which we put the intentions of human nature together so that we can understand the *why* between the sequence of events in a story.

Telling us *why* is Freud's main aim with his case histories. All his narrative skills are assembled only for the sake of plot. Freud devised a plot that fits all his stories. Although the plot itself is simple enough, it requires complication, mystification, and fantasy. Freud's artfulness is necessitated by his theory. We have to have concealments and flashbacks to early reminiscences and screen memories. The plot has to thicken with the intense complications of transference and resistance, regressions in the development of character, and critical junctures in the forward thrust of the story. All this richness which results from the plot structure makes demands on our memory and intelligence—faculties which Forster says are essential to plots. And Freud's plot was absolutely economical; no loose ends. This economy in plot is called elegance in theory.

Nonetheless, basic plot in Freud is simple. Every Freudian narrative comes out the same way and can be taken apart to show one answer to the question *why*. The mystery is repression (in one of many varieties), followed by passions, crimes, and miseries (symptom formation), the involvement of the author (transference of the repressed), lifting of the repression through prolonged recognitions (psychotherapy), and the denouement of ending therapy.

When Jung charges Freud with too simplistic a causal schema, he is faulting Freud for his plotting. Plots in human lives do not unfold side by side with one's story. The development of my life and the development of its plot are two distinct unfoldings. *Why* can be answered only by Freud in terms of time sequences, what happened first and what happened after that.

Why has other answers than material and efficient causality; it asks also *what for* (final cause) and *why* in the sense of what archetypal idea, myth, or person (formal cause) is at work in the story. Jung says we must look at the intentionality of the characters and where they are heading, for they are the main influence upon the shape of the stories. Each carries his own plot with him, writing his story, both backwards and forwards, as he individuates. Jung gives far more weight to individual character than either to narrative or to plot.

If "plot is emergent from the selective logic of the writerly act,"[13] then Jung considers Freud too selective and too logical, shaping all shoes on one last. Everything may be founded on human nature, but human nature itself is founded on things beyond human nature. Jung's plot (his theory of archetypes) is inherently multiplistic and variegated. Individuation shows many forms, has no prescribed momentum, and may come to no end. Jung's cases pick up many colorful but extraneous threads. They don't make as thrilling reading as Freud's just because his plot has less selective logic and therefore less inevitability. Only when it is cast, or when we read it, in the model of a heroic quest or a pilgrim's progress does the individuation plot grip the reader. But that is only one archetypal mode of individuation, one mode of selective logic.

A reason that Alfred Adler's writings haven't the same fascination as Freud's is that Adlerian plot eliminates complexities. Adler's plotting—monistic like Freud's, one plot for all persons—does not allow as much secondary elaboration: symbolization, defenses, disguises, displacements, reaction formations, coded messages, and censoring. The main antagonists of the psychomachia (ego, id, superego) are done away with, so that much less demand is made upon the reader's intelligence and memory.

Of course Freud had to present his plot of human nature in the form of a theory, and this theory has its medical, biological, empirical language of libido. His double style of writing required that what was plot and myth on one level was theory and science on another. But for us who read him, it is important to bear in mind that our fundamental unease with Freud's theory is not that it cannot be verified but that it does not satisfy. We fail to fall for it not because it empirically fails as a hypothesis about human nature, but because it fails poetically, as a deep enough, embracing enough, esthetic enough plot for providing dynamic coherence and meaning to the dispersed narratives of our lives.

Freud's one plot is named after a myth, Oedipus. With this move, Freud returns to the very beginning of poetic theory, to Aristotle's use of mythos in his *Poetics*. When we open that book to read in English about *plot* we find that wherever that term appears the original Greek work is *mythos*. *Plots are myths;* the basic answers to "why?" in our work are to be discovered in myths.

So we see that Freud too placed mind on a poetic basis. He understood that the entire narrative of a human life, the characters that we are, and the dreams we enter, are structured by the selective logic of a profound *mythos* in the psyche.

But a mythos is more than a theory and more than a plot. It is the tale of the interaction of humans and the divine. To be in a mythos is to be inescapably linked with divine powers, and moreover, to be in mimesis with them. Once Freud and Jung took the step into understanding human nature in terms of myth, they moved from human nature to the nature of religious powers. The poetic basis of mind must be taken in the classical sense of *poesis,* as a *mimesis,* a making in the shapes of the Gods, and a making of our lives mimetic to them. The selective logic that operates in the plots of our lives is the logic of the mythos, mythology.

3. *The Empirical Fiction*

There are two other long case histories essential to the empirical foundations of Freudian psychoanalysis—"The Phobia in a Five-

Year-Old Boy" (1909) and "Comments on a Case of Paranoia" (1911). Like the first one, "Dora," these two have grown their more fictional titles, "Little Hans" and "The Schreber Case."[14] Here Freud leaves the requirements of case history as an empirical anamnesis and moves freely into his new genre. Here he has become an interpretive commentator, outside the scene of actual therapeutic operations. Freud did not analyze little Hans nor Daniel Schreber. He analyzed the story told him by Hans's father and the story written in Schreber's memoirs.

We are now at that point in Freud's movement where he does not need to found his writing upon persons from his practice—or upon any practice at all. He essayed this style in three works: on Jensen's *Gradiva* (1907), on Leonardo (1910), and on Michelangelo's Moses (1914), the last published anonymously, with a deceptive editorial disguise. (The dates show these essays written parallel with his main case histories.) The *Gradiva* study is the analysis of wholly fictional dreams, dreams in a novel. But Freud's main ventures into the realm of wholly invented story are *Totem and Taboo* and *Moses and Monotheism*. These are religious fictions presenting Freud's science (in distinction to the scientific fictions presenting Jung's religion in his works on flying saucers, synchronicity, and alchemy). For *Totem and Taboo* and *Moses and Monotheism* no evidence can ever be empirically produced. Freud drops the empirical disguise and reveals himself as a writer of pure fictions.

I am not scoring Freud for what he did or should have done differently; rather I am emphasizing that when one reads Freud one must bear in mind throughout his writings, and especially in his constructions through the use of "case material," that he has created a new style of writing complete with the mask, so necessary to the writer, as Thomas Mann laboriously insisted, behind which the author must conceal himself in order that he may reveal himself.

I am using *fiction* and suggesting that case histories are *fictions* in three senses of the word:

1. Case history as factual history, a true account or knowledge about the "succession of events through which anything passes"[15] is a fiction in the sense of a fabrication, a lie. But it is only a lie

when it claims literal truth. Early on in the taking down of case histories, Freud found that he was not recording a true account of historical events, but fantasies of events as if they had actually happened. The material of a case history is not historical facts but psychological fantasies, the subjective stuff that is the proper domain of fiction in the sense of Alain and Forster above.

Case histories even today when we use tape recorders and public information from whole families still cannot claim that what is told in the tellings is a true account of the succession of events through which a thing has passed. This is supposedly so for history of any sort, and especially so for case history for these reasons: (a) case material must be solipsistic—about dreams, passions, fantasies, wishes, pains, none of which can be witnessed by the writer firsthand; (b) the material is particularly *fictive* (unbelievable, implausible) because it belongs to those surrealist and bizarre categories of events we clinically call hysterical, paranoid, hallucinatory, etc.; (c) external corroboration of a case history (by another clinician or a family member) is possible only in regard to limited circumstantialities; (d) anything referred to as "history" must be yoked to chronicity, but psychic realities, as both Freud and Jung insisted, do not follow laws of time.

2. Case history is a fiction in the sense of an invented account of the imagined interior processes of a central character in a narrative story. Its writer is not the main character, that is, it is not autobiography; nor is it biography since the narrative events are severely selected by the demands of the plot. Essential to this fictional form is the empirical disguise.

Much could be said about "empiricism" in psychotherapy. I want only to touch it and only in one respect. One of the reasons for empiricism in philosophy, according to A. J. Ayer,[16] is "the egocentric predicament." Empiricism prevents solipsism; it gets us out of the circle of our minds by pointing to public demonstrable events for corroboration. Empiricism is not only a defense against Platonism (innate ideas, universals, deductive idealism), it is, psychologically, that fantasy which makes us feel safe from solipsism, its isolation, its paranoid potentialities. Therefore, since psychological material is essentially subjective and the therapeutic situation a reinforcement by mirroring or doubling (the closed vessel) of this isolated subjectivity, *the appeal to empiricism of therapy is a direct consequent of the solipsism of therapy.* The empirical disguise in case histories is an inevitable defense against the solipsistic power of the fictions with which therapy is engaged.

3. Case history as the presentation of literal statements transposed to a key where they cannot be controverted or verified is a fiction in the philosophical sense, i.e., a formula that must necessarily posit itself as beyond criteria of true or false, the as-if fictions of Vaihinger.[17] Here fictions are mental constructs, fantasies by means of which we fashion or "fiction" (*fingere*) a life or a person into a case history.

We will be touching again upon these three kinds of fictions and their relevance for psychotherapy. But first we need to be impressed by the full actuality·of this new kind of fiction invented and developed during the twentieth century, written by thousands of hands in clinics and private practices and welfare centers, sometimes published but often not, mainly stored in the archives of asylums and the attics of analysts. At night, in the *Schreibstube* like Freud, the lonely therapist sits, recording, dictating, typing these accounts, in the grip of the stories of his patients and of their common therapuetic fantasy. All these stories, wherever and by whomever they are written, whether having a Freudian plot or a plot derived from any number of different myths, have one and the same leitmotif: *the main character enters therapy.* Therapy may appear as the denouement (the classical anamnesis leading up to—"and that's why I came to see you, Doctor.") Or therapy may be the beginning of the story: as Freud's cases which open with the character's arrival in the consulting room, e.g., the Rat Man case of 1909. Hence I call our genre "therapeutic fictions."

As a detective story requires the discovery of the murderer, a heroic tragedy the death of the principal, and comedy a pleasing resolution of conflicts, so therapeutic fiction is the story of a person who comes to therapy, and, more often, the story of the therapy than the person. Therapy is either the whole content or the story leads up to therapy. Roth's *Portnoy's Complaint* is therapeutic fiction in genre, even as it differs from it mainly because Roth does not use the empirical disguise.

Usually therapy is the theme on which the narrative incidents are hung together, as the Dora story. Usually, too, therapy provides the means for focusing and selecting incidents, like a political novel chooses politically relevant events. And usually, the story leads out of therapy at its ending into cure and world (or, for an antitherapeutic denouement, a "failed case"). Freud ends his Dora story with these words: "Years had gone by since her visit. In the meantime the girl has married . . . and had been reclaimed once more by the realities of life." As the tales of this genre are written with a therapeutic eye, they are read with that same eye by a new genre of reader, who can, in fact, read even Shakespeare, Faulkner, or his own biography as pieces of therapeutic fiction. How this has come about in Freud we have seen. Now, what does it imply?

4. *Stories in Therapy*

The sophisticated "therapeutic class" who come to private therapy have their stories already formed into the therapeutic genre, that is, the story is self-reflective and focused upon the "problems" of the main character. With the "hospital population" the shape of the story often requires coaching from the listener. There are too many main characters (projections); incidents are not selected according to the economical requirements of a therapeutic plot; time sequence, basic to the definition of story, may be altogether missing. Although the listener shapes the tale into the therapeutic genre, the condition of the teller—that which makes him a hospital patient—plays a large part in the form of the tale, especially its stylistics.

Patients use their stories in different ways. Some tell stories as entertainments to while, or wile, away the hour, others are reporters, others are prosecuting attorneys building a plaint. Occasionally a tale becomes wholly metaphorical in which every aspect of "what I saw yesterday"—the large building site, the hard-hatted foreman in a control booth, the little girl in a shiny silver rain puddle in danger from a bulldozer, the passerby who intervenes—all refer as well to figures within the patient's own psyche and their interplay.

A clinician is supposed to note the way stories are told. Old textbooks of psychiatry, such as Eugen Bleuler's, referred to style for aid in diagnosis. The psychiatrist was encouraged to note florid expansiveness, rambling, alliterations, punnings and bizarre word associations, hyperbole, archaicisms, mannerisms —terms we may find in literary textbooks on style. A diagnosis is partly made on the basis of a person's style with his tale.

A psychological diagnosis too is a "telling about the patient." It is a caricature, an abbreviated character sketch—Szasz and Goffman might say "character assassination"—in the language of a clinical specialist to be read by other clinical specialists. (It's definitely not for the patient.) A psychological diagnosis does not say what a person has, or what a person is. It describes his *Zustandsbild,* his clinical picture. It tells about the presentation of self to the clinical writer.

The clinical writer tells one into a diagnosis, into an "abnormal story." I mean abnormal in two ways: first it is a story written with an eye for the morbid, deviant, and bizarre—like a Gothic novel or a tale by Poe, presented with the naturalism of Zola. But, unlike a Gothic novel, a tale by Poe or Zola—and this is the second meaning of abnormal—this story takes itself literally, believes itself as factual history and thus deviates from the norms of a story. Diagnoses are wholly literalistic in their historicism—and of course it is wholly necessary that they be told in this way in order to organize the character about whom they are written into precisely the style of fiction that the writer is empowered to create. Diagnoses are highly creative acts of writing. The force of their literalistic stories is overwhelming (as are all literalistic writings where imagining is disguised as the truthful mirror of "real facts"). Literalism is anyway the main instrument of the clinical mind.

The force of diagnostic stories cannot be exaggerated. Once one has been written into a particular clinical fantasy with its expectations, its typicalities, its character traits, and the rich vocabulary it offers for recognizing oneself, one then begins to recapitulate one's life into the shape of the story. One's past too is retold, and finds a new internal coherence, even inevitability, through this abnormal story. A diagnosis is indeed a *gnosis:* a mode of self-knowledge that creates a cosmos in its image.

In each case the story leads into therapy, as we said. But this also means that I the therapist have now entered the tale, in fact become a key figure in a story whose beginnings, development, plot, and style have had, until this meeting, nothing to do with me. I have never known and probably will never know any of the other characters, take part in any of its other scenes, or be apprised of "what happens next" or what clinics call the "follow-up."

A colleague once told me about a new patient walking out on her when she challenged the thematic mode of the patient's story. The patient presented himself as a rather sick case, having been more or less steadily in therapy for fifteen of his thirty-six years, that things had not that much changed (alcohol, homosexuality, depressions, money worries), and that he had tried many kinds of therapy. My colleague said: "For me, you are a new case, and I don't accept that you are as sick as you believe you are. Let's begin today." By refusing his web of constructions she also cut him off from his supporting fiction. He did not return.

A second case, this one from my practice (do you believe me?): A story of psychotic episodes, hospitalizations with medical abuses, seductions, and violations of rights, shock treatments and "helpful drugs" by which I mean those authorized by the institution (and not the "harmful drugs" which make a person a patient). All this had gone on for years in many places.

I took this story like the past another woman might tell of falling in love in high school and marrying the boy next door, of having a loving husband, children, and a spaniel, a story of making it. In other words both are consistent accounts exposing a thematic motif which organizes events into experience. Both of these women, this one from her percale sheets and the other from her canvas strait jacket—to put the fantasy figuratively—might come in equally desperate, saying precisely the same thing: "It doesn't make any sense; I've wasted the best years of my life, I don't know where I am, or who I am." The senselessness derives from a breakdown in the thematic motif: it no longer holds events together and gives them sense, it no longer provides the mode of experiencing. The patient is in search of a new story, or of reconnecting with his old one.

In the first case—the man whose tale was refused by my colleague—his story still made sense to him: an incurable, but still a dues-paying member of the therapeutic traffic. He wanted analysis and the analyst to fit into his story. In the third case—the woman with the spaniel—there is clearly going on a reorganization of the sustaining fiction of her life. She is modern woman in search of her mythos; she is without a plot, even though events go on narrationally in a time sequence.

In the second case, mine, I believed her story to be her sustaining fiction, but that she had not read it for its hermetic possibilities, its covert meanings. She had taken her story literally in the clinical language in which it had been told her, a tale of sickness, abuse, wastage of the best years. The story needed to be doctored, not her; it needed reimagining. So I put her years of wastage into another fiction. She knew the psyche because she had been immersed in its depths. Hospital had been her finishing school, her initiation rites, her religious confirmation, her rape, and her apprenticeship with psychological realities. Her pedigree to survival and diploma was her soul's endurance through, and masochistic enjoyment of, these psychological horrors. She was indeed a victim, not of her history but of the story in which she had put her history.

You will have noticed that my colleague contested a story of sickness and I confirmed one, but that both of us clashed with the presenting fiction, thereby beginning the battle of stories which is an essential aspect of one-to-one therapy and of clinical case conferences. We saw this already in Freud with Dora. He took her story and gave it a new plot, a Freudian plot: and part of this plot is that it is good for you; its the best plot because it cures, which is the best denouement of the therapeutic genre.

The talk going on in depth analysis is not merely the analysis of one person's story by the other, nor is it an embodied critic working over an embodied history, nor is the talk one between two partners in a dialectic; whatever else is going on in this story—ritual, suggestion, eros, power, projection—it is also a contest between singers, reenacting one of the oldest kinds of cultural enjoyments that we humans know. This is partly why therapy pretends to being creative, and I use that word advisedly to mean originating of significative imaginative patterns, *poesis*. Successful therapy is thus a collaboration between fictions, a revisioning of the story into a more intelligent, more imaginative plot, which also means the sense of mythos in all the parts of the story.

Before we burst the bounds of this section by going into the archetypal plots in our stories—which means nothing less than invoking the classical pantheon, the nymphs and heroes, the titans and tricksters whose tales our lives enact—let us stick with the idea of therapy as a contest between singers or collaboration between fictions.

Unfortunately we therapists are not aware enough that we are "singers." We miss a lot of what we could be doing. Our ways of narration are limited to four kinds: epic, comic, detective, social realism. We take what comes—no matter how passionate and erotic, how tragic and noble, how freakish and arbitrary—and turn it all into one of our four modes. First, there are the cases showing the ego's development, especially out of childhood, through obstacles and defeats: heroic epic. Second, the tales of tangles, the confused identities and uncertain genders, the impossible bumbling inadequacies of the foolish victim, but which come out with a happy end of adjustment: comic. Third, unmasking hidden plots through clues and crises, indefatigably tracking down what went wrong by a taciturn but twinkle-eyed, pipe-puffing analyst, not too unlike Holmes or Poirot: detective. Fourth, the detailed descriptions of small circumstances, true to life, the family as a misfortune, environmental conditions as another, historicism as verbatim accounts of the actual milieu, all presented with lugubrious sociological terminology and the heavy-handed panned shots of tendentious importance: social realism.

Psychology would do better to turn directly to literature rather than to use it unawares. Literature has long been friendly to us, openly incorporating a good deal from psychoanalysis. Those in literature see the psychology in fiction. It's our turn to see the fiction in psychology, which could enrich our repertoire.[18]

For instance, we might look at the picaresque mode. Its central figure does not develop (or deteriorate), but goes through episodic, discontinuous movements. His narrative ends abruptly without achievement for there is no goal; so the denouement can neither be the resolution of comedy nor the fatal flaw of tragedy. Rather than using such large programmed scales, success and failure is measured by the flavor of daily experiences. (There is enormous attention paid to eating.) There are tales within tales that do not further a plot (for there is no plot), showing that psychic history goes on in many places at once—"meanwhile, back on the farm, in another part of the forest"—and in many figures at once. Other personages of the story are as interesting as the main character, just as the other figures within our dreams and fantasies often bear more upon our fates than does the ego. There are no lasting relationships, and much emphasis upon personae, the garbs and masks of life at all levels, especially the shadow world of pimps, thieves, bastards, charlatans, and pompous dignitaries. These figures, in us each, are the realm of picaresque reflection, of seeing through every established stance, yet without moral implication. And though the picaresque character suffers defeat, depression, and betrayal, he does not progress by means of suffering into the light.

From the tragic perspective such a way of framing a case history is a waste; soul demands something more metaphysically important. From the comic viewpoint there would have to be a resolution, some sort of accepting awareness and adaptation to the society which to the picaresque person is always hostile. From the heroic standpoint, the picaresque mode is a psychopathic parody of the individuation epic—but then individuation might be a paranoid organization of the picaresque. The same tale told as social realism would turn into a political tract, as indeed anarchism and the picaresque thrive best in Spanish soil.

But I have made my exhibition: case histories have different fictional styles and may be written in a variety of fictional genres. And therapy may be most helpful when a person is able to place his life within this variety, like the polytheistic pantheon, without having to choose one against the others. For even while one part of me knows the soul goes to death in tragedy, another is living a picaresque fantasy, and a third engaged in the heroic comedy of improvement.

5. Genre and Archetype

A German Jungian, Wolfgang Giegerich, while exposing the archetypal pattern within the writings of Erich Neumann, makes the remark:

> Something (some "factor") obviously keeps us from the truly psychological orientation and makes our thinking unpsychological by making us wish for, or even need, empirical verification, scientific truth, and systematizations. This "factor" is our containment in the Great Mother/Hero myth, whose nature is to create the (mythic!) fantasy of the possibility of heroically breaking out of myth, into "fact," "truth," "science."[19]

He then develops the theme, showing that a narrative account in evolutional terms is a genre which belongs to the perspective of the Hero/Great Mother. This implies that when we conceive our life story as a Battle for Deliverance from the Great Mother—as Jung called it—we are engaged in heroics; these heroics reflect in such concepts as ego development, ego strength, and personal identity, and the theory emerging from this archetypal perspective is that of Neumann's *Origins and History of Consciousness*. That book is not a statement of *faith* in progress or a work of *science* in evolution. Nor is it, as Giegerich shows, a *history* in any sense of that word but story. It is an archetypal fantasy held together by a captivating plot: the development of Ego, an Everyman, with whom we each can identify. Its persuasiveness rests upon this same archetypal foundation—the rhetoric of the archetype—which in this example casts each of us readers into an ontogenetic recapitulation of the heroic battle of deliverance from maternal uroboric claustrophobia.

Giegerich links a genre of psychoanalytical writing with an archetype. In a short paper of my own I also tried to show that a certain style of presenting psychology, Jung's in particular, by means of diagrams, numbers, and crystals, by references to introversion and slow patience, and by images of the Old Wise Man and uses of ancient wisdom and magic, belongs to the senex consciousness of Saturn.[20] Again, the rhetoric of an archetype. Again, a genre which determines our plots and our styles in writing case history.

The relationship between archetype and genre has been worked out most famously by Northrop Frye in his *Anatomy of Criticism,* where the four classical genres of literature are each given a season in the year, so that literature follows the cycle of the corn god. Actually Frye's system, though fourfold, remains still within the single myth of the Great Mother, the God-Hero her son, and the cycle of nature.

More fundamental than any of these attempts at the problem of genre and archetype can be extrapolated from a paper by Patricia Berry. She considers that narrative as such cannot help but reflect the ego's concerns, because narrative is essentially the genre of the hero archetype. She writes:

> Narration is also reinforced by therapy. As we tell our dreams, so we narrate our life stories. Not only the content of our dreams is influenced by analysis but the very style of our remembering. . . . Since the narrative style of description is inextricably bound with a sense of continuity—what in psychotherapy we call the ego— misuse of continuity because of the ego is also close at hand. . . . The most important difficulty with narrative: it tends to become the ego's trip. The hero has a way of finding himself in the midst of any story. He can turn anything into a parable of a way to make it and stay on top. The continuity in a story becomes *his* ongoing heroic movement. Hence when we read a dream as narrative there is nothing more ego-natural than to take the sequence of move- ment as a progression culminating in the dreamer's just reward or defeat. The way story encapsulates one into it as protagonist cor- rupts the dream into a mirror in which the ego sees only its con- cerns.[21]

This same thought has been put succinctly in Roger Fowler's dic- tionary: "The narrative without a hero remains a critical fiction."[22] Even the "antihero" is what we in psychology would refer to as a negative inflation of the ego. Whether invoked or not, ego is always present. If we are going to tell tales in narrative form we are going to come out with ego theory. Berry implies that the genre of nar- rative itself determines the plot by which we form our case history and understand it.

The question now arises: is our style of case-history writing, even of interpreting individual dreams and situations, the result of ego psychology, *or* is it possible that ego psychology—as presented first by Freud, then by one division of his school, and now by the therapeutic establishment—is the result of our style of case-history writing? Have we produced ego psychology through our way of writing cases? And are our case histories not so much empirical demonstrations of the way the psyche works but actually empirical demonstrations of the way that poesis works in organizing our vision?

This means we would begin to read case histories with an archetypal eye toward their form; we would be interested in the genre in which the case is fantasied, even the rhythm, the language, the sentence structures, the metaphors. For we find the archetypes not only in the content of a case history. Form too is archetypal. There is an archetypal psychology of form. Thus we would open ourselves to the idea that were the story written in another way, by another hand, from another perspective, it would sound different and therefore *be a different story*. I am suggesting the poetic basis of therapy, of biography, of our very lives.

Perhaps the examples of the heroic ego and the picaresque are not enough to show what I mean. Let us return to the abstractions of senex consciousness where we move away from narrative altogether, both epic and episodic.

We find in this style of writing, both Freudian and Jungian, an emphasis upon reductions, either downward to castration anxiety, omnipotence fantasy, primal scene, etc., or upward to wholeness, self, fourfoldedness. The work of analysis is presented less in terms of what happened next than in terms of descriptive states of being, basic abstractions of powers at work in the soul. The abstractions and reductions can be theoretical in terms of libido and its quantifications, or historical, numerical (quaternio), or configurative (mandala). The images of a dream, instead of being primary and irreducible as Jung's own theory itself states, become representations of something more abstract. The lady in the shop window repairing carpets is not that precise image and its metaphorical implications, but is a representation of a nonrepresentational and abstract mother imago to which it can be reduced. The scenes of childhood are not taken either as images, or linked into developmental narrative, but become exemplars of theoretical universals, anal or Oedipal. Events do not tell a story but expose a structure. This structure is then applied to other events across time and to images regardless of context—attempts to be best in school, obsession with changing underwear, fear of the dark forest in camp— uniting them together as manifestations of the one root principle.

No longer is it a question of what happened next and how did one move through this situation into the next one. Rather it is a question of instances exemplifying principles, images as allegories, scenes as enactments in time of eternal verities. In this style of examining a case—and I say examining deliberately—the function of consciousness, represented by the writer-analyst, is that of seeing abstractions, a keen-sighted perspicacity into structures and laws.

Here the connecting function of consciousness is defined, not hermetically in terms of significances, or martially in terms of activation, or erotically or Dionysianally, but systematically, through a paranoid ability to see defenses and resistances as mechanisms (not as obstacles in the heroic course of progression). Finally, the denouement in this genre is less in terms of a goal in the patient (improvement, say) which belongs to the narrative style and to ego development, than the denouement is an instruction in the science of analysis, a contribution to theory, adding another stone to its monument. Saturn, the senex.[23]

You will have noticed that I threw in a few alternatives that we have not yet discussed: hermetic writing where connections do not close up but open and reveal; aphroditic where the eye is on sensate value, personal relatings, perhaps, or sex; Dionysian where flow matters most. I also have left only as a hint the point of view of the anima which, as I see it, would stay with images and fantasies themselves, never translating them or organizing them into narrative or through plot at all, but responding to them in a metaphorical style where consciousness is one of innuendo, reflection, echo, tone, and elusive movements.

The idea that there is a God in our tellings and that this God shapes the words into the very syntax of a genre is not new in literary studies even if it might come as a shock to my colleagues who believe they are really only writing clinical accounts of facts.

Annabel Patterson,[24] for instance, has taken up again "The Seven Capital Stars" or description of the seven ideas of style employed in Renaissance compositions. There we see how different Gods can be linked with genres, i.e., gravity with Saturn, speed with Mercury, beauty with Venus, vehemence with Mars, etc. One-to-one parallels, as in all things polytheistic, are not forced literally, but imagined suggestively as perspectives towards writing and reading.

My point in this section has already been put in that same article by Berry: "The way we tell our story is the way we form our therapy." The way we imagine our lives is the way we are going to go on living our lives. For the manner in which we tell ourselves about what is going on is the genre through which events become experiences. There are no bare events, plain facts, simple data—or rather this too is an archetypal fantasy: the simplistics of brute (or dead) nature.

Rhetoric means the art of persuasion. And the rhetoric of the archetype is the way each God persuades us to believe in the myth that is the plot in our case history. But the myth and the God are not something set apart, to be revealed in numinous moments of revelation, by oracle, or through epiphanies of images. They are in the rhetoric itself, in the way we use words to persuade ourselves about ourselves, how we tell what happened next and answer the question *why*. To find the Gods in psychology we ought to look first at the genres of our case-history writing.

Our reflection needs to turn to psychoanalytic literature as *literature;* that is, I am suggesting that literary reflection is a primary mode of grasping where one is ignorant, unconscious, blind in regard to the case because one has not differentiated the Gods in one's work.

6. *Soul History vs. Case History*

Before we go any further we need to come back to a distinction made above by Alain between history as stories of outer events and fiction as stories of inner events. This same distinction was crucial to my argument in *Suicide and the Soul* where I held that suicide can be understood, if at all, only from the viewpoint of soul and its inner history. Outer events of the case record are not enough. Let me repeat what was said there:

> Outside and inside, life and soul, appear as parallels in "case history" and "soul history." A case history is a biography of historical events in which one took part: family, school, work, illness, war, love. The soul history often neglects entirely some or many of these events, and spontaneously invents fictions and "inscapes" without major outer correlations. The biography of the soul concerns experience. It seems not to follow the one-way direction of the flow of time, and it is reported best by emotions, dreams, and fantasies. . . . The experiences arising from major dreams, crises, and insights give definition to the personality. They too have "names" and "dates" like the outer events of case history; they are like boundary-stones which mark out one's own individual ground. These marks can be less denied than can the outer facts of life, for nationality, marriage, religion, occupation, and even one's own name can all be altered. . . . Case history reports on the achievements and failures of life with the world of facts. But the soul has neither achieved nor failed in the same way. . . . The soul imagines and plays—and play is not chronicled by report. What remains of the years of our childhood play that could be set down in a case history? . . . Where a case history presents a sequence of facts leading to diagnosis, soul history shows rather a concentric helter-skelter pointing always beyond itself. . . . We cannot get a soul history through a case history.[25]

The subsequent softening of this radicality takes more pages than can be reprinted here, but nonetheless the distinction remains sharp. Case history is brushed aside as "the achievements and failures of life with a world of facts." It is merely a relic of the medical model, incidental to the concerns of the soul.

But this won't do. What about case history, not only as a written document but as an actuality of each existence. We each have our stories—parents and schools, sicknesses and diplomas, jobs held and loves lost. Are these so trivial and accessory to the soul? The job on case history in this paper carries on from that job on suicide: what *does* case history tell us? Why have it at all?

As long as the problem is locked into the old mechanical dualities of soul and world, inner and outer, psychological and medical, we chug on down the same old ruts. Instead we have to see the inner necessity of historical events, out there, in the events themselves, where "inner" no longer means private and owned by a self or a soul or an ego, where inner is not a literalized place inside a subject, but the subjectivity in events and that attitude which interiorizes those events, goes into them in search of psychological depths.

The core mistake of mechanism in psychology is that it literalizes functions and actions as discrete moving parts, separated from each other. The core mistake of my two sorts of "histories" was this mechanistic separation of soul and case, the latter further becoming wholly hardened into literal facts. The passage above puts that strongly enough. By being so tough-minded about case history as hard facts, I could free soul history to be wholly inner, important, and symbolic.

That model of two histories embraces the mistake that historians are supposedly aware of, the mistake of historical literalism, that what is written in a history is what actually happened, a report of the facts, a verifiable account of actual events as they actually were. Alain too makes this mistake, placing history all on one side and fiction all on the other. This separation ennobles case history with literal reality which then must be equaled by overemphasizing—as I did above—that soul history has the same sort of reality: "they too have 'names' and 'dates' . . . like boundary-stones. . . ." Having literalized the outer, I had to literalize and harden the inner.

What I missed there and want to correct here is that a case history—no matter how "outer" its style—is also a mode of imagining. I would take case history anew, as one of the ways the soul speaks about itself, as a case and with a history. Then we can respect case history for the genre of fiction that it is, one cast in literalisms and that necessarily does not recognize itself as such, because, as we shall work out in this round, this kind of literalism is necessary to the soul. It wants its literal case history, adding to it as it engages in life.

Above all we cannot claim inner certainties of the soul against the flux of outer facts. What we tell ourselves about our "true" identities and landmarks of the soul are as subject to dissolution, misapprehension, and shifting boundaries as are any "outer" events. We can be as deluded about ourselves as about the world's facts. The distinction between a case history of outer events and a soul history of inner experiences cannot be made in terms of indelible permanence and literal truth. Neither is more "real" because it is more solid. We have to affirm psychic reality in another way —not by copying the literalistic metaphors, the fantasies of fixity and hardness, that we use for outer reality.

To make the distinction between inner and outer on other grounds, means seeing the movement between soul and history to be a process that is continually internalizing and externalizing, gaining insight and losing it, deliteralizing and reliteralizing. Soul and history are names we give to this more fundamental operation going on between what Hindu thought refers to as *suksma* (subtle) and *sthula* (gross), between the fictional metaphorical viewpoint and the literalistic historical viewpoint, between inwardness and outwardness. It is not that there are two kinds of events, or two places of events, but two perspectives toward events, an inner psychological one and an outer historical one.

Now we come to a fundamental in the relation between soul and history. An event becomes an experience, moves from outer to inner, is made into soul, when it goes through a psychological process, when it is worked upon by the soul in any of several ways. Plato gave us main ones: dialectic, kinds of mania including love and ritual, and poetry to which we can add sickness or pathologizing as the thanatological activity of the psyche. (In other words we can take in the world by putting it through sickness; by symptom making we can turn an event into an experience.) But a simple narrative, just a story, is not enough to make soul.

A love story is but an *histoire,* one of *mille e tre,* only the outer history of emotional events, like a crowd of yellow daffodils, unless it be recollected in tranquility, put through a psychological operation, such as the soul itself compels to—love letters, anxieties, poems, confidences, assignations, fantasies. Dreams, visions, and feelings—so entirely inner and mine—have nothing to do with soul unless they be recollected, recorded, enter into history. Inner images and feelings (so-called soul-stuff) are free for grabs, nightly at the oneiric fair, simply giveaways from the tunnel of love and the chamber of horrors unless they be put through the qualifying intelligence, the history-making, of the psyche, sifted and weighed in the disciplined reflection of loving, of ritual, of dialectics, or an art—or of a psychological analysis with its therapeutic plot.

You see that here I am speaking of "history" in another way, as an equivalent for soul-making, as a digestive operation.

These two ways of "history" reappear in the opposition between soul and case. The case kind of history is the story of outwardness, raw gross matter, unfermented, undigested, unworked. And this case material (as it is just as well called) can be as much the intense private fantasies of an LSD high or a religious epiphany, as dull public papers from my files—so long as this material has not been worked over and ingested to become experience. Outer means simply we are outside looking at it; it is closed in its factual literalism. This and this happened, and then this. Inner means we are taking it in; it is open to insight. Ingestion slows down the happenings for the sake of the chewing.

So I am saying that history can be seen from the soul viewpoint. By carefully collating what happened, history is a major mode of digesting events, moving them from case material to subtle matter.

Hidden in this fantasy is a tenet of my faith: soul slows the parade of history; digestion tames appetite; experience coagulates events. I believe that had we more experiencing there would be need for fewer events and the quick passage of time would find a stop. And then I believe that what we do not digest is laid out somewhere else, into others, the political world, the dreams, the body's symptoms, becoming literal and outer (and called historical) because it is too hard for us, too opaque, to break open and insight.

What we do not experience becomes only case material or world history, hastening the pace of events both in my soul and in the world. All haste comes from the devil, as an old saying goes, which psychologically means that one's devil is to be found in one's indigestion, in having more events than are experienced. What we do experience by putting through an imaginative process such as history (in the soul sense) is taken off the streets of time and out of the ignorant sea of my mental turbulence. We beat the devil by simply standing still.

For this reason I worship psychologically especially at the altar of the God of historical time and slowness, Saturn, the archetypal swallower, who teaches us the art of internal digestion through the syndrome of his magistral depressions.

It is curious to find that analysis does not regard history in this beneficial manner. Deep psychotherapies go into a person's past with the desiring of altering that past, even shedding it. A person is a case with a history *because* of history. Therapy is a kind of *opus contra historiam*. It works against the historical influences of childhood and society in order to uncover a "true" ahistorical self and free it. So we find deep therapies invoking ahistorical principles, such as instincts, timelessness of the unconscious, rebirth, archetypes, and other eternal universalities such as the Oedipus complex or the self. *Deep* tends to mean beyond or outside of history. These therapies also try to give the soul a history that is independent of its case material, a soul whose history recapitulates phylogeny or religious individuation.

But I come at this history question from another angle. I see the opposition between the two kinds of history as a necessity of the therapeutic plot. Therapy requires the fiction of literal realities as the primary material to work on. It must have the raw in order to cook. So we begin with a classical anamnesis. But this move is not so as to be grounded in facts, but because these factual stories are the primal matter in which the psyche of the patient is stuck. He is immersed in these literal attachments and identifications, the clinging circumstantialities of *physis*. Here is the apparently soulless abyss, the unformed, unpsychological material full of sibling data, economic figures, passage through welfare centers, aches and pains and needs, not yet "worked up" into a plot, prior to fermentation.

This level of the fiction must present itself literalistically. The therapeutic plot needs opaque events in order to make insights. What is more, the therapeutic plot as a continuing process continues to need new materials in order to go on making soul. So a case history and its material runs along contiguous with soul history and makes soul history possible. Therapy profits from keeping the borders between "outer" and "inner" in order to move things back and forth between them with its art of interpretation.

Have you glimpsed toward whom I am pointing? Hermes. He is God of borders and hermeneutics, of connections between sorts of worlds. One does not catch him by himself, but in his dealings. One recognizes where he has been by the mound of stones erected to mark his intervention. And these boundary stones go on being erected in the psyche as part of its soul history (as mentioned above) after a bit of deft hermeneutical work has been done on a dream or a story.

If Hermes is to function as guide of souls we must have some things for him to turn into a message. No material, dreams, or associations, no therapeutic insights. There must be something to move across the threshold and exchange for an insight. When Hermes is at work in an analysis, one feels that one's story has been stolen and turned into something else. (My woman colleague who "cheated" her new patient by not giving him what he wanted for his story: that was a Hermes move, even if it didn't work.) The patient tells his tale, and suddenly its plot has been transformed. He resists, as one would try to stop a thief—no, this is not what I meant at all, not at all. But too late: Hermes has caught the tale, turned its feet around, made black into white, given it wings. And the tale is gone from the upperworld historical nexus in which it had begun and been subverted into an underground meaning.

Freud and Jung each began with these hermetic tricks. "Something crazy happened to me yesterday" became for them hermeneutic messages. They took the slips of the tongue, jokes, and the oddities of word associations right out of their innocent *prima facie* context and into the vast caverns of psychic significance. They were both masters of hermetic conversion, turning case material into soul.

7. *Jung: Child of Hermes?*

Besides the genres we have pointed to—hermetic, heroic, picaresque or episodic, erotic, Saturnian, and that of the anima—we can find the seeds for another in Jung.[26] But we must look in the right place. For, although Jung made several contributions to the relations between psychology and literature (*CW* 15), these belong among the more conventional depth psychological approaches to the subject. They are general, and they put the whole matter in terms of opposites: personal/collective unconscious, esthetic/psychological, creativity/normality, form/content, etc. Jung's observations on fiction, with the exception of his piece on Joyce's *Ulysses* and his affinity with Goethe's *Faust*, refer in the large to second-rate writers like Rider Haggard. His real contribution, like Freud's, is in the fictions he himself constructed, his very way of writing psychology. *Answer to Job* is the most evident of these; but even more interesting analogies to literary productions are his phenomenologies of different archetypes—trickster, Mercurius, child, anima, mother—which are the creative invention of fictional personalities, biographies or character descriptions of archetypal persons.

Like Freud's, much of Jung's published case material (excluding his early psychiatric and Freudian papers, i.e., work done before age thirty-seven when Jung became what we now call "Jungian") is a giant step removed from clinical empiricism. When he refers to cases, as he does all through his written works, it is not in the clinical empirical sense, but as anecdotal fillers, or as instances of a point. His cases are secondary illustrations often prefaced with the remark: "I would like to illustrate this by an example" (*CW* 8, §§477, 809, 451, 843, 457, 303; *CW* 7, §§44, 75, 206; *CW* 16, §§91, 307, 335, 464; *CW* 10, §§29, 627).

"Miss Miller," his most famous long case, though "an analysis of a prelude to a case of schizophrenia" as he subtitled *Symbols of Transformation* (*CW* 5), is, like Freud's Schreber case, an analysis of a printed document, originally written by an American, the French translation of which Jung worked through in German. His second most important published case (*Psychology and Alchemy* [*CW* 12]), like Freud's Hans, was material from a patient who did not work analytically with Jung. Jung expressly chose a case not his in order that the demonstration of his theory by means of the case be yet more objectively empirical, i.e., less subject to his influence (cf. *CW* 11, §38). Even that notorious Burghölzli patient, upon whose spontaneous fantasy of the solar-phallus creating wind became the "empirical" base of Jung's hypotheses of the collective unconscious and the archetypes, turns out to have been not his own case, but that of his pupil Honegger who told Jung about it.[27]

When Jung introduces the one volume of his collected works embracing his papers on empirical analysis and empirically entitled *The Practice of Psychotherapy* (*CW* 16), he says: "This book may serve to give the reader a good idea of the empirical foundations of psychotherapy." The pedestrian reader expects "case material." But the eleven cases mentioned in the book—except for the short posthumous one appended by the editors in the second edition after Jung's death—are *en passant* anecdotal references, or are patients' *dreams* serving as material for Jung's method of interpretation.

The way in which the later Jung uses "empirical" is worth a study in itself for he refreshes a term that has shrunk into an encrusted cliché of scientism. I think that his use of the word refers to a subjective process in himself and is more in keeping with the poet's use of empirical. The empirical event—the solar-phallus image in a patient—releases a movement in the mind setting off a hypothesis (or an image, a line of verse). One then points to the empirical event as the efficient cause, for indeed the hypothesis did start up from an empirical fact, with a time and a place, like a poem may start in a concrete perception. And, like the poet, Jung returns ever and again to the concrete world of perceptions (cases, dreams, religious fantasies, ancient texts). In this sense he is empirical. Further he is empirical in accumulating instance to support his hypotheses; and third, in the pragmatist sense of valuing hypotheses in terms of practical therapeutic heuristics. But he is not empirical, not even in the clinical sense of the single case as paradigm, because the case is not the indispensable source of his insights or the place of their proving.

Except—the case of his autobiography. This came at the end of his twenty-volume cosmology and was not intended to belong to the evidence for his much earlier theories, although it subsequently turns out to have been the main empirical vessel of his entire work.[28] For Jung's work, like Freud's theory of dreams, repression, and the unconscious, results from one principal case history and is demonstrated by it, the author's own.

In sum, Jung's presentation of cases is decidedly not medical empirics—reports on the interactions between physician, patient, pathology, and treatment—but rather his case material presents spontaneous psychic fictions and their interpretations. (The relation of these dreams and fantasies to the "case" and to the doctor [Jung] is barely sketched and usually incidental.) His cases are also not anamneses, biographical presentations of life, or even soul histories. He expressly abjures this mode:

> The accusation has been made in certain quarters that the newer psychotherapy is concerned too much with philosophical problems and not enough with the minutiae of case-histories. This accusation must be emphatically rebutted, because philosophical problems belong in the highest degree to any empirical study of the psyche, as fit subjects both for research and for philosophical criticism. The empirical intellect, occupying itself with the minutiae of case-histories, involuntarily imports its own philosophical premises not only into the arrangement but also into the judgment of the material, and even into the apparently objective presentation of the data. If psychotherapists today are beginning to talk about a *Weltanschauung,* a philosophy of life, this merely proves that they have discovered the existence of certain broad assumptions which were formerly overlooked in the most ingenuous manner. What is the use of even the most accurate and punctilious work if it is prejudiced by an unavowed assumption?[29]

So what are we left with? The interpretation of and commentary upon spontaneous psychic imaginings. The stuff is fiction though it be called "unconscious material." Where Freud was a writer of fictions, in the sense above, Jung is a writer on fictions. And, for Jung, the more fictitious and far-out the better (hence, alchemy, Tibet, Zarathustra, astrological aeons, schizophrenia, parapsychology) for such "materials" obliged him to meet them on an equally imaginative level. But—both Freud and Jung assumed an empirical posture, subjected themselves to empirical criticisms, and attempted to reply with empirical defenses. They would have been better served had they turned for help to the field in which they were themselves working, the field of the literary imagination.

Jung's style of writing psychology takes various forms, sometimes exhortative and apocalyptic as a heretical preacher, sometimes with the charts and figures of a Wundtian experimentalist, sometimes with the whacky systems, impenetrable language, and arcane references of an early Gnostic from the Near East. Like Hermes whose winged feet touch down as well in Hades as on Olympus and who carries messages from every one of the Gods, Jung's hermeneutic knew no barriers of time or space—Chinese yoga, Mexican rites, contemporary historical events, hospital patients, modern physics—he would interpret anything; anything was *prima materia* for his psychological operations. His psychology presents itself as a continuing essay, *Versuch*. No more than any other great essayist, Montaigne or Emerson for instance, Jung too, as he always insisted, did not write a system. That his second generation of followers quickly showed the buried cosmology within the unsystematic essays—complete with maps and figures —still does not make Jung himself any less hermetic. The one work (volume 7 of the *Collected Works*) which did "essay" a systematic approach was written originally before his main works on science, religion, myths, alchemy, and psychic reality had even been conceived. (That this book is still used as primer to Jung's work shows how desperate we are for explanatory *systems* of psychology and not insightful *essays* in it.)

So Jung's way of writing psychology seems to have been under the tutelage of Hermes who is most active in borderline conditions of the psyche, where fields touch on each other. Jung's work is a hermeneutic that does not build a new cosmology but resignifies this one in a Hermes style, that is, by connecting it with psyche and psyche with death. All things bear messages for the soul from the Gods. Hermes appears in Jung's concern with the myth of meanings, his attraction ever and again to Mercurius, whether in schizophrenia, synchronicity, transformation, death, or in the hermetic art, alchemy. Hermes also is the trickster who can twist a word, like "empirical," to carry the message needed at the moment, so as to slip another meaning through. In the center of his Bollingen stone carving surrounded by the glyphs of the planets is the sign of Mercury.[30] Mercury among other things, is the God of writing.

But in my own mercurial way the God I want to point to in Jung is not Hermes, but Dionysos, and in order to do this we must turn to Jung's discussion of the dream.

8. *Dream, Drama, Dionysos*

Jung did not accept Freud's fiction of the dream; it was both too contrived and too simplistic. So he had to offer one of his own which would have required constructing a reasoned system equal to and in the manner of Freud (something out of the question for a "child of Hermes"), or he had to imagine the dream altogether hermeneutically, i.e., as manifesting the Gods *primae facie,* in the images themselves.

For Jung the dream was not allegorical—"a narrative description of a subject under guise of another,"[31] in which "characters, actions and scenery are systematically symbolic."[32] The dream was metaphorical, speaking two tongues at once, or, as he put this hermetic duplicity, the dream is a symbol, a throwing together of two dissonants into a unique voice. The difference between Freud and Jung is the difference between allegory and metaphor. And the difference between allegory and metaphor is more profoundly determinant of the true schools of psychology and the understanding of the soul and its speech than are differences derived from the plots or theories of Freud and Jung.

Allegory and metaphor both start off saying one thing as if it were another. But where the allegorical method divides this double talk into two constituents—latent and manifest—and requires interpretative *translation* of manifest into latent, the metaphorical method keeps the two voices together, hearing the dream as it tells itself, ambiguously evocative and concretely precise at each and every instant. Metaphors are not subject to interpretative translation without breaking up their peculiar unity. "The man has a wooden leg," is no longer a metaphor if one says: see, under his trousers, one of his legs is artificial; or if one takes the other tack, saying: I mean only figuratively that his style is similar to one with a wooden leg. It is fake, hollow; it limps, drags. Since symbols and metaphors cannot be translated, another method for understanding dreams is needed, a method in which masks, disguises, and doubleness inherently belong, a method that is itself metaphorical.

This metaphorical mode of speech is for Jung the voice of nature itself; Jung's favorite metaphor for the dream was that it was nature itself speaking. By this he meant, at least to me, both *natura naturans* (the primordial force of nature) and *natura naturata* (the primordial forms of nature, the ambiguous but precise archetypal images). By turning to dreams for the creative nature in the soul, Jung was also turning to the God of this nature, Dionysos. He is both the life force, *zoe,* and he is also the ambiguous flow of primordial fantasy, always a child, bisexual, and the Lord of Souls, the psychic life of transformation through half-hidden events. Jung pointed to Dionysos also by stating that the dream had a dramatic structure. Dionysos is the god of theater: the word *tragedy* means his "goat song."

When Jung said the dream had a dramatic structure and its nature could be read as theater, he made the same sort of move as Freud. Both projected onto the dream the idea by which they were viewing the dream. Freud said the dream contained repressed sexuality, whereas he was viewing it and deciphering it by means of that idea, which, by the way, is not just an "instinct theory" or a "biological model" but an archetypal plot expressing Aphrodite, Eros, Priapos, and Dionysos-Liber too in another way. Jung said the dream had dramatic structure, whereas he was using the perspective of drama to read the dream. This confusion between what we see and how we see is another example of the effect of ideas. An *eidos* means originally that which one sees and that by which one sees. Actually we can see the dramatic structure only if we see by means of it. We see what our ideas, governed by archetypes, allow us to see.

You have by now caught on to why I have drawn to such length the contrast between Freud and Jung. Jung's step into drama was another of his literary moves. Again he took a crucial step approximating psychology to poetics. Moreover (to put this thought as a hypothesis, and in italics for staggering your mind): *if the dream is psychic nature per se, unconditioned, spontaneous, primary, and this psychic nature can show a dramatic structure, then the nature of the mind is poetic.* To go to the root of human ontology, its truth, essence, and nature, one must move via the poetic mode and use poetic tools. To understand the structure of dreaming we turn to drama; poesis is the via regia to the via regia. The unconscious produces dramas, poetic fictions; it is a theater.

Jung lays out the four stages of dramatic structure (Statement of Place, Dramatis Personae, Exposition; Development of Plot; Culmination or Crisis; Solution or Lysis) in a work (*CW* 8) not published until 1945. I won't repeat it here; you will enjoy reading it for yourself. It is instructive, useful—and misleading. For the dramatic structure is not true on the level Jung posits it: the dreams one sees in practice can rarely be discerned into four clear-cut stages, because dreams are mainly abrupt and fragmentary or hysterically swollen and meanderingly long. Moreover, the dramatic structure idea is misleading in a deeper sense: the dream is primarily an image—*oneiros* (dream in Greek) means "image" and not "story" (cf. Berry, p. 69f on the relation between narrative and image in dreams). We may see the dream narratively, allegorically, or dramatically, but it itself is an image or group of images. When we see drama in it, we are always, in part, seeing our own hypothesis.

The Dionysian hypothesis has been valuable for seeing the *dream* in another way; it will be even more valuable for seeing *Dionysos* in another way.

Dionysos has been written off, or adulated, for his hysteria. He has come to mean simply the opposite of Apollo,[33] and has thus become in the popular, and scholarly mind too, a creature of raving maenads, communal ecstasy, lost boundaries, revolution, and theatrics. Logos has to be brought in from elsewhere, e.g., Apollo. But when Jung says the dream has a dramatic *structure* he is saying it has a dramatic *logic,* that there is a Dionysian logos and this is the logic of theater. The dream is not only psychic nature; it also presents psychic logic. (Freud of course presented the first grammar of this logic in part seven of his *Traumdeutung*. But that work can also be seen as a perverse turning of poetic rhetoric into pathological mechanisms. The terms Freud uses for the dream work—condensation, displacement, symbolization, and the like—are the very ways of poetic diction.)

I believe what Jung is suggesting is this: If psychotherapy is to understand the dreaming soul from within, it had best turn to "theatrical logic." The nature of mind as it presents itself most immediately has a specific form: Dionysian form. Dionysos may be the force that through the green fuse drives the flower, but this force is not dumb. It has an internal organization. In psychology this language speaks not genetically, not biochemically in the information of DNA codes, but directly in Dionysos's own art form, theatrical poetics. This means the dream is not a coded message at all, but a display, a *Schau,* in which the dreamer himself plays a part or is in the audience, and thus always involved. No wonder that Aristotle placed psychotherapy (catharsis) in the context of theater. Our lives are the enactment of our dreams; our case histories are from the very beginning, archetypally, dramas; we are masks (*personae*) through which the Gods sound (*personāre*).

To put dreams with drama and Dionysos means not to put them with prophetics and Apollo. Jung's move invalidates the entire oracular approach to the dream, an approach Jung himself often fell for, reading the dream as a prophetic message of what to do and how to behave: dream interpretation as counseling for daily life. Again: not messages; masks.

If the structure of Dionysian logic is that of drama as given in works on this subject from Aristotle onwards, the particular embodiment of Dionysian logic is the actor; Dionysian logos is the enactment of fiction, oneself an as-if being whose reality comes wholly from imagination and the belief it imposes. The actor is and is not, a person and a persona, divided and undivided—as Dionysos was called. The self divided is precisely where the self is authentically located—contrary to Laing. Authenticity is in the perpetual dismemberment of being and not-being a self, a being that is always in many parts, like a dream with a full cast. We all have identity crises because a single identity is a delusion of the monotheistic mind that would defeat Dionysos at all costs. We all have dispersed consciousness through all our body parts, wandering wombs; we are all hysterics. Authenticity is *in* the illusion, playing it, seeing through it from within as we play it, like an actor who sees through his mask and can only see in this way.

Failure to understand this Dionysian logic, that our dramas are filled with form and dynamic coherence because they are plotted by myths in which the Gods participate, drives one outside. We attempt to see through what is going on from the viewpoint of the detached observer. Then we have Pentheus up his tree, the schizoid Apollonic movement out of hysteria, depriving logic of its life and life of its logic. Both are mad.

The essence of theater is knowing it is theater, that one is playing, enacting, miming in a reality that is completely a fiction. So, when Dionysos is called Lord of Souls it means not only the metaphysical sense of death and the mysteries of the underworld. It means also Lord of psychic insight, the psychological viewpoint which sees all things as masks in order to see through all things. For where masking is essential to a logic then seeing through is implied. Dionysian logic is necessarily mystical and transformational because it takes events as masks, requiring the process of esotericism, of seeing through to the next insight. It is his logic that necessitates his attributes of movement, dance, and flow. His is the viewpoint which can take nothing as it is statically, nothing literalistically, because everything has been put literarily into dramatic fictions. All the world's a stage, we are such stuff as dreams, said Elizabeth's court psychologist.

We have been long led to believe that logos can be defined only by Olympian structures, by children of Zeus and Athene, or by Apollo or Hermes or Saturn—logos as form, as law, as system or mathematics. But Heraclitus told us it was a flow like fire; and Jesus that it was like love. Each God has its logos, which has no single definition but is basically the insighting power of mind to create a cosmos and give sense to it. It is an old word for our worse word, consciousness.

Dionysian consciousness understands the conflicts in our stories through dramatic tensions and not through conceptual opposites; we are composed of agonies not polarities. Dionysian consciousness is the mode of making sense of our lives and worlds through awareness of mimesis, recognizing that our entire case history is an enactment, "either for tragedy, comedy, history, pastoral, pastoral-comical, historical-pastoral, tragical-historical, tragical-comical-pastoral,"[34] and that to be "psychological" means to see myself in the masks of this particular fiction that is my fate to enact.

Finally, too, to view ourselves from within a drama refers to the religious origins, not only of drama, but of the mythical enactments that we perform and name with the mask of "behavior."

9. *The Need to Historicize*

Freud's crucial discovery that the stories he was being told were psychological happenings dressed as history and experienced as remembered events was the first recognition in modern psychology of psychic reality independent of other realities. It was, further, a recognition of the independence of memory from history and history from memory. There is history that is not remembered—forgetting, distortion, denial, repressing; there is also memory that is not historical—screen memories, confabulations, and those tales told him of early sexual trauma and primal scenes that had not occurred in the literal historical past.

The separability of history and memory—that memory is not a reliable guide to history and can falsify it—is old hat to historians. Hence their insistence upon objective documentary evidence. No document, no event. But that history is not the very substance of memory, and that memory not only records but originates and presents its productions as reproductions, throws open wide windows to a view of the mind, to reminiscence, and to the sense of time.

Platonists find nothing startling in Freud's rediscovery of what they had always said. From the *Meno,* through Augustine's *Confessions,* the Art of Memory in Guilio Camillo, to Swedenborg, Romantic philosophy, and Rudolf Steiner, "reminiscence" is never only of facts that happened in your or my lifetime, imprinted on the wax tablet of the mind, stored and retrieved through links of association. Memory for Platonism is a vast potential of all knowledge written not by the hand of events but by the signature of the

Gods; all images and the mental activity that summons them is in some direct but obscure relation with the mind of God. To remember in the Platonist sense was to move right through history into gnosis.

I prefer calling this sort of remembering *imagining,* this sort of memory, *imagination.* This restores to memory the term *memoria* which did once refer to an activity and a place that we today call variously memory, imagination, and the unconscious.[35]

Psychology has performed a vivisection upon memory, turning the word to mean only what suits associationist theory of mind. Memory is now a functionary of the positivist notion of history, a bureau for recording vital statistics, "what really happened." By severing memory and imagination, modern psychology also bled imagination dry. No longer could our images provide entrance to the *mundus imaginalis.* One could no longer say with Blake: "Jesus the Imagination." For it had become a realm of unconscious fantasies, inferior representations of repressed instinctual wishes, criminal, dirty, sexy, personal. It loses its descendence from Mnemosyne, Remembering as Mother of the Muses, so its musings become mere fantasies, trivialities in a madhouse. Similarly, memory without imagination has only to do with the past, an inactive repository, a dump.

I don't want to go on with this. It is not our main theme, but belongs to a prolegomena for the resurrection of imagination, a beginning of which is the reconnection of it with memory, that is, with history, which does take us to our theme, to Freud, and to the question arising from his recognition that productions of memory present themselves as reproductions of history. Why does the psyche need to present experience dressed in the costumes of the past, *as if it were history?* Why does the psyche historicize?[36] What does historicizing do for the soul?

This seems to me the most important psychological question, and maybe historical question too, arising from Freud's insight into the historical "falsification" of memory. For this "falsification" is nothing other than the historicizing activity of the psyche itself, a history "making" that is altogether fictional, the poesis of Clio proceeding as an archetypal and autonomous activity.

It has been argued, and I confess to having once taken this line, that placing events in the past is a defensive maneuver. It shows split feelings: one cannot stand for a shame and so one puts it into the past tense. When I say: I used to lie to my former analyst; I used to masturbate; I used to hear voices, but no longer, not now —this puts distance between myself and the action. By placing the scandal in the past, it no longer presses me so closely. I disown it. Historicizing is a cover-up.

But I now regard these moves into history to be means of detachment. To call them defenses returns us to the ego who is accused of not taking stands, of splitting, of not owning up. But not the ego makes these moves, the psyche does. It spontaneously historicizes, even in dreams, and it does this, I believe, to gain a particular kind of distance as a means of *separating an act from actuality*. Lying, masturbating, hallucinating become psychic events not ego events, something for reflection rather than for control. They are now less affective and personal, more collective and general, part of a story rather than a report. Because they have been disowned, they have moved from confession into fiction where they can be looked at in another light.

In this sense the cover-up of history is for the sake of discretion, maintaining an event intact but removed, in a glass vessel so that it can be puzzled over without being identified with. It remains my crime, but the crime is no longer me. I can move about it, whereas were it happening here and now I would be at its mercy, without insight, only recriminations and defenses. The move into past tense in analysis is a signal that the psyche wants analysis. It has put an event into another time so that it can be treated in another style, such as we would use to treat any historical event, with a certain quality of respect, bemused curiosity, and dispassionate inquiry—and above all by gathering its cultural context. Historicizing is less a sign of psychological defensiveness than of the psyche getting out from under the ego's domination.

Historicizing, moreover, puts events into another genre. Neither here and now, nor once upon a time, but halfway between. Yet this "between" has a precise locus in history and an event placed there requires treatment in this style.

Not all psychological complexes appearing as dream figures and symptoms are up to date, asking for a today kind of therapy. There are parts of me that live in old-fashioned stories, stories told even before I was born. They shrink at Rolfing and Esalen, might even fall into a faint, have an attack of vapors, or dry up in *acedia,* were they forced to weekend. Some of these parts live still on the frontier in a fundamentalist stockade, or at Versailles before the revolution, or betray attitudes of nineteenth-century colonialism or the stealthy upholstered eroticism of Freud's Vienna. The historical fictions that the psyche uses to tell us where we are at also tell the kind of therapy called for. Full-blown hysteria in the classical sense of Charcot, Janet, and Freud only exists in that historical context, and should it appear in a contemporary patient that historical context is likewise reappearing complete with its suffocating stage-set. Symptoms are a way of entering history: other times, other complaints. History is a way of entering symptoms.

There is still more to historicizing. Why is history about kings and decisive battles and declarations, about great inventions, ages, and empires? The past is presented as a monument, things that have gone down in history, and we may assume that only what matters is historicized, is given the dignity of history.

History enhances, dignifies. When the Renaissance turned to the past[37] it was part of their concern for dignity; the past was a means of dignifying the present. We historicize to give the events of our lives a dignity that they cannot receive from contemporaneousness. Here historicizing moves events halfway back toward the once-upon-a-time, toward the sacred and eternal. Any petty event of merely personal life, Napoleon's breakfasts, Luther's farts, when historicized immediately takes on another significance, echoes with metaphor, moves from description to symbol. History dignifies because it moves events onto the stage of history, becoming thereby tragic, epic, and imaginative. Historians, however, often lose the imaginative function of their work. For them history is a giant supersonic complexity constructed in a darkened hangar by hundreds of workmen organizing millions of parts. But once wheeled on the tarmac it is an image, and was an image all along. The nuts and bolts disappear into a silver vision.

It is this approach to the case history that revitalizes it. My

story is a complexity of grey nuts and bolts, all the metallic tedious-
ness of what went wrong and who was right, and yet in it is my
dignity, my monument. And in it is history itself: my mother had
a mother and behind her an ethnic ancestral stream; the son with
whom I battle is today, and tomorrow too. There is no part of my
personal record that is not at the same time the record of a community, a society, a nation, an age.

The implication is: if history dignifies, then case history as a
form of historical writing does so too. In our case history is our
human dignity even if that history be written by Zola, Genet,
Spillane, or Dickens. Even if it is a tale of degradation and written
with sentimentality, even if presented as a wholly literal rope of
facts to hang one up in a clinical diagnosis, a case history, because
it is history and therefore fiction, is a move into imagination.

For it is the imagination that gives distance and dignity, allowing us to see *events as images*. It is the imagination that stands
halfway between the world of now and the imperceptible eternal-
ities of the spirit. Back of history is Mnemosyne (Memoria), the
imaginal, mother of historicizing, the soul's archetypal, *sui generis*
process of musing in terms of history.

History is a way of musing upon oneself, and case history which
too is an expression of Clio, is one of the ways the therapeutic
profession and the patients can muse therapeutically. That it does
not succeed, that it creates degradation and diagnosis rather than
detachment and dignity only points again to the power of story in
determining who we are. But the possibility for revisioning and
enhancing who we are is within the events of each case history, if
we learn to read it as a fiction and its events as images of Memoria,
who needs to historicize in order to create.

10. *The Gift of Case History*

I have found that the person with a sense of story built in from
childhood is in better shape than one who has not had stories,
who has not heard them, read them, acted them, or made them up.
And here I mean oral story, those depending mainly on speech—
and reading too has an oral aspect even when one reads alone in

silence—rather than story watched on screen or in a picture book. (The preference for word over eye I will explain in a moment.) Story coming on early puts a person into familiarity with the validity of story. One knows what stories can do, how they can make up worlds and transpose existence into these worlds. One maintains a sense of the imaginal world, its convincingly real existence, that it is peopled, that it can be entered and left, that it is always there with its fields and palaces, its dungeons and long ships waiting. One learns that worlds are made by words and not only by hammers and wires.

Screened, watched stories are different because they enter imagination via perception, reinforcing the confusion between perceptual pictures and imaginative images. Pictures we perceive with our sense perceptions; images we imagine. Or, as Edward Casey[38] puts it: an image is not a content that we see but a way in which we see. We may see pictures as images, and a filmed picture may be imagined and become an image; but these images usually remained linked with the visualities in which they first appeared. Word-image, however, are immediate property of imagination, which in turn may visualize them in a mock-perceptual way (like visualizing scenes to music, or faces for fictional characters, or locations in novels); but the essence of word-images is that they are free from the perceptible world and free one from it. They take the mind home, to its poetic base, to the imaginal.

Again it was Freud who rediscovered the difference between perceptual and imaginative images. Actual pictures—Mom and Pop in bed on Saturday afternoon—did not have the recollecting power, the symptom-making force, of the story and images of The Primal Scene. To paraphrase Casey: a trauma is not what happened but the way we see what happened. A trauma is not a pathological event but a pathologized image, an image that has become "intolerable" as Lopez-Pedraza puts it.

If we are sick because of these intolerable images, we get well because of imagination. Poesis as therapy.

The person having had his stories early has had his imagination exercised as an activity. He can imagine, and not only think, or feel, or perceive, or learn. He recognizes that he can *imagine life,* and not only think, feel, perceive, or learn it. And he recognizes that imagination is a place where one can be, a kind of being. Moreover, he has met pathologized images, fantasy figures that are maimed, sexually obscene, violent and cruel, omnipotently beautiful and seductive. Therapy is one way we can revivify the imagination and exercise it again. Of course we have to go back to childhood to do this, for that is where our society and we each have placed imagination.[39] Therapy has to be so concerned with the childish part of us (not for empirical developmental reasons) in order to recreate and exercise the imagination. The entire therapeutic business is this sort of imaginative exercise, and it picks up again the oral tradition of telling stories. Therapy is a restorying of life.

Of course if one still holds to the rationalist and associationist theory of mind and the positivist theory of man then it will be argued that there can be too much fantasy, that it is a flight from reality, and that the task of therapy is precisely the reverse of what I have sketched. Therapy, they would hold, is the gradual trimming of imagination and bringing it into service of realistic goals. What makes a man or woman insane, they say, is precisely being overwhelmed with fantasy. Too much story, story confused with history, realities gone.

But the imaginative schools of therapy, sensitively discussed by Mary Watkins in her pioneering book *Waking Dreams,* move straight into fantasy. They take quite literally that therapists are workers in story. Unfortunately this then leads them to dispense with case history as only outer, forgetting that this history too is a piece of imagination and all the figures in it, including those ever present traumatic figures, Mom and Pop, are not pictures in memory but images of memoria, with archetypal echo, progenitors in my genealogy myth, who continue to engender my soul by the fantasies and emotions they continue to cause. Case history is not the place of hang-ups to be left behind; it too is a waking dream giving as many marvels as any descent into the cavern of the dragon or walk through the paradise gardens. One need but read each literal sentence of one's life metaphorically, see each picture of the past as an image.

Finally, we recognize that the case history in psychology is a genuine psychic event, an authentic expression of the soul, a fiction created not by the doctor but by the historicizing activity of the psyche, and that this genre of telling corresponds with the re-emergence of soul in our age through depth analysis. As depth psychology invented a new kind of practitioner and patient, a new language, a new style of ritual, and of loving, so it shaped a new genre of story, one that is neither biographical nor medical, nor confessional witness, but a narrative of the inner workings of the soul through time, a history of memories, dreams, reflections, sometimes disguised, but not necessarily, in empirical realities. No matter who writes them, they remain documents of the soul.

The lonely analyst in his lamplit *Schreibstube,* the social worker chain-smoking, typing under pressure—the very urge to write these tales though they go unpublished and unread is a psychological gesture, itself a telling. For this new form of fiction enters our age driven with fierce compulsion. We want to get it down; there is so much to tell about. This craven trivia is so momentously important because history is now taking place in the soul and the soul has again entered history. Therapists are the new historians.[40]

It is in this sense that case histories are fundamental to depth psychology. Not as empirical fundamentals or residues of the medical model, nor as paradigmatic examples demonstrating one or another theorist's plot do they earn our attention. They are subjective phenomena, soul stories. Their chief importance is for the character about whom they are written, you and me. They give us a narrative, a literary fiction that deliteralizes our life from its projective obsession with outwardness by putting it into a story. They move us from the fiction of reality to the reality of fiction. They present us with the chance to recognize ourselves in the mess of the world as having been engaged and always being engaged in soul-making,[41] where "making" returns to its original meaning of poesis. Soul-making as psychological poesis, the making of soul through the imagination of words.[42]

Perhaps our age has gone to analysis not to be loved or get curied, or even to "know thyself." Perhaps we go to be given a case history, to be told into a soul story and given a plot to live by. This is the gift of case history, the gift of finding oneself in myth. In myths Gods and humans meet.

NOTES

1. Giovanni Papini (1881–1956), Italian pragmatist philosopher and writer. Cf. *The Encyclopedia of Philosophy* (New York: Mac-Millan, 1967) vol. 6. *See* "Papini."

2. G. Papini, "A Visit to Freud," reprinted in *Review Existential Psychology and Psychiatry* 9, no. 2 (1969),: 130–34.

3. J. Hillman, *Re-Visioning Psychology* (New York: Harper & Row, 1975).

4. S. Freud, *Collected Papers III,* "Case Histories," trans. A. and J. Strachey, 3rd ed. (London: Hogarth, 1946). For some recent discussions of Freud's cases as literature, *see* S. Marcus, "Freud und Dora. Roman, Geschichte, Krankengeschichte," *Psyche* 1974 (28), pp. 32–79; L. Freeman, "Bibliography" in her *The Story of Anna O.* (New York: Walker, 1972).

5. Roger Fowler, ed., *A Dictionary of Modern Critical Terms* (London and Boston: Routledge & Kegan Paul, 1973). *See* "technique."

6. E. M. Forster, *Aspects of the Novel* (1927; reprint ed., Harmondsworth: Penguin, 1962), pp. 37–38.

7. I have heard that the last work Freud read as he was dying was Balzac's *Peau d'chagrin*.

8. Quoted by Forster, *Aspects*, p. 54.

9. Freud, *Collected Papers III*, p. 24. Freud's defense of the patient's defenses (timidity and shame) also provides him the occasion to intervene as narrator between the story and the reader. This device is fundamental to storytelling: "In imaginative literature the nature of the link between the reader and the text is crucial, and here the *narrator* becomes important. Narrative has two overlapping aspects. One is a question of content, the assemblage of material; the other is rhetorical, how the narrative is presented to the audience." Fowler, *Critical Terms. See* "narrative."

10. Cf. my "Methodological Problems in Dream Research" in my *Loose Ends—Primary Papers in Archetypal Psychology* (New York/Zürich: Spring Publications, 1975), pp. 196–98.

11. Quoted by Forster, *Aspects,* p. 54, from Alain's *Système des beaux arts* (Paris: 1920, pp. 314–15).

12. Forster, *Aspects,* pp. 93–95.

13. Fowler, *Critical Terms. See* "plot."
14. Also in *Collected Papers III*. The best discussion and bibliography of the Schreber case is that by Roberto Calasso appended to the Italian translation of Schreber's *Memoirs* (Milano: Adelphi, 1974).
15. First definition of history from J. M. Baldwin, *Dictionary of Philosophy and Psychology* (New York: MacMillan, 1925). *See* "history."
16. A. J. Ayer, *The Foundations of Empirical Knowledge* (London: MacMillan, 1969), p. 79.
17. Hans Vaihinger, *The Philosophy of 'As If'*, trans. C. K. Ogden (London: Routledge & Kegan Paul, 1935); cf. the relevance of as-if fictions for archetypal psychology in my *Re-Visioning Psychology*, pp. 153ff.
18. One who has explored fictional modes for the *vision* an analyst has toward a case is Roy Schafer, "The Psychoanalytic Vision of Reality," *International Journal Psycho-Analysis* 51 (1970): 279–97, 1970. Schafer finds four basic visions in psychoanalytic writing: comic, romantic, tragic, and ironic (acknowledging his debt to Northrop Frye who in turn acknowledges his to Jung).
19. Wolfgang Giegerich, "Ontogeny = Phylogeny?" *Spring 1975* (New York/Zürich: Spring Publ.), p. 118.
20. My "On Senex Consciousness," *Spring 1970* (New York/Zürich: Spring Publications), 146–65. Also on Saturn from the psychological viewpoint, A. Vitale, "Saturn: The Transformation of the Father," in *Fathers and Mothers: Essays by Five Hands* (New York/Zürich: Spring Publications), pp. 5–39.
21. Patricia Berry, "An Approach to the Dream," *Spring 1974* (New York/Zürich: Spring Publ.), p. 69.
22. Fowler, *Critical Terms. See* "hero."
23. On Saturn and reduction, see P. Berry, "On Reduction," *Spring 1973* (New York/Zürich: Spring Publ.), p. 82 and my "The 'Negative' Senex and a Renaissance Solution," *Spring 1975* (New York/Zürich: Spring Publ.), pp 88ff.
24. Annabel M. Patterson, *Hermogenes and the Renaissance: Seven Ideas of Style* (Princeton: Princeton Univ. Press, 1970).
25. J. Hillman, *Suicide and the Soul* (1964; reprint ed., New York: Harper Colophon, 1973), pp. 77–79.
26. All references to Jung, unless otherwise indicated are to *The Collected Works of C. G. Jung* (Bollingen Series 20) translated by R. F. C. Hull and edited by H. Read, M. Fordham, G. Adler, and W. McGuire (Princeton: Princeton Univ. Press), hereinafter *CW* with volume number and paragraph.
27. H. H. Walser, "An Early Psychoanalytical Tragedy," *Spring 1974* (New York/Zürich: Spring Publ.), p. 248n.
28. On the relation between Jung's ideas and his case history, see

A. Jaffé "The Creative Phases in Jung's Life," *Spring 1972* (New York/Zürich: Spring Publ.), pp. 162–90.

29. *CW* 10, §1042. Cf. *CW* 9, §319f. for further reason why Jung does not go into case history in the usual sense.

30. On Jung and Hermes, see D. C. Noel, "Veiled Kabir: C. G. Jung's Phallic Self-Image," *Spring 1974* (New York/Zürich: Spring Publ.), esp. pp. 235–40.

31. Gay Clifford, *Transformations of Allegory* (London: Routledge, 1974).

32. Fowler, *Critical Terms. See* "allegory."

33. On the history of the Dionysos/Apollo contrast, see J. Ritter, ed. *Historisches Wörterbuch der Philosophie* (Basel/Stuttgart: Schwabe 1971), "Apollonische/dionysische," vol. 1, p. 422. On Jung's ideas of Dionysos see my "Dionysus in Jung's Writings," *Spring, 1972;* on the Apollo-Dionysos contrast my *The Myth of Analysis,* part 3 (Evanston: Northwestern, 1972); Gerald Holton, "On Being Caught between Dionysians and Apollonians," *Daedalus,* Summer 1974, pp. 65–81; on the Greek god himself the indispensable works are W. F. Otto, *Dionysus,* trans. R. B. Palmer (Bloomington: Indiana Univ. Press, 1965), and K. Kerényi, *Dionysus,* trans. R. Manheim (Princeton: Princeton Univ. Press, forthcoming). Modern works on the theme are often misleading because they do not give a full enough picture of either Dionysos or Apollo, and this because they are themselves caught by these Gods in their polarity and thus they express archetypal-stereotypical views. For instance, P. E. Slater, *The Glory of Hera* (Boston: Beacon, 1968), M. K. Spears, *Dionysus and the City* (New York: Oxford Univ. Press, 1970). As I pointed out in my paper on Jung's Dionysos, our general image of this God is Nietzschean, Wotanic, Germanic. For a collection of material on this Germanic Dionysos, see: J. H. W. Rosteutscher, *Die Wiederkunft des Dionysos* (Bern: Francke Verlag, 1947).

34. *Hamlet,* II, 2.

35. The classical difference between memory and imagination is only that "remembered" images have the quality of time added. This distinction comes from Aristotle, cf. Frances Yates, *The Art of Memory* (London: Routledge & Kegan Paul, 1966), pp. 32ff.

36. Cf. K. R. Popper, *The Poverty of Historicism* (London: Routledge & Kegan Paul, 1969). Popper takes the first step into a discussion of history as a psychological need. But he is speaking of a particular view and use of history: historicism. We are opening the question further: why the historical mode at all?

37. Peter Burke, *The Renaissance Sense of the Past* (London: Arnold, 1969), p. 105.

38. E. S. Casey, "Toward a Phenomenology of Imagination," *J. British Society Phenomenology* 5 (1974), p. 10.

39. I have discussed at length the relation between imagination and childhood in my "Abandoning the Child," *Eranos 40—1971.*

40. Differences in case-history writing follows old conventions. Social realism's interest in craven and trivial detail requires the low style for writing of things of everyday life. The Jungian style is "high" with its archetypal resonances to heroic, racial, and mythic events; it follows the Classical and Renaissance idea of history which "excluded 'low' people, things, or words" (Burke, ibid.).

41. The term "soul-making," and the idea of its taking place in the "vale of the world," is from John Keats; *see* my discussions in *The Myth of Analysis* and *Re-Visioning Psychology.*

42. For an excellent presentation of soul-making and psychotherapy through words, *see* Pedro Lain Entralgo, *The Therapy of the Word in Classical Antiquity,* trans. L. J. Rather and J. M. Sharp (New Haven: Yale Univ. Press, 1970).

VI

"Story" and Experience

MICHAEL NOVAK

WHEN PAUL TILLICH was transplanted from Germany to the United States, the tenor of his thinking changed profoundly. When Reinhold Neibuhr moved from Yale to become a pastor in Detroit, and again after he had visited Germany and seen the rise of Hitler, the content of many of his concepts shifted. Basic experiences often alter one's cognitive life. It does not follow that one's ordinary cognitive methods suffice to give a full account of these experiences.

One of the functions of "story" in philosophy is to meet this gap in our cognitive methods. "Story" articulates a change in experience. It is a particularly apt method for expressing the sort of experience that alters one's fundamental "standpoint" or "horizon."

Story, then, is a method. It is an ancient and altogether human method. The human being alone among the creatures on the earth is a storytelling animal: sees the present rising out of a past, heading into a future; perceives reality in narrative form.

During every high tide of rationalism—a phenomenon as recurrent in its way as the rising of the oceans—story is not a highly valued method. In rationalistic periods, the human subject is self-effacing. What counts is not the experience which occasioned insight, nor the moment (if one has occurred) of conversion, nor the altogether individual, unique, and contingent details of autobiographical narrative; no, what counts, in the rationalist self-image, is that the mind be conformed (1) to *universal* principles, (2) to *general* rules of evidence, and (3) to *clear* and *distinct* concepts accessible to any inquiring and adequately disciplined mind. As a method, story runs against the grain of these criteria. Elements of the universal, the general, and even of the clear and the distinct idea figure in almost all stories. But whereas in a story these elements are recessive and implicit, in a more rationalistic method they are salient, explicit, ruthlessly dominant. Elements of story are an embarrassment to a fully rationalistic period; rationalism attempts to "demythologize." When encountered in undigested form, not fully imagined, not utterly concrete, not thoroughly experiential, elements of the universal, the general, and the conceptual are an embarrassment to a good story.

Story is not an easy method to master. There are not many master storytellers, nor master philosophers. Story can be learned; it requires the development of specific skills; it demands frequent practice. All of us tell stories from time to time, and can improve our timing, insight, exactitude, and cumulative power. Such skills do exist. They cannot be faked. Their demands are exceedingly high. People have been criticizing stories for as many generations as they have been criticizing arguments. It is not easy to tell a story well.

One of the moments in philosophic thought that is of the highest interest is that critical point at which the thinker undergoes a "paradigm change," a shift in his or her intellectual "horizon," a fundamental "passing over" from one standpoint to another. It is hard enough to mark out exactly the parameters of the "before" and the "after." Did Reinhold Niebuhr really change his mind on several key matters between 1934 and 1936? What precisely did he hold before that time? What was his exact position later? Or consider Wittgenstein between the *Tractatus* and the *Investigations*. Simply getting the differences straight is, I say, difficult enough.

But of even more absorbing interest is the question, *Why* did these changes come about? In order to understand them, the student must recreate in himself the elements of experience that so dramatically separates the one period in his subject's life from the other. It is precisely here that a well-developed method of storytelling plays a helpful role.

Thinking takes place under two imposing constraints. The first constraint is the "world" of images, symbols, and mythical forms by which we each structure our experience. The second constaint, then, is our inner *intention:* our drive, our will, our interest, what we are looking for and working toward. Often during a career, we read the same classical text every year. Each year, we find something new in it, something that had been there all the time without our having the interest that now brings it to light. Our *intention,* then, our interest, constrains our thinking.

But so also does the fund of images within whose context we inquire into concepts. Frequently, students cannot understand a simple point, not because they lack intelligence, but because their perceptual set has them looking in the wrong direction. A good teacher proposes a counterexample which turns their attention to another set of images: suddenly the idea becomes transparent. A shrewd use of apt examples is the essential instrument of teaching, the midwifery of the imagination.

All thinking makes use of images, more often than not implicitly. Images are not exactly presuppositions of thinking, in the way that axioms are presupposed in further steps of implication. Rather, images are the backdrop, the structurings of experience, into which we peer, seeking insight. Given happy dispositions of the imagination, thinking grasps connections, sees relations, comprehends wholes. All thinking makes use of images.

But all thinking is also part of a narrative form, occurs within an autobiography, has a place in a tradition, participates in an intention. Prior to thinking is storytelling, in at least these two respects: reliance on the imagination and upon intention.

To make ourselves conscious of the storytelling in which our own thinking has its actual roots is liberating. It teaches us to observe the connections between our real experience and our thinking. Sometimes what we regard as personal and limited turns out to be virtually universal. At other times, our most intensely reasoned and carefully qualified generalizations do not actually apply to concrete cases; they may even prevent us from perceiving what is right in front of our eyes. Many an academically trained mind is hopelessly confused in practical situations—a political scientist in a political campaign, for example.

It is time, now, to cease talking about story, and to tell one. A story may express more fully why I changed my interpretation of radical politics among college youth than any of my essays. For between 1968 and 1972 I did change my mind rather remarkably, and I also tried to explain why, as I went along. The basic text of the earlier period of my thinking is *A Theology for Radical Politics* (1967, 1968). The basic texts of the transition period are collected in *Politics: Realism and Imagination* (1971).

One of the essays in this latter collection, on the birth of radical politics at Stanford from 1965 to 1968, provides a sharp contrast to the story I tell below. The ideals, concepts, and symbols of the earlier period at Stanford are still active in this story.

Disasters at one place should not lead one to think less of ideals which are realized elsewhere in a more healthy way. But such experiences do force one to think harder. They have a marvelous capacity, like a blow over the head with a plank, to grab one's attention. They make one look for the presuppositions that differentiate place from place, and to estimate the reliability of those presuppositions. I began to see . . . well, a story may help you to see what I saw.

The Experimental College
at Athensbury

A FICTION

THE STARS were right. Youth was in ascendance, nay, at zenith. The hour for experimental education struck. Athensbury, long existent in the Master Plan of the State University and the Cosmic Plan of God, was ushered into life.

Alasdair Henry Armstrong III, diplomat, government officer, modern Socrates, was Athensbury's president. He would make possible for one hundred dedicated students a renewed Socratic search. Not for every person in his college: for one hundred. Southern Methodist, he was also a realist. One hundred stout-hearted, gadfly-bitten followers of Socrates would be quite enough. They would remake the face of higher education.

Armstrong had never approved of the elective system. His very bones told him the only academic revolution worth having combined synthesis and action. With their professors, students would walk in the gardens, not to say the ghettoes, of the world. A community of scholars would reappear. Students and faculty would have full power in the college. No divisions, no departments. Only full partners in the quest—that ancient restless question—for truth.

Carefully Alasdair had gathered his staff. He had met the dean of an upstate college on a bus once, and immediately hired him as his first (and only) Ph.D. for the planning staff. Alasdair didn't trust Ph.D's. "What American higher education needs," he told his wife, "are legions of gifted amateurs, men of wholeness and roundness, men of swift intelligence and astute public relations. You need to change *attitudes* towards things, the *image* of things, the *feel:* we have to get the country moving again."

The two years set aside by the state for planning for the first one

179

thousand students of Athensbury were not really needed. Three of the four great intuitions through which Athensbury would revolutionize higher education in America were already dimly known to its president. *Full partnership to students*—that would capture the Berkeley syndrome. *The whole world as campus*—that would capture political revolutions and relevance. *Each man his own teacher*—that would capture "Do your thing," and lead serious, intense young people from the smorgasbörd of electives to independent study in the great tradition.

Alasdair's staff added the notions of *community* and *person*. "Athensbury," they resolved with liberal righteousness, "will not be a factory. We will not put together another institution; we will build a community. What the world lacks is *community*. No more 'Do not fold, mutilate or spindle.' No more College Board scores or other numbers games. We insist that people be treated as people: all equal, each responsible, each a mature adult." On these principles Athensbury was founded.

The first students arrived three months ahead of time, in June. The gates of high schools clanged open, and in their VW's the chosen raced immediately to college. They were not happy at home. Summer camp was out. So was earning money. They came, saw, remained—a dozen in the Stable House, one in a tepee.

The estate on which Athensbury's new communal dormitories would soon rise, courtesy of youth-oriented taxpayers of a fascist State, was verdant and exquisitely landscaped. There was lots of grass.

Athensbury was a sleepy Republican town of well-manicured estates zoned for a minimum of five acres, close to sailing, boating and water skiing: an ideal setting for a relevant education. In Athensbury one could draw deep, sweet breaths.

The first faculty, all eleven of them—modest, utopia-inclined—came in August. Five had Ph.D.'s. The others had proven skills: men and women, as it were, of the world. Those without Ph.D.'s, among them Jane Parker, who had a master's in comparative literature, deeply resented being classed among President Armstrong's "gifted amateurs."

They were a surprise to one another, as a faculty. None of them had ever met before. They all knew Pinker, of course, the psy-

chologist and former dean, since he had been the chief faculty re-
cruiter, but their relative inexperience startled them. Each had
privately thought he or she wanted to be associated with an experimental college. But each had counted on the others being
professionals of that sort of thing. To their dismay, each learned
that those enticing phrases that had brought them to Athensbury—
"full partnership," "university of the world," "each man his own
teacher," "community and person"—were the *only* phrases any
of them knew about experimental education. No exegetes were
present. No one had a full-blown theory. Nearly all were privately
skeptical about the few sentences they did know, but fell back
upon the sacred word "experiment." All relished the sweet humil-
ity of "not having all the answers." Each thought it would be
intriguing to see how far intelligent people could go under optimal
conditions: three million dollars for the two completed planning
years—open to eighty-five students. Then, the official opening and
the full one thousand students, and millions more from the op-
pressive State.

The first meeting of the new college was, in retrospect, a disaster.
The first plenary meeting of the faculty was assembling to plan a
curriculum for the autumn; classes were to begin in six weeks. Several of the faculty and students were sitting on the grass outside the
meeting room. It was twenty minutes past the hour when the meeting was to have begun and urgency had not yet bestirred them.
(Athensbury, they used to say, is on Italian Savings Time.) President Armstrong, sitting crosslegged, was holding forth.

"When we were in Rio de Janeiro . . ." he reminisced mod-
estly. He blinked his eyes against the sun and looked towards
Miss Parker. "Fantastic city! The sweep is unbelievable! Anyway,
we had this cook—Gregorio or something like that—everyone
had them there, even poor people. We felt sort of funny, but—*he*
was a riot!" Alasdair Armstrong broke up. "Every day he would
come in and take the ice cubes out of the refrigerator and proceed
to boil them! We couldn't get him to stop. . . ."

The academic vice-president was hovering over the group.
President Armstrong held up his wrist. "Is it time? Sorry I won't
be able to stay." His face fell in sincere disappointment. The father
of the college would miss his very first faculty meeting. "But it's

for a good cause. The Police Investigators Group—PIG—is holding a conference on drugs." He raised his handsome eyebrows. "With *all* the college presidents and deans. Be good to be there, don't you think?"

Two of the girl students nodded.

"Well, take care of my college for me. Wish me luck." With a wave, Armstrong was gone.

Miss Parker had to excuse herself before the start of the meeting and told Pyotor Pninski, the philosopher, she'd be along in a minute.

The faculty meeting, then, which President Armstrong could not attend, was late in starting. Quite obviously, the full partners had a right to be there too. Twenty-eight minutes past the scheduled hour, students and faculty were still filing in. Miss Parker entered, searched for a seat, hesitated. All the chairs at the table were taken, one of them by Susan Ponsonbee's college, whose tongue was hanging out pathetically in the August heat. Miss Parker sank willingly onto the floor in a corner.

Miss Parker was just straightening out her skirts (she seemed a little more self-conscious than the lass beside her, whose spread-eagled legs exposed blue panties to air and light) when vaguely the sound of her name rose across the table. A sudden crick in her trick back seemed to prevent her from looking up immediately. Hiding the grimace of fleeting plain, she turned toward the sound, and her trusty thick lenses picked out a focus. It was the gentlemanly Professor Pninski.

"Here, Jane," he offered, "Vould you like to sit up here?"

Instantly she caught his indecision. It was considered bad form at Athensbury for women to be granted special courtesies. On the other hand, those coming in from other cultures could possibly be excused from strict observance. Wedged between imperatives, Professor Pninski raised his buttocks a little and swept one arm around.

"No, no!' she remonstrated. "I'm fine._ This is fine. I always sit on the floor at home." At home, of course, she had cushions, not to mention a raised fireplace, and she only sat there on winter evenings, three or four times a year.

The girl with rose glasses, across from Miss Parker, beamed

with admiration. Miss Parker felt as close to virginal sainthood as it had been her privilege to feel. "We are going to be, quite obviously," she thought, "a very sweet community. Of equals."

That prospect did disturb her a little. It would require of her a little readjusting to feel the full-bodied equal of the boy with the torn khaki shirt and the dirty hair, for example. Through some strange deficiency she'd never despite twelve years of analysis discovered, she could not tolerate the sound of someone loudly chewing gum. The slow grinding of this boy's jaws was, to her ears, deafening. What made her position intolerable was that he was black. Middle-class prejudices! Swift squirts of acid hit her intestines; she tried to calm them with a mental replay of the beautific smile she had just received.

"The subject for today," Blaise Kendall began. He was the academic vice president, a dear sweet man and, as events were to prove, a well-oiled mariner's compass of direction: place him between four or five conflicting pressures and he would unerringly locate the vector of reconciliation and objectively, patiently, calmly, explicate its necessities. He was objectivity personified. Mr. Quaker as scientist (nuclear physics).

"The subject for today," he cleared his throat and smiled sweetly.

A large girl, who wore no bra under her sweaty tee shirt, was loudly whispering across the room for a boy with shaggy eyebrows to throw her a cigarette.

"The subject for today is curriculum. Very soon now we must talk about governance, evaluation, field programs and"—he gestured inclusively—"a whole host of other problems. But today I thought—"

"Blaise, one minute!" The boy with the shaggy eyebrows, having thrown one damaged cigarette across the room, interrupted with authority. "One damn minute. Is it true that students are full members of this meeting?"

You could hear people sweating in the silence.

"No one, I think, had denied it." The beautiful cautiousness of the canons of evidence: Vice President Kendall never affirmed too much.

"Well, I mean, like that sign, man. It said *fac*-ulty meeting." David "Bull" Connor (that was his name) was very bright, but he had a slight stutter. Second syllables of some of his words, the longer ones, tended to get lost. "I just wanted to be sure you meant we're *all* fac-ulty. I didn't want to start the year gettin' screwed."

"C'mon!" said the one well-dressed boy in the room, with contempt. He was a transfer student from Harvard.

Bull fought to keep on top. "Yeh, well, I know it's goin' to happen. Sure it's gonna happen. We'll get screwed. The whole fuckin' country's getting screwed. I thought maybe *here* we could get through a day or two before it happened."

One quality Blaise was jealous of, his fairness. "I thank you. But I'm sure"—you could see him ready himself for the effort, like a pole-vaulter about to lift himself out of his accustomed level— "I'm sure I know of no one who is trying to—screw you." The word came painfully, and Blaise attempted a silly grin to disguise it but en route around the room his eyes caught Pninski's and he blushed.

A few giggles covered the awkwardness. The girl with rose glasses beamed with admiration. The language of the young, as well as their seating arrangements, had been blessed.

Jane Parker stirred uncomfortably.

"Blaise!" This time it was a tall pretty girl standing against the walls of the room where they joined at the corner. She had large, soft eyes like a deer or a calf. All the more striking was her gravelly Long Island City voice. She even waved a finger. "How do we know how decisions are being made around here? Who decided how to decide? Like, who called this meeting? Who picked this time? this place? I didn't even find out about it until I went into the john. I still wouldn't know about it if Amy hadn't told me. Are there privileged classes here?" For a pretty girl, she had a mean, snarling lip. "Are some partners here more equal than others? Like getting information others don't get? We haven't even started yet, and already the administration is playing tricks."

Jesus Christ! Jane Parker thought to herself. *So that's what Jewish mothers are made of.* The juices squirted again: another Waspy prejudice. *Jane darling,* she told herself. *Janey Parker. Old Jane. You're going to learn a thing or two here. Like nowhere you've ever been. Man.* She had a headache and she felt confused.

The meeting ended in disarray. Blaise was trying to say, "Now just a minute, just a minute—there's a lot of work we have to accomplish this morning." But some people were groaning, others looked at the ceiling, and others buzzed angrily and busily. A critical moment in the credibility of the school had obviously come.

"Blaise . . . Blaise . . ." A calm voice said from the other side of the table.

"Shh! Shh!" the rose-tinted girl said.

"Mister Pratt, you have the floor," Blaise said.

"Look, it's too hot in here. Why don't we go outside on the lawn and get to know one another a bit. I don't agree with some of the allegations that have been thrown around in here. But it's clear we can't make any headway until we talk about some preliminaries." He laughed slightly, "Like trust."

It was a sensible speech. Miss Parker tried to remember who he was. Oh yes, Pratt, the philosopher from Yale. Yes, an obviously sane and intelligent man. Well, at least there were some allies around.

By general consent we pushed and crowded out the doorway into the lawn. Unwillingly, Miss Parker had her first sensory experience with Athensbury students: an intense whiff of wet, sweaty straw on the clothes of one of the boys who was sleeping in the tepee. The eyes of the girl on his arm were so deeply circled, however, she wouldn't have wagered a nickel they were getting any sleep on the straw. *When I was in school,* Miss Parker thought back (God! how many generations ago), *it was the jocks who looked and smelled and loved like that; at Athensbury the hippies are the sexual athletes?*

The meeting on the lawn did not go a whole lot better. Miss Parker felt dismay after telling one boy—it was a shocking explosion, for her—"No, goddamit, I am not your servant!" She did not often use profanity, certainly not at public meetings, not even at the hottest editorial board meetings she had attended. But *that slimy lad* as she called him later made her absolutely "livid."

"You're not special people," the boy had jabbed at the faculty. His name was Carl Sherman. "You don't know anything about my life or how I want to live it."

At that Point Miss Parker was on the verge of saying: "Your life would bore me to tears." The effort to choke it down was her undoing.

"I'm a faculty member," the boy asserted. "Equal to you. Even superior, because schools are meant for students. I'm a faculty member: I'm my own teacher. But I'm a student, too. And you people—" he pointed a thin, dirty-nailed finger, "are functionaries. You help me when I need you."

"Then why are we paid, and you're not?" Ralph Portly, the bearded sociologist from Penn asked very gently.

"Because you're functionaries," Carl Sherman—Miss Parker always saw him thereafter on some flaming march—replied triumphantly.

That's when she exploded. "I am not your functionary. You're crazy if you think my life revolves around you."

"Then why are you here?" the girl with the rose-tinted glasses asked.

Miss Parker really didn't want to lose the girl's rosy beatific glance. She didn't feel at all like trying to justify herself. But she found herself thinking: *How can there be an experiment, unless all our assumptions are examined?*

"Like," she said, "to teach." Instantly, she hated herself for saying "like." She hurried on. "But you're mistaken if you think my life is exhausted by my life with you. Students are only part of my life. I'd be of no use to you, or to myself, if I let you devour me."

The girl did not seem to be reasurred. Miss Parker thought she saw traces of famine in her cheeks.

"People who have degrees can't be trusted," a young man in a blue-striped polo shirt mumbled. He sat crosslegged, pulling blades of grass and throwing them into the air.

"What was that?" Ralph Portly said. He was quite heavy, and leaned forward sympathetically. "No, I didn't get it. Please repeat it."

The boy's head tossed nervously as he spoke. Speech in public, around adults, was a victory for him. "They've done stuff to your heads. By the time you've got your degree, who can trust you?"

"Yeh, there's some truth to that," Portly nodded. "Graduate school socializes you."

"What doesn't?" Jane Parker asked no one in particular. She was finished at this place, she could tell. "Even grooving in the grass is a form of socialization. My God, you can't escape it."

"Good point," Portly agreed. His chunky hands formed a little square in front of his knees. "You see," he addressed the polo-shirted boy, graphically bracketing his case with his hands. "Youth culture is socialized, too. Everybody has their own bag."

The boy was nodding. He didn't see at all. "Yeh, that's what I mean," he said. "How can we trust you?"

"Oh, well," Portly laughed, shrugging merrily but looking at me with puckish eyes. "They're only kids."

Kids, Jane thought! Eels. She could feel them, already, sucking her life away.

The whole group ate lunch together on the lawn beside the Stables House. Jane's headache had gotten worse. She was ashamed of herself for losing her temper. Who was she to be so self-righteous? After all, she had never taught before. Besides, Athensbury was an *experiment*. Old standards didn't apply. She was probably falsifying the discussion from the very beginning, by trying to impose some outmoded structure of her own upon a fresh, delicate organism. *You should be old enough to be detached and to observe: you should be flexible enough to learn a new set of standards,* she admonished herself.

"Hi," Professor Pratt said shyly. "Wild place, isn't it?"

He wore Madras shorts and white tennis shoes. He had the legs of a cyclist, which probably prompted her to keep her eyes above his belt.

"Interesting," she said, delicately. Her tongue caught the bit of sandwich clinging to her lip. She coughed slightly. *Interesting:* the famous Manhattan word. By now she knew that when she used it she felt defensive. *Why?* she wondered. "Say, I appreciate your remarks at the meeting."

He shrugged with pleasure. "Oh, you should have been here last spring."

"Were you on the staff earlier?"

"I was just down for four days as a consultant. You didn't miss anything. Christ! It was incredible."

"What do you mean?"

"Well, you saw it. These fuckin' kids think they're so goddamned smart." He said the words so quietly and politely it made her realize how gentle Free Speech could be.

"Still, I'm ashamed of myself."

"Why ashamed?"

"It's an experimental school, and what do I know about teaching?" She gestured toward the kids sitting, standing, kneeling on the lawn, tossing a red frisbe. "They're such genuine kids. A little nervous and lonely. They do look a little ratty—I'd like to see some of those girls in evening dress just once. But on the whole they look like fairly gentle types. I wish I hadn't been so hard on them."

"You were reacting genuinely. They respect that. You were engaged."

"Well, I've always had a rather sharp tongue. I'll have to control it better."

"Good luck!" he said mischievously. "Say, would you like to take a little walk? We have a half hour."

"Sounds lovely."

They walked down the gravel walks of the estate—over red gravel, white, gray-blue—past marble statues of romantic satyrs and Greek goddesses, past tall dark hedges precisely contoured, past an absolutely stunning walk of summer roses. Under the grape arbor, they stopped to test the early grapes.

"A little sour yet," Pratt said.

"Um, I got a good one."

They spat out the seeds.

Pratt talked about his philosophy classes at Yale. He was a logician, skilled, Jane could see, in all those modern symbols that gave her such a fright. But he seemed like a decent man, even-tempered and cool. He also let it be known that he was Jewish, which surprised her, and he mentioned in passing that he almost never had guilt feelings. "An analyst once said I was the healthiest guy he knew," he said. He wasn't boasting; the fact pleased him, but it was a fact like, say, the angle and warmth of the sun upon his face at that particular moment. "I just don't spend time worry-

ing about things. I just don't. I don't think I've ever lost five minutes' sleep over anything."

She was inclined to believe Pratt. There was something altogether mysteriously attractive about him. He was about forty,
sandy-haired, stocky—perhaps a trifle paunchy. He was an incredibly factual man—one wanted to say value-neutral but that
wasn't it at all. He had practiced an objective look so long, perhaps, that he automatically distanced himself from things, even
from his own fantasies and feelings, which he would quite freely
report on, without inhibitions, when it seemed fitting to do so. He
had made his consciousness into as stable a screen as he could,
and over it impressions and ideas passed, vivid and pale alike, to
his constant and quiet entertainment. It unsettled Jane at first.
How hard she struggled for equilibrium, for control, for insight into
a thousand clusters of dark feelings and impulses that sometimes,
quite plainly, tore her apart. And here was this man beside her, the
epitome of what one part of her was struggling to be. And yet she
did not altogether like what she saw. Pratt was to her mind a little
like David Hume or Philip Rieff, whereas she emulated Nietzsche's
three heroes: Socrates, Goethe, Jesus. A trace of turbulence, a
precarious tension of Apollo and Dionysus. No Dionysus in Pratt,
unless it was a fierce love of clarity, a passionate effort at balance:
but "fierce" and "passionate" somehow did not apply. Pratt in-
trigued her. She had decided to try teaching in order to learn something from her colleagues, and her first peripatetic exercise was a
good one.

By the time they returned for the afternoon session, her headache had disappeared. She greeted Bull Connor with unfeigned
warmth when he tried to step through the door in the same rhythm
as she. Perhaps she would learn to extend her own confined per-
sonality, which had long been a source of dissatisfaction, through
all these people. Both hesitated, but she gestured Bull in, effusively,
ahead of her. He had the good manners to blush, which further
gratified her.

There was a seat at the table and, looking around to be certain
of not trespassing, and feeling perhaps a little guilty to be taking
a chair that symbolically might mean so much more to some uncertain, shy kid, Jane lowered her weight into it. The walk with

Pratt had made her sweaty as well as fatigued, and she reached into her purse and tore open a moist freshener, proceeding, out of sight, under the table, to wipe her fingers carefully and then to dab quickly at her forehead and cheeks. Looking for a place to deposit the freshener, she felt a hand on her shoulder. It was Oliver Cretin, the tepee-dweller. He smiled, wiped the freshener broadly on his own hands, which had gotten sticky from a glazed doughnut, and deposited the soiled tissue with a true one-handed push into the wastebasket five feet away, where it fell with a conclusive *pang!* The meeting began.

"Now that we have gotten to know one another, at least a little," the academic dean began again with a truly charming smile, "perhaps we had better turn to curricular planning."

"What if someone wants to do all independent study?" a dark-haired, sleepy-eyed boy, heretofore silent, asked with only a trace of defiance. (Trace of insecurity, I noted in my notebook.)

"Shall we talk about independent study first?" Blaise asked sweetly. "We have four topics: humanities seminars, social science seminars, field projects, independent study. Shall we begin with the last? Professor Pratt, do you have anything to say?"

"Not really. I mean I didn't know I would be called on. I didn't bring my statement. I have it in my office, just in some notes, if you want me to go get it."

"Professor Pratt is in charge of Independent Study," Blaise explained to the braless girl, who had pulled his arm.

Louder to Professor Pratt: "No, I don't think that will be necessary. We have whole days set aside for the discussion of each of these topics, and I believe you're due up next Tuesday."

"That's what I thought."

"Today a once-over will suffice."

"Can a student do anything he wants for Independent Study?" Bull Connor asked archly. His tall, thin friend, in frayed dungaree shorts and no top, whispered something to him.

Blaise directed the question to Pratt with a look.

"With the consent of his faculty advisor," Pratt said. "And within reason."

"You won't trust the faculty advisors?" Pettibone asked incredulously. He was the youngest faculty member, a new Ph.D. in political science.

"Trust them, yes. But I have the final responsibility."

The buzzing, blooming confusion of reality exploded.

"Order, order!" Blaise pounded the table, a candle in the dark. "Professor Pratt has the floor."

"I haven't made my whole presentation yet. But I certainly don't intend to be a rubber stamp. I'll use my own head in certifying Independent Study Projects."

"Who do you think you are?" Oliver Cretin asked gently. "I mean, why should I give jurisdiction over what I want to do to someone else's head?"

The whole room nodded.

"We've been fucked over enough in high school," Bull Connor commented. He was twenty-five and had led sit-ins at three different colleges, and was expelled from all three. Athensbury was going to show there was at least one school where such independence of mind was not perceived as a threat.

"Yeh!" the tall pretty girl whispered. "I've been fucked over enough already." A few of the other girls smiled.

"Well, I want everybody to know," Pettibone announced, "that as a faculty member I intend to sign for any project any student wants to do."

There was a significant silence. Then he continued: "These are all mature, adult kids. I intend to treat them as adults. A project may sound silly to a lot of people, and still be important to the individual. When Columbus sailed west, people laughed. People always laugh at new ideas. In order to get one percent of creativity, you sometimes have to support a lot of seemingly wacky ideas. I underline *seemingly*."

"Suppose someone proposes to lay matches end to end across the Brooklyn Bridge," Pratt began calmly. Jane was pleased to see his cheeks reddening. "I'm not going to approve of that."

"Why not?" Pettibone said. "I would."

"Because it's silly."

"Well, it's easy to pick out something silly," Portly entered as a grave, moderate mediator.

"But even in an example like that . . ." Pettibone was inspired and shifted his weight in his chair. "Even in a case like that, a given individual might learn a lot. Would he try to get permission, or just do it as a kind of sit-in? How far will the establishment go in allowing academic freedom? And suppose the kid went to jail. He'd learn a lot about our society."

The whole room was nodding.

"Look," Pratt said slowly. "Everything in the world is educational. But there are some forms of education I intend to support, and others—"

"Who the hell died and left you judge of my education?" a short, heavy girl broke in with indignation.

"So long as I have the responsibility, I intend to exercise it. Making distinctions is one-half the business of education. I'm sorry, but I intend to make distinctions."

"Yes, but not for other people," the girl said. She seemed ready to cry.

"Look, Alfred," Portly addressed Pratt. "In my view we're making too many assumptions. I think Athensbury should select only students who are college material—bright, mature, responsible. Then, give them their degrees the first day they arrive and turn them loose. I'm convinced they'll do better work."

"No one in America," Pinker the psychologist added, "has tried the Summerhill approach. I think we should keep standards, guilt, evaluation, clubs over people's heads, sanctions *out* of education. No one is going to try to lay matches end to end across the Brooklyn Bridge."

"I think it would be a great idea," Pettibone rose to the challenge. "They'd learn a lot about American society. In practice, not from books by liberal ideologues."

("I confess," Jane Parker said afterwards, "my emotions were spinning." She admired Pratt's brave attempts at reason, but felt he had chosen a poor example. She hadn't expected the enormous —truly enormous—revulsion against standards and evaluations. *Why,* she had thought, *these kids are scared to death of failure. But why on earth does the faculty support them?*)

"Well," said the Academic Dean lamely, "maybe it's just my

hang-up. But I still feel as though there has to be some procedure of evaluation."

"Pass-fail," one student said.

"Pass-No," another contradicted.

Pinker added; "There's no need to label anyone a failure. A lot of people have been destroyed that way. Parents ridiculing their children—it's only in America that that happens. 'No pass' would mean they don't get any credit. They can take as long as they want to get through school; they just need enough 'Passes.' "

"But then you fall into the trap of the credit system," Frederick Poole added. He came to Athensbury from a Great Books tradition. "Once you do that, you're sunk."

"Give them their degrees the day they arrive," Portly said emphatically, boxing the issue with his thick hands. "Let them do what they want to. I'm sure it will work. They're all intelligent kids." He summed them up with his eyes, while each of the kids grew an inch under his gaze.

"I guess I just have a hang-up," Blaise was reduced to giggling to the girl next to him. Louder: "We can settle grading and credit later. Right now the subject is Independent Study."

"Can I study lovemaking?" a very quiet feminine voice said from the floor. Everyone turned.

"That would have to be a Field Project," Pratt said without blinking an eye. "Probably not for credit."

"What could be more relevant?" Portly laughed, framing another box.

The laughter eased the tensions in the room.

"I don't intend to submit my Independent Study to anybody," Oliver Cretin said slowly and genuinely. "If I did, it wouldn't be independent."

"Wait a minute," Pratt said. "Logically, Independent Study does *not* imply there won't be any supervision. The *work* is independent, and the choice of project is largely independent. But I am certainly not going to run an unsupervised, chaotic program."

"Unsupervised does not logically imply chaotic," Pettibone mimicked.

"True, but experience counts for something in the use of logic."

One face at the meeting captivated Jane. One of the faculty
members had been unusually silent and wore an expression that
was most often severe but also often ironical and pained. When
finally he spoke—she knew his name was Pickering, and that he
had come from Santa Barbara—his voice was whispery soft. She
didn't trust him, for some indefinable reason.

"Aren't we going around in circles?" he asked. Since everyone
was indeed dizzy, everyone strained to hear his voice. "We have to
make a decision. Some people want the school to certify whatever
anyone wants to do. Others want some definition of standards—
perhaps any definition, even an entirely revolutionary definition,
but some definition of standards. We can't do everything at once,
we have to limit ourselves to one form of education. What will it
be?"

He took a deep breath. "I don't see how any group of human
beings can avoid having standards, even if they try not to. Raised
eyebrows, intonations, sympathies—all of these tell you who is in
and who is out. We're going to have standards, all right, the only
thing is, are we going to choose them consciously or just allow
them to happen?"

"It's all right for you cultivated people to talk standards," Bull
Connor said. "I can tell you in advance what they're going to be.
You're going to make us over into people who are like you and
some of us, at least, are saying 'no thanks.' "

"Then it's a little hard to see," Pickering said sadly, "why you
have chosen to study with us or—"

"We didn't choose it. We have no choice. The draft, remember?
That little war somewhere—where is it now, somebody help me to
remember."

Pickering pushed on very softly: "—or why we have chosen to
teach you."

That was a mistake. Jane could recognize it because it was
exactly the sort of thing she had done earlier. The temperature of
the room flowed cold in Pickering's direction.

"The point is," Pickering picked up in a barely audible whisper.
His hands were shaking. "We came here for the sake of experimental education. We don't think we're gods or anything, and we
don't mean to inflict ourselves upon you. But we can only teach

you what we know as success and failure, good or bad or me-
diocre."

"Don't you see the ideology in that?" The tall pretty girl's voice
had authentic despair in it. "Can't you understand that we despise
you and your society? We're not asking you to teach us. We just
want to be left alone. We want some space to educate ourselves."

"Then there's not much point in being a teacher here, is there?"
Pickering asked.

"That's childish, Pickering," Portly said calmly. "She's not saying that. She's overstating the case a little. What she means is, these
kinds are unusually intelligent and mature. I was on the Admis-
sions Committee. I can assure you that these are the very cream
off an incredibly good bundle of applications. What they want is a
new kind of education. That's what 'experimental' means. They
just want a chance. I think we should give it to them."

Pickering was stung, and somewhat contemptous of Portly's
playing to the crowd. But the crowd was loving it. Jane Parker
seemed to be looking over the kids and thinking that they should
be given a chance.

"But Roger," Pickering was saying quietly to Portly, "we can't
abdicate our own experience and intelligence. Naturally, these kids
are bright and mature—outstanding even. But they can't ask us to
lie down and play dead. I'm willing to argue with them all they
want. But when I think they are wrong I intend to say so. I think
that they are running away from possible failure. And failure just
isn't that terrible. I don't think it's right to give way to their prejudices, just because so many things are wrong with American education. They have a right to expect adults to stand and fight."

"I'll stand and fight," Pettibone smiled. "But I'm on their side.
I'm probably just young enough and just old enough to see both
sides. I worked hard for my Ph.D. and I got it in record time. But
I think I was cheated. I hated every minute of graduate school and
thought that nine-tenths of it was bullshit. Yes, bullshit." He looked
around the room uneasily, sorting out his roles. "I don't want to
inflict on other young people what was inflicted on me. And that's
why I'm here."

There was a revivalist, testimonial character to Pettibone's
speeches. To give them well, he needed an audience easily moved

by the baring of his soul. He was the kind of boy one wanted to
mother. *He's a hurt boy,* Jane Parker kept thinking to herself. *He
hurts.*

"Well, I still have my hang-up, I guess," the academic dean
laughed. "We certainly haven't decided much but it seems to have
been a fruitful discussion."

"*I* think we've decided," Pettibone said.

"Decided what?" the academic Dean asked.

"Well, if I can read the sentiment of this room, the vast majority
is in favor of *independent* Independent Study. That is, no faculty
advisors, no supervision. Except for record keeping."

"You mean everybody just passes, automatically?" the academic
dean asked.

"That would be my inclination," Pettibone shrugged. "But I
know you have the State to worry about. So I'll compromise. I'm
a realist to that extent. I'd say that students should evaluate themselves. If they do passing work, they know it. If they don't, they'll
be honest about it."

"*Nemo judex in causa sui.*" Pickering barely parted his lips.

"What was that?" Pettibone's eyebrows went up, above his smile.

"Never mind. It's useless," Pickering waved.

"Shall we have a vote?" Pettibone encouraged.

"Well, this is a faculty meeting . . ." the Dean began.

"I thought we've agreed we're all faculty," the students said.

Some one shouted derisively: "Full partner-ship! Full partner-
ship!"

"It's a participatory democracy," Pettibone added. "One man—
one vote. Isn't that what the whole nation stands for now? Isn't that
what democracy is?"

"Let's not get into that one now," the academic dean grimaced.
"We discuss governance next week."

"How can you distinguish curricular questions from governance
questions?" Pettibone asked. "Every political scientist and social
scientist knows that the form of education conveys more than the
content."

"That's a point worth debating," the nuclear physicist dean said
impatiently.

"Look!" Pratt requested the floor, closing this meeting as he had the last. "I haven't made my presentation yet. Can't we hold voting until we discuss this in an open, full, and formal manner? The informality of this place is getting me down. I don't mind feet up on the table and things—even without shoes—but I think you, Blaise, ought to run meetings a little more tightly. Otherwise, school will begin and we still won't have a curriculum worked out. We need an agenda and we should be forced to stick to it."

Blaise slapped the table with a smile. "And I'll begin right now." Then he gave his characteristic fadeaway laugh. "Meeting adjourned."

Further Thoughts

IT WOULD BE EASY to resume the genre of the critical essay and to analyze the meanings of this story. But a story, once told, no longer belongs solely to the storyteller. It has existence independently of his will, intentions, or analysis. It is an object accessible to others. Others may see in it what the storyteller does not. Story is not narcissism or subjectivity, but its opposite: the making of an independent object.

More than ten years ago, in an essay called "Philosophy and Fiction," I suggested that a story is related to a philosophical analysis as experience is related to cognition. A story is not pure experience; it is itself a kind of abstraction; it does not represent the whole texture of experience; it is a highly selective lifting out of some details, designed to create the illusion of a whole. But just this effort to create the *illusion* of experience requires the storyteller to veer away from too much abstraction, too much selectivity, and to veer toward the ambiguities and complexities of actual life. Although both the storyteller and the philosopher are concerned about the concrete and the universal, they tend to complement one another by their opposing tendencies.

The storyteller (generally) insists upon the particularity of his materials; the philosopher (generally) insists upon the generality of his. Yet in order to be cherished by a wide audience, the storyteller must touch upon universals in human experience; while in order to have his theories touch ground, the philosopher must have a sharp nose for the nuances of the particular. Often, followers of the one vocation employ the skills, techniques and perceptions of the other: often, as in Camus, Sartre, Santayana and many others, the two vocations coinhere.

It is obvious to anyone who has tried to tell a story that the insights into action required to make a story plausible are numerous and subtle. Faced with a blank white page, how does one know which characters, which incidents, which narrative distance and point of view make a scene come to life? How does one capture just those elements of experience one wishes to render accessible to others? There are thousands of ways to fall short of one's intention, to simplify or to distort the experience.

The highest form of art is to disguise one's art. (First, one must acquire it.)

Philosophers and theologians still in training who wish to gain an understanding of human motivation and human action might try their hand at storytelling. If they attempt to create facsimiles of human action, they will notice concrete elements that have heretofore escaped their ken.

They will come face to face with unexpected gaps in their understanding.

Biographical and Bibliographical Notes

STEPHEN CRITES is professor and chairman of the Department of Religion at Wesleyan University. A philosopher of religion, author and editor, Crites is a well-known person in nineteenth century European philosophical and theological studies. Kierkegaard and Hegel have been the foci of some of his major work. As editor of the monograph series of the American Academy of Religion, Crites is influencing decisions to make available publication of serious and substantial shorter works which might not find commercial outlets. Crites is author of a number of books and of articles particularly significant regarding religion and story studies. Among the latter are: "Myth, Story and History," in *A Meeting of Poets and Theologians to Discuss Parable, Myth and Language* (Cambridge: The Church Society for College Work, Fall, 1968); "The Narrative Quality of Experience," *Journal of the American Academy of Religion* 39, no. 3 (Sept. 1971); "Pseudonymous Authorship as Art and as Act," *Kierkegaard: A Collection of Critical Essays,* Josiah Thompson, ed. (Garden City, N.Y.: Doubleday Anchor Books, 1972).

WILLIAM G. DOTY has taught at Drew University and for the past several years at Douglas College of Rutgers University. He is a biblical scholar who has frequently enlivened professional and learned society meetings such as the Society for Biblical Literature, The American Academy of Religion, the Society for Religion in Higher Education with scholarly presentations of a great variety. Author and editor of substantial works in New Testament studies, he has also developed competence in mythology, Amerindian studies and history of religions. Among his writings are *Contemporary New Testament Interpretation* (Englewood Cliffs, N.J.: Prentice Hall, 1972) and *Letters in Primitive*

Christianity (Fortress Press, 1973.) He is currently editing a reader on myth and ritual, and one from the writings of Mircea Eliade to be published by Harper & Row. He has written articles on parables, genre in literary analysis and eschatological language.

GILES GUNN is Associate Professor of Religion and American Studies at the University of North Carolina in Chapel Hill to which he recently moved after several years in the Divinity School and English Department at Chicago University. A scholar specializing in religion and literature, Gunn has concentrated in American letters. He has recently assumed the chairmanship of the Publications Committee of the American Academy of Religion after serving as chairman of the Arts, Religion, and Literature Section for two years. Gunn's works include his editing of *Literature and Religion* (New York: Harper & Row, 1971) and *Henry James Senior: A Selection of His Writings* (Chicago: American Library Association, 1974.) He is at work on a forthcoming book on the critical achievement of F. O. Matthiessen.

JAMES HILLMAN, born in the United States and resident of Switzerland, did his academic degrees in the humanities and philosophical psychology at the Sorbonne, Trinity College Dublin, and the University of Zurich. In recent years his radical and seminal contributions to psychological thinking (for which he has been quoted in *Time, Newsweek, Look, Harper's Bazaar,* etc.) have been presented mainly at the Eranos meetings in Ascona, Switzerland, in small symposia, and universities. He has given the Dwight Harrington Terry Lectures at Yale, was a visiting lecturer there and at the University of Chicago. He edits *Spring: An Annual of Archetypal Psychology and Jungian Thought.* His own books include *Emotion, Suicide and the Soul, Insearch, The Myth of Analysis, Re-Visioning Psychology* (The Terry Lectures), and *Loose Ends: Primary Papers in Archetypal Psychology,* in which the checklist indicates thirty other publications to date. He is in private practice in Zurich after having served for ten years as Director of Studies at the C. G. Jung Institute, Zurich.

MICHAEL NOVAK has taught at several universities including Stanford and the State University of New York at Old Westbury. Most recently he was Director of the Humanities Division of the Rockefeller Foundation. Novak has been a prolific writer. His *Belief and Unbelief* (1965) was subtitled "A Philosophy of Intelligent Subjectivity," and this line of thought led naturally enough toward the concept of "story."

In *The Experience of Nothingness* (1970) Professor Novak explored the notion of "a sense of reality" while in his novel, *Naked I Leave* (1970), he argued for the return of "story" in fiction. *Ascent of the Mountain, Flight of the Dove* (1970) is one of the first works constructed entirely around the concept of "story." In a monograph for the Council on Religion and International Affairs called *"Story" in Politics,* Mr. Novak began a line of inquiry which he has continued in *Choosing Our King* (1974), an examination of five American civil religions through the use of this concept. *The Rise of the Unmeltable Ethnics* (1972) represented his attempt to convey the cultural story which formed the context and starting place of his own inquiries.

JAMES B. WIGGINS is a professor in the Department of Religion at Syracuse University. Historical theology, history of western religion and theologies of history have been his primary areas of research, teaching, and writing. Currently on the Board of Directors of both the Society for Arts, Religion and Culture, and the American Academy of Religion, he has long been interested and involved in interdisciplinary studies. He is the author of "Narrative," in *Echoes of the Wordless Word,* Daniel Noel, ed. (American Academy of Religion, 1973), "Eschatological Consciousness," *Journal of the American Academy of Religion* 43, no. 1 (March 1975), and "History as Narrative: Remembering Creatively," in the forthcoming publication of the proceedings of a seminar of the American Academy of Religion on myth and history. He is a coauthor with Bruce Burke of *Foundations of Christianity* (Ronald Press, 1970).

4 14 89